Parent Education
for Early Childhood

Child-Rearing Concepts and Program Content
for the Student and Practicing Professional

Parent Education for Early Childhood

Child-Rearing Concepts and Program Content
for the Student and Practicing Professional

Christine Z. Cataldo

Teachers College, Columbia University
New York and London

Published by Teachers College Press, 1234 Amsterdam Avenue,
New York, N.Y. 10027

Library of Congress Cataloging-in-Publication Data

Cataldo, Christine Z.
  Parent education for early childhood.

  Bibliography: p. 255
  Includes index.
  1. Parenting—Study and teaching—United States.
2. Child rearing—United States. 3. Child development.
I. Title.
HQ755.7.C38   1987   649.1'07   86-14573
ISBN 0-8077-2797-0
ISBN 0-8077-2796-2 (pbk.)

Manufactured in the United States of America

92 91 90 89 88 87   1 2 3 4 5 6

To Claudia, Jason, and Jerry, with love.

—We love you, too.
Claudia,
Jason,
and Jerry

Contents

Acknowledgments   x

Foreword   xiii

Preface   xv

Part I: Families and the Parent-Education Process

1:   The Development of Parent-Education Programs   3
    The History of Parent Education   3
    Types of Parent-Education Programs   7
    The Effectiveness of Parent Education   15
    The Triad: Child, Family, and Professionals   20
    Program Suggestions   25

2:   Inside the Family: Relationships and Parenting Skills   26
    Family Organization and Function   26
    Parenting as a Role   29
    Parenting Skills   32
    Family Relationships   42
    Program Suggestions   48

3:   The Child, Family and Others   49
    Families and Society   49
    Parents' Peers   52
    Children's Peers   57
    Grandparents   63
    Schools and Families   65
    Program Suggestions   71

4: Models of Parent Education and Child Rearing   73
        Approaches to Child Rearing for Parents   73
        Models of Parent-Education Programs   84
        Program Suggestions   93

5: The Conduct of Programs with Parents   95
        Programing Procedures   95
        Program Formats   109
        Problems in Programs   119
        Program Suggestions   123

Part II: Content Areas for Parent-Education Programs

6: Child Care: Activities, Developmental Issues, and Problems   127
        Child Care Within the Family and Center   127
        Supplementary Child Care   133
        Developmental Patterns, Transitions, and Problems   137
        Family Crises and Uniqueness   147
        Children's Rights   149
        Program Suggestions   150

7: Children's Play   151
        The Nature of Play   151
        Types of Play   154
        Adult Roles in Play   161
        Toys and Play   167
        Program Suggestions   171

8: Children's Behavior at Home and School   172
        The Meanings of Behavior   172
        The Purposes of Discipline   180
        Systems for Managing Behavior   189
        Program Suggestions   199

9: Feelings and Personality   201
        Children's Emotional Well-Being   201
        Children's Personality Development   207
        Feelings: Their Expression and Management   219
        Summary   229
        Program Suggestions   231

10: Families and the Child's Education   232
        The Educational Home Environment   233
        Basic Skills   236
        Social Skills   241
        Attitudes Related to Learning   245
        Special Challenges   247
        Families' Relationships to Schools   256
        Summary   252
        Program Suggestions   252

References   255

Index   265

About the Author   272

Acknowledgments

I very much appreciate the cooperation and assistance of the families, students, and staff at the Early Childhood Research Center, State University of New York at Buffalo. My activities with them have enriched the content of this text and have helped me to develop material that addresses their needs and salutes their competence.

I affectionately thank my husband, Jerry, and my children, Jason and Claudia, who have provided understanding and insight throughout my career, but especially for a project that reflects so many of our experiences as family members and professionals.

CHRISTINE Z. CATALDO

My darling Christine died on April 27, 1985 at three o'clock on a Saturday afternoon. It is a tragedy beyond my ability to understand.

Christine was a fantastic lady. She was a fine teacher and an exceedingly effective and productive professional. She accomplished a great deal in a short time—as it turned out she had to. But most of all, she was a wonderful and caring mother, a terrific and loving wife, and my friend. She did it all, very, very well. She had limitless enthusiasm and enjoyed her work, her friends, and her family to the fullest. Christine had a crystal-clear sense of self, and never lost it. She was that rare person who was totally committed to her work, yet who never lost for a moment her strong sense of family. Jason, Claudia and I were never deprived. Christine did it all!

The caliber of Christine's friends also says a lot about the person she was. And it is one of Christine's dear friends, Teresa Rosegrant, to whom this acknowledgment is addressed. As emotionally painful and upsetting as the task was, Terri took responsibility for responding to the editor's initial and subsequent comments that Christine never had the opportunity to review and saw to it that this book was published. She painstakingly tried to respond to the editor's comments while at the same time preserving Christine's intent. Terri did it beautifully, and I know that Christine would have approved. I want to thank Terri from the bottom of my heart for all that she has done, and most of all, for her devotion to Christine. She did this out of love and nothing more. She, too, is a fantastic lady!

JERRY F. CATALDO, PH.D.

Foreword

This work is an important book for education professionals who assist parents, and for parents seeking information. It conveys insights, understanding, and concrete information about parent-education programs and topics particularly relevant to such programs. The author, Dr. Christine Z. Cataldo, has demonstrated her expertise as a professional in early childhood education, as a seasoned director of parent-education programs, as an experienced teacher of parenting courses for other professionals, and as a parent of two quite remarkable children. Her untimely and tragic death in April, 1985 was truly a loss for the early childhood community, her students, the children and parents at the Early Childhood Research Center at State University of New York at Buffalo, and her friends and family.

This book reflects Christine's energetic and optimistic approach to parenting and the need to assist parents in their everyday efforts. At a time when parents—and mothers in particular—are finding it difficult to balance their professional and parental responsibilities, Christine felt that parent education programs provide a unique means for parents to gain information, support, and guidance. This text will benefit early childhood professionals in their efforts to establish and maintain parent education programs. With Christine, we share a common belief that our commitment to children is conveyed by our efforts to assist those who are primarily responsible for fostering children's growth and development—their parents.

TERESA J. ROSEGRANT, PH.D.

Preface

Parent education is a part of raising children and a method for helping them to grow and develop. The study of child rearing and the design of programs are relatively new to the field of education. In the early childhood years, mothers and fathers are increasingly responsive to educational efforts that help them to acquire information and skills and make their child rearing more satisfying and effective. Professionals from education, child care, social work, health care, and psychology are interested in providing parents with organized activities to meet these needs. This text has been designed to help such parents and professionals to nurture the development, personal growth, and learning of children from earliest infancy to the beginning primary grades. It focuses on parent education as a process that can take place in a variety of settings with differing groups of families.

The approach taken here to parent education for early childhood emphasizes the value of programs that are well designed and responsive to the needs and concerns of mothers, fathers, and children. Parenting is viewed as a home responsibility that benefits from the supportive activities of early childhood professionals. Child development and education are the specialties of professionals, from whom families can gain information they may apply to their child-rearing attitudes and practices. Each can contribute to the other through the parent education process. To design and maintain programs of different types, using specific formats and models, or to understand better the content and scope of child rearing and parent education, this text will examine a wide range of issues and topics. The student of the early years and the practicing professional who works with families raising young children will be able (1) to study child rearing and the process of parent education and (2) to apply the material to the conduct of a program.

The text contains two major sections, which examine (1) families and the parent-education process and (2) content areas for parent-education programs. The chapters in Part I deal with the history and development of programs, relationships and practices inside the family, the child and family in relation to society, models of parent education and child rearing, and the administration and conduct of programs. Chapter 1 describes historical trends, types of educational programs, the effectiveness of programs, and the triangular relationship involving the child, family, and professional.

Chapter 2 covers family organization, parenting roles, specific parenting skills, and relationships among family members. Chapter 3 includes discussions of society, parents' peers, the children's peer group, and schools and families. In Chapter 4, eighteen approaches to the child-rearing process are described and specific models of six types are presented. Chapter 5 is designed to help the professional establish and maintain a program. It includes procedures and formats and explores some problems to be expected.

Part II of the text provides the reader with five content areas for parent-education programs. These will be valuable to the practitioner and the student, in part because the topics form the basis for work with families. The areas were selected for their potential for organizing information and suggestions that parents often request when children are young. They will help any early childhood specialist to deal with the needs of children and families. The topics discussed are child care and problems, children's play, behavior at home and school, feelings and personality, and the education of children by families. Chapter 6 presents child care requirements, day care, and developmental patterns and problems. Chapter 7 describes types of play, adults' roles in play, and toy elements and quality. In Chapter 8, children's behavior is examined in relation to its meanings, the purposes of discipline, and systems for managing behavior. Chapter 9 contains a discussion of children's emotional needs, personality development, and feelings. Chapter 10 completes the section with its focus on the child's education in terms of basic skills, socialization, attitudes toward learning, and relationships to schools.

There are some special features of this text that deserve mention. Each chapter has two aids for the reader. The first is a table that summarizes a significant theme or content area of the text and can be used to simplify, review, or extend the material. Second, at the end of each chapter is a list of eight program suggestions that can be very valuable for use in programs and courses. The professional will be able to present the activities to parents who are involved in the program, while the college or inservice instructor can use the items for course projects. The photographs in the text, taken during actual parent-education activities, add emphasis. Finally, since parent education occurs in several disciplines, the text often refers to centers, schools, and agencies and refers to the reader as a staff member, teacher, or helping professional. This practice reflects the expectation that interest in this field extends to students and practitioners in education, child care, social work, health care, and psychology. It is hoped that the text will help them all to work with families and young children, whether they conduct formal programs or deal with individual parents seeking information.

PART I

Families
and the Parent-Education
Process

1

The Development of Parent Education Programs

Children are raised in families, child care programs, and schools. The adults in these settings are responsible for meeting children's developmental needs and preparing them for a future in society. In the early years, from birth through the lower primary grades, children's personal, physical and learning requirements are managed by parents, with supportive efforts from professionals. Each contributes to the understanding and skills of the other, making parent education one of the most fascinating specialties in early childhood and elementary education today.

In recent years formal programs of parent involvement, education, and counseling have increased in frequency and scope. While parent education does have a history dating back to colonial days, today's programs are more organized and far reaching. There is a belief in the potential of the early years when families can consciously aid the developmental and educational processes. Many parents have joined professionals in seeking information and advice on how best to proceed, and issues concerning their roles, curriculum content, and program impact continue to be in the forefront of discussion.

In a sense, we are at a crossroads in our work with families and children. Program staff members and resources can make significant contributions to the child's development and the family's functioning in relation to growth and learning. There are challenges, however, in designing and conducting programs in school and child care settings. The student and practicing professional require a perspective from which to view their efforts. In this first chapter the history of parent education and trends leading to recent theories and practices will be explored.

THE HISTORY OF PARENT EDUCATION

The term *parent education* has come to be regarded as one that encompasses a wide variety of home and school relationships. In many ways, it is a

3

misnomer because it implies that relationships with parents are, or have to be, educational. In truth, when they communicate, it is often the case that professionals learn as much about children and homes as parents do about the school or the child. Yet most of what educators do in relation to families does appear to focus on learning. Program goals may refer to communication and other two-way processes, and mothers and fathers may contribute significantly to the content or materials in a particular setting. But learning is the business of schools, and it is only natural that their special programs be expected to do the same. Hence, parent education has come to be the general phrase used for a variety of programs involving home-school relationships.

The history of parent education has been carefully described in the opening chapter of a parent-education text by Berger (1981). From primitive societies, where beliefs and practices were transmitted orally; to Greek and Roman cultures, in which Plato and Aristotle argued for child education by the state; through the middle ages to the 1500s, the education of children was carried out privately by families and through apprenticeships. The first "advice" book, on teaching children to talk, was dated about 1500, and the first book directed to parents was printed in the seventeenth century. It described the teaching of letters and behavior. Strict discipline was emphasized for children, including good manners and adherence to rules and responsibilities.

A shift in views regarding the child began toward the end of the seventeenth century. Locke and Rousseau argued for work schools and children's freedoms. Pestalozzi was given the title of Father of Parent Education in the early 1800s. He stressed the vital role of parents in nourishing the child's body and mind. His notions about children's natural goodness and their learning through concrete experiences and self-activity signaled the beginning of early childhood education philosophies. With Froebel's curriculum, designed to parallel the child's natural unfolding, the kindergarten and child study movement began.

The first parent magazines and books date to 1820, when meetings of parents' groups were already occurring and mothers' study groups were developing. Such groups were heavily supported by the Women's Christian Temperance Union, and the Child Study Association was organized in 1888. Following the White House Conference on Children in 1909, federal support and university-based centers were launched, as was the PTA. By the 1920s parent education and programs for young children were well established. Child-rearing practices had emphasized character, strict discipline, and finally mental health. Since the 1930s it can be said that parental understanding of the child's development and behavior came to be considered as an important contributor to academic and social success (Clarke-

Stewart, 1981; Croake & Glover, 1977). Programs emphasized ways of improving the relationships among children and other family members. The child's behavior seems to have received the greatest attention. Other content areas included child-rearing techniques, general personality functioning, and practical care-giving tips. Norms of development, discipline strategies, and emotional growth were described by program group leaders and in the mass media. Each authority or program attempted to teach parents how best to aid the child's development along the lines described by those individuals. Methods included conferences, school participation, directed observation, and the use of special devices. Group methods of teaching parents, however, came to be synonymous with the overall concept of parent education (Croake & Glover, 1977). Varied agencies and professionals also were in evidence, although school-based mental health programs and early childhood professionals seem to have remained the most involved. The early childhood years appeared to be the most popular time for parent education, and there was an apparent consensus that this was the most appropriate period in which to initiate programs.

This brief historical backdrop serves to explain some of the trends in evidence today. Although the enthusiasm for parent education was quieted by other events in the 1940s and 1950s, the interest in providing information to parents and helping them to manage this role in relation to the child's welfare has persisted (Pickarts & Fargo, 1971). Parents themselves have encouraged this trend, at least in terms of their purchase and use of mass-market books and articles (Clarke-Stewart, 1981). The most recent professional interest and activity in parents' roles in education was stimulated in part by the early intervention movement in the 1960s and 1970s (Bronfenbrenner, 1974). During this period, programs were developed for certain young children, aimed at reducing the disadvantage with which they seemed to begin their schooling. Poor and minority children, and later handicapped children, were provided with educational treatments during their early years that were expected to improve their achievement in school, prevent predicted declines in IQ, and help families to understand how to support their children's growth and progress. The educational models used by authorities to design, implement, and evaluate these programs varied widely. Parent involvement and education was employed exclusively in some programs, but even where children appeared to be the sole focus of attention, staff members attempted to communicate or work with families to at least a minimal degree (Gordon, Olmstead, Rubin, & True, 1979; Zigler & Valentine, 1979).

The variety of roles fulfilled by parents in these programs reflected the interventionists' views of how children are well or poorly prepared for their schooling. Parents served as bystanders, liaisons, participants, or policy makers (Cataldo, 1980). Every programmer seemed to acknowledge the influence of the family on the child's development, but each had somewhat different notions of how to help parents to improve the children's functioning. Nonetheless, parents gradually came to be viewed as valuable allies in the educational process (Leichter, 1975). The emerging position was: If parents were able to serve as *teachers* of their children, it seemed reasonable to expect them to assume the role of *learner* in relation to the program, especially since parenting and teaching in the earliest years were considered to be quite similar (Gordon, 1976). "We teach them, they teach their children," was the predominant view by the end of the Head Start and Follow Through decade (Cataldo, 1980). Programs still varied, however, in their approach to parent education and their basic respect for the family's own teaching accomplishments and cultural preferences. Issues such as teacher-parent role distinctions still have not been resolved (Katz, 1981).

In the late 1970s and early 1980s the concept of *high risk for developmental difficulties* was emerging. The term represents a broadening of the intervention population beyond the poor or minority preschool child (Tjossem, 1976). Infants and toddlers began receiving a great deal more attention from educators because many remedial programs were considered to be too late if initiated at the three- or four-year-old level (Bronfenbrenner, 1974). Programs for the handicapped also were proliferating during this decade, and virtually all of them began treatment at birth and involved parents in formal ways (Caldwell & Stedman, 1977; Lillie, Trohanis, & Goin, 1977). Child abuse and neglect prevention became a part of education, in response to new techniques of studying the earliest parent-child relationships and because some patterns of developmental delay were produced by these factors. In managing the needs of the very young high-risk child it became clear that parents' own perspectives, difficulties, and abilities had to be considered, particularly when program staff members worked in the home setting or with individual families (Gary & Wandersman, 1980). Group education methods used with middle-class families and school involvement practices employed in poor or minority neighborhoods seemed inappropriate for many high-risk multiproblem families and for parents just beginning to feel the impact of a child's handicapping condition. Hence, more clinically oriented parent-support and counseling programs that focused on family and adult development as well as child development began to emerge (Bromwich, 1981; Huntington, 1979). Parents' own abilities to obtain support from their families' personal and social networks (Cochran & Brassard, 1979) is part of this emphasis. Such programs use a more indirect and parent-centered approach to the child's development than programs oriented toward the child.

As parent education moves into the 1980s several distinctions can be made from the years of preceding activity. Recent child-rearing practices, while still emphasizing mental health, have taken account of the need to stimulate children's intellectual development. Together these point to a trend toward more wholistic child rearing that includes learning and personality. The family's role appears to be more important than ever before. Early intervention programs led to greater advocacy for parent responsibility and decision making. A sense of partnership between families and professionals seems to be emerging, with educators recognizing the value of youngsters' emotional and developmental ties to the home, and parents valuing the knowledge and techniques of professionals.

Today's parent programs expand upon previous ones. There is a greater variety of method and content, more emphasis on specific developmental markers, more organization of curriculm, greater concern over risks to early development, a distinction between comprehensive and brief programs, and greater emphasis on the family as an interactional unit. Two major themes are important: (1) program contributions to children's development and education and (2) program support for adults in creating a good home situation. The child's development and well-being are the ultimate goals in all types of programs included in this text, whether children or parents are the primary participants. Program types, effectiveness, and issues will be discussed in the sections that follow.

TYPES OF PARENT-EDUCATION PROGRAMS

Programs that are designed to promote parent involvement, education, and support can be examined in relation to their type, format, goals for parents and schools, and objectives for the child. The degree of participation of the child, parent, or family; the program's home or center/school setting; and the primary orientation of the program designer (education, mental health, health care, social work) also are useful dimensions along which formal parent-professional relationships can be described (Cataldo, 1980). In this section, general program styles will be presented along with authors who reflect them and the general content areas that are used. In other chapters, strategies and formats for working with parents, model programs, and techniques used to build child-rearing skills in families will be explored.

General Parent Education

The delivery of information and child-rearing advice on a very wide range of topics characterizes general parent-education programs. Child development, behavior, learning, and child care guidelines are presented and discussed, usually in group meetings. Media materials such as books, magazines, newspapers, films, and television also can be placed in this category, since their orientation is to provide parents with information and advice. General parent education is expected to enhance children's development and behavior. The assumption is that an informed parent can better handle child-rearing activities and responsibilities. The professional uses didactic teaching methods and suggestions for new strategies and resources.

The specific content of general parent-education programs and media materials may depend heavily upon the sponsoring agency or the background of the author. Health care, nutrition, and family management tend to be emphasized by nursing and well-child agencies. Dr. Spock's book (1976) on baby and child care primarily focuses on the child's physical well-being, although behavior and parent-child relationships are discussed by both Spock (1976) and Brazelton (1969, 1976, 1981). Nevertheless, overall physical well-being and normal development tend to be the themes. In social service settings, family relationships within and outside of the home are usually emphasized, along with role responsibilities, cultural differences in child-rearing patterns, and the use of community services. The integrity of the family or home unit is typically the focus of attention and assistance from social workers. In schools, general parent education frequently takes the form of presenting topics such as the school curriculum, school-related projects, behavior codes, peer relationships, neighborhood activities, and children's affective development. Outside consultants may present special programs, where parent groups request these, and specialized schools may provide information about the children's distinctive handicapping, behavioral, cultural, or talented characteristics. Learning about the child as a member of the school community, obtaining support and assistance, and extending learning into the home are the concerns of most home-school parent-education programs.

By far the most predominant sources of general parent-education information and advice are mental health authorities, particularly developmental and child psychologists, and recently, early childhood education specialists. Their materials deal almost exclusively with the child's socioemotional development and, to a certain extent, intellectual growth. Most books, articles, and other media presentations are directly addressed to parents.

Mental health and learning-oriented programs frequently include a focus on child, family, and school-related behavior, signs of disturbance, and techniques for managing children's needs, especially in relation to others. Normal developmental milestones and sequences of growth are often presented. Detailed exercises might be outlined for improving parents' abilities to deal with behavior and learning, to the child's and their own benefit. Such programs have focused upon communication, intelligence, values, problem solving, behavior control, and parent-child interaction. In some, the perceptions of mothers and fathers in relation to children are thought to be improved through greater understanding of the characteristics of children, how they progress in learning and self-awareness, and how they are similar to and different from others.

Some materials are more sympathetic than others, expressing to their audience a genuine respect for the difficult task of parenting. Others present a rather straightforward script or set of procedures that seem to promise success in child rearing when followed conscientiously. Still other authors emphasize factual, developmental, and behavioral information; or one aspect of growth receives their full attention, such as self-esteem, reading, or toys. In the first three years of infancy and toddlerhood, books often focus directly on parent teaching with babies and preschoolers, sometimes with the emphasis on healthy, overall competence, or on raising IQ and encouraging precocity.

General parent education, then, is characterized by efforts to advise, teach, inform, and otherwise educate mothers and fathers. The populations served by these programs may vary considerably. High-school students, middle-class families, special groups of teenaged mothers, high-risk parents, schools for the handicapped, specially funded low-income or minority programs, new-parent groups, community center projects, and active PTA's all frequently rely upon general parent education for their primary orientation and content.

Parent Training

Sometimes the child or parent needs to gain experience and skills that are rather detailed and more clearly and narrowly defined. It may be that an infant must be physically handled in a particular way, that a family wishes to know exactly how to teach a set of preschool skills, or that a mother will benefit from having specific language and social interactions modeled for her that will help her baby learn and develop normally. Parent-training programs are more focused and formal than those of general parent education. They contain a series of instructional goals and procedures and are usually conducted by trained professionals. Sometimes the parent learns skills for herself that are expected to benefit the child, such as using elaborated language or advocating for services for the youngster. In other programs parents are taught how to teach their infants and children particular tasks such as self-feeding, identifying shapes, or reading successfully. In each case, the specificity of the program makes it distinctly different from general parent education. The preset curriculum content means that the program designer has already made primary decisions regarding goals and outcomes to be expected when parents participate. The formality in procedures often creates a kind of script, a step-by-step guide to achieving particular behaviors. In a sense, it is an all-or-none proposition for the parent. The program is a package, to be accepted or rejected in full. In most cases of parent training, however, this very specificity can be a strong asset to families. A clear set of goals and strategies keeps the program on target, keeps staff members focused upon an available, predetermined content, and gives parents measurable skills. For families who wish to gain such competencies or for parents whose children may be at a disadvantage educationally or developmentally, parent training can provide important assistance within a clear-cut structure using advanced planning and outcome evaluations.

There are several settings in which such programs are likely to be conducted. Special education schools have recently placed a great deal of emphasis upon building parents' abilities to handle their handicapped infants and toddlers within their first year of life. Such early intervention is thought to prevent or reduce the degree of later difficulties that occur from the confounding of early medical problems, developmental delays, or physical deficiencies. In this setting, parents are taught how to hold and feed their child, how to create learning activities, and how to work with professionals. Training programs for high-risk families are important when there appears to be some risk of difficulties as a result of premature birth, illness, parenting failures, maltreatment, or overwhelmingly negative home environments. Programs for adolescent parents, for example, have taught specific child-care, play, and social-interaction skills to mothers. Parent training also has been popular with middle-class families who wish to learn techniques for working with their child's behavior or learning. Curriculum packages have been created for mothers and fathers of infants to help them, with a step-by-step set of directions, to build their child's intellectual, physical, communication, and social skills. In some circles, parent effectiveness training has come to be synonymous with parent education.

Parent Participation and Observation

In traditional early childhood education programs such as nursery schools and parent cooperatives, and more recently in programs such as Head Start for low-income preschoolers and in daycare situations, parents have assumed responsibilities in the daily program. They may participate as dependable assistant teachers or irregular volunteers; they may observe the program directly or through meetings and newsletters. They may handle transportation or arrange for visiting community representatives. The distinguishing characteristic of this kind of formal or informal parent involve-

ment/education program is that families are direct participants and observers in the school program. They contribute in some way to the child's
school experiences and see firsthand the child's activities, environment, and
relationships. From this involvement parents often become familiar with
teachers, curriculum, and school policy. They may gain a rather wide range
of information and understanding that could help the child with anything
from homework to relationships with a teacher or playmate.

In some school situations, if not many, parent participation/observa-
tion seems threatening and difficult for the busy teacher. Indeed, often there
is a strong need for backup staff members to help with visiting mothers and
fathers. In today's economic period where both parents may be working,
this involvement can be hard to manage. Yet, some daycare centers and
schools, with a combination of flexible scheduling and gentle pressure, are
able to help parents find ways of becoming familiar with their child's
program. For many families and schools parent involvement in, or observation of, the child's learning is an effective way of building vital bridges
between the child's life at home and in the world outside the family. When a
mother or father has shared a child's classroom experience it is possible to
talk about materials, tasks, and friendships in a more meaningful way. This
exchange can provide ideas for new toys or a way of handling a work
assignment and can balance the parent's perception of the child's place in
the peer group.

Parents as Policy Makers and Advisors

School boards are one example of how parents serve as advisors in the
conduct and content of school programs in which their children are taught
the skills and values society views as necessary for citizens. The advisory role
for parents is one of the most common historically, dating back to the
colonists and settlers who hired frontier teachers and extending to today's
PTA. In some programs parents participate in employment, financial, evaluation, and even curriculum decisions. In Head Start programs, for example, parent advisory committees have continued to play a part in such
decisions. The goal has been to ensure that cultural values are considered
within the child's curriculum. This is still the case in some minority communities where black, Hispanic, Indian, and Oriental families attempt to advise
professionals about their children's heritage, in the expectation that school
programs may be more meaningful and less in conflict with their own
standards. Active PTA's, traditional nursery schools, and, to an even
greater extent, cooperative programs where parents serve as assistants, have
tended to inform parents about what their children require to be more fully
prepared for later schooling. Where infants and toddlers are enrolled,

parents' advisory activities may significantly shape the staff's behaviors with and arrangements for the babies. In programs for the handicapped, parents often need to function as advocates for their children, thus their input into the child's school program is frequently sought.

Parents' roles as policy makers are considered by many to be at the highest level of parent-school relationships. Family members who formally provide advice or influence program administration through committees would fall into this category. But mothers and fathers who visit the director or principal, who are outspoken with teachers, and who regularly visit the program also are bound to achieve some shifts in school policies and practices. On occasion this influence has been viewed as a negative one, such as when parents insist on schools teaching skills to children before they appear to have acquired needed prerequisite abilities or when they object to specific instructional goals or materials. For the most part, however, recognizing the perspective of parents with respect to children's development and education has benefits for both schools and families.

The education of parents in their roles as advisors and policy makers is a broader one than that of gaining general information or specific skills. Parents learn to deal with schools as systems and with programs in terms of what they are seeking to achieve across several years of education. Such insights are quite important if schools are to be responsive to the real needs of children growing up in a particular time and place, with a set of cultural norms and priorities. Parents learn to examine and work with these issues when they assume this role in a parent-education program.

Parents as Home-School Liaisons

Perhaps the most traditional view of family-school relationships is that in which parents function as liaisons between the child and the program. They interpret and in some cases help to maintain goals and activities the child has experienced. They provide a communication link between home and school, teacher and child, society and family. As they fulfill this role, they become informed and experienced in managing these interfaces, generally to the child's benefit. They learn to examine the needs and priorities of each and to determine how to help one or the other in achieving particular goals. The teacher who, at a conference, points out the child's interest in counting and the parent who informs a director about the child's previous school experience are maintaining a continuity between home and school that supports the educational process.

Formal programs in which parents serve as liaisons are seldom described in the literature. It might be more appropriate to say that families are encouraged to attend to this role by particular supportive individuals, either friends or family members or school-related or other professionals. Nevertheless, some programs do consciously support parents in the role of child or school advocate. Certainly newsletters, visits, parent meetings, parent-teacher conferences, and the use of other family resources are attempts to teach parents the value of "being involved" from outside of the school setting. This would apply to regular help with teachers' assignments and requests as well as communicating any concerns or impressions of family members about the school program. For the very young child, the parents' exchanges regarding adjustments and care-giving needs are vital to the program. So are any consequences relating to new school experiences, for example, schedule changes, adjustment to the program, and fears. In specially funded or private school settings, parents often are inclined to assume this active role to be certain the child's participation is enthusiastic and beneficial.

General Parent-Support Programs

In this type of parent education the orientation is toward helping families to provide stable, nurturant, and healthy environments for children. Parent-to-parent materials are particularly important as resources for mothers and fathers in the ongoing tasks and challenges of parenthood. Information about toy buying, daycare centers, nursing, coping with predictable crises, role conflicts, parent needs, and so forth are typical of the material that is intended to aid families as they, in turn, help their children to grow and learn. In a sense, emotional and social support also are provided through such activities. Parents come to feel that they are not rearing their children in isolation, that there are people and programs to which they can turn for information and a shared sense of the challenges and satisfactions of child and family development.

Programs designed to facilitate parent-to-parent relationships, provide family resources, and promote healthy family functioning are often rather independent from a host agency or school. A coordinator may arrange for reading resources, space, use of a telephone, and mailings but the parents themselves are expected to contribute significantly to the design, content, and conduct of the program. They may borrow heavily from the school, using staff and curriculum suggestions that are closely tied to the children's program. Or they may pursue content more related to home and family matters and may arrange their own workshops, meetings, or rap groups. The results of these activities can be expected to have a positive effect on the child, family, and school. The sense of support that parents can feel when schools share their resources and value their families enough to help them build a network of friendships can be expected to produce a good deal of commitment to the child's education. The information that may be provided also should serve an important educational role, especially when it is sifted through the feelings and knowledge base of other parents.

Child care programs are in some sense another example of parent support, whether or not there is a formal set of parent-oriented arrangements. Working families rely upon daycare and nursery school staff for a variety of child and family assistance. This would include health care guidelines and advice on child learning and behavior as well as the capacity for detecting and remediating any early development or social difficulties. Centers are meeting places for mothers and fathers and sources of new playmates for children. Parents are relieved of child care responsibilities for part of the day and are freed to attend to their own personal and economic needs. The children's center thus provides parent support as a byproduct of its child care/educational role. Staff members can expand this function markedly if they arrange for parents to meet regularly with one another or utilize resources that keep them informed about common interests.

Parent Counseling

Children who are at high risk for developmental problems and family members who are not able to parent their children successfully may need a parent-education program that provides some counseling. The degree of therapeutic value of any type of program tends to be significant for at least some families, so it is sometimes difficult to separate the two. Counseling is needed, however, for mothers and fathers who cannot manage their infants or young children, as determined either by their behavior as witnessed by others or by their own feelings about themselves and their children.

To be sure, parent counseling is a process both of education and therapy. In some cases, teachers, principals, child care workers, and others are quite skilled in bringing about successful changes in parents' feelings and behaviors, just through sympathy and information. Attention to parents' concerns, paired with a few simple insights about normal child development and typical family pressures, are often effective buffers between minor problems and the need for a full psychotherapy program. Such simple forms of family counseling most likely occur during the normal course of the child's progress through school. An organized program is somewhat more difficult to implement. Groups of parents might meet with teachers, while individuals could arrange confidential discussions on a regular basis. However, the more serious counseling needs of families do require mental health professionals. In some situations specialized services could be conducted by agencies outside of the school setting. This appears to be especially appropriate for high-risk or problem families, for very young parents, and for any mother or father who feels unable to provide nurturance and guidance to children. In any program, though, the educational element of parent counseling helps parents to understand and work effectively with the child and gain in personal and family development as well.

THE EFFECTIVENESS OF PARENT EDUCATION

When parents are involved in educational and support programs it is expected that there will be positive outcomes for both the child and the family. That is, children's development and the family's well-being are thought to be enhanced by this type of activity. Proving that this is indeed the case, however, has been somewhat problematic. The relationship between what the program contributes and how parents and children react is not very clear. We do not know, for example, how parents use the information they may acquire to help their child. Often subtle shifts in mothers' and fathers' attitudes and understandings, produced at least partly through programs, cannot be detected. Results may be far reaching yet elusive for the professional or the parent to identify on such evaluation measures as questionnaires, behavior scales, or observations of child-rearing activities.

The outcomes of programs are to a certain extent taken on faith. Somehow common sense, professional judgment, and testimony from parents, when combined with some research evidence and the current social policy, all serve to convince participants that their efforts are worthwhile. In the end what develops in the field is a set of beliefs or theories that influence programs, many of which have emerged from practical experience as well as research. In this section some specific evidence and current conceptions of effective program procedures will be explored to identify both the achieved and potential outcomes of parent programs.

Research on Parent Programs

The most frequently reported outcomes of early child-parent programs consist of direct gains in *children's* development, intelligence, achievement, and socioemotional well-being (Beller, 1979; Brown, 1978); that is, greater gains for children have been associated with parent involvement in their preschool (see Table 1). In these situations activities for parents may be conducted concurrently with the children's program or parents may be present in the program itself. Such approaches have been associated recently with the early childhood intervention projects of the 1960s and 1970s. In a report of evaluation studies of twenty-eight preschool educational programs for children that also involved work with parents, preschoolers emerged

Table 1
Summary of Research Findings on Potential Benefits of Parent-Education Programs

	Areas of Improvement	*Supporting Reference*
BENEFITS FOR CHILDREN	Intelligence Achievement Well-Being	Beller, 1979; Brown, 1978; Goodson & Hess, 1978
	Grades Adjustment	Goodson & Hess, 1978
	Perception & thought Task completion Independence Self-Concept	Cochran & Brassard, 1979
	Language Curiosity & resourcefulness Cooperation Home environment	Stevens, 1978
	Family mental health	Croake & Glover, 1977
BENEFITS FOR PARENTS	Family management Emotional relief	Cataldo & Salzer, 1982
	Attitudes & effectiveness	Croake & Glover, 1977
	Supportive information	Powell, 1978; Stevens, 1978
	Career development	Gordon et al., 1979; Zigler & Valentine, 1979
	Marital satisfaction	Belsky & Steinberg, 1978
	Extended social relations	Galinsky & Hooks, 1977
BENEFITS FOR SCHOOLS AND AGENCIES	Fewer grade retentions Fewer remedial classes	Lazar et al., 1977
	Home-school relations Community involvement	Gordon et al., 1979; Zigler & Valentine, 1979
	Planning for child	Lillie et al., 1977
	Child-adult relations	Croake & Glover, 1977

with both immediate and long-term advantages in school-related skills (Goodson & Hess, 1978). Higher intelligence, achievement, grades, grade placement, and teachers' ratings of social adjustment were associated with parent as well as child programing. The evidence seems to suggest that parent participation increases the power of the early educational experience to contribute to the child's growth. In their discussion of family networks, Cochran and Brassard (1979) enumerate developmental outcomes for children that appear to be mediated by parents, including (1) intellectual gains (perception, task completion, thinking) and (2) social benefits (attachment, independence, role expectations, self-concept). Stevens (1978) also reports studies that have documented parent program effects upon children's cognitive functioning, language development, curiosity, cooperation, and resourcefulness.

Developmental benefits for children, which seem in many cases to be quite significant, thus appear to be associated with relationships between the program and the parent, whether the family is actively involved in the child's activities or attends meetings or consultations apart from the children's program. Regardless of the procedure used, parent and child are both targeted for treatment in these activities. Parent-child program effects appear to indicate that the mother or father is able to support the child's learning more effectively when there is a formalized relationship to the school. Perhaps the parent adopts one or more roles already described, for example, serving as a more effective liaison in helping the child to generalize school learning to the home, or participating regularly in school and becoming familiar with the child's curriculum. Parents may gain information that helps them deal more effectively with the child's behavior at home or in school, or they may feel a general sense of support from program professionals that, in turn, improves their attitudes about taking their children to special community events or reading nightly to them. Each of these kinds of program results may appear to be rather small or isolated, but there is a potential for extending the parent's activities with the child beyond that first success into a pattern of more educational child-rearing practices at home.

Indirect effects on children resulting from parent education that is conducted apart from child-centered programs also are reported. Some parents make observable changes in the home environment, such as the provision of play materials, stimulation, and a warm emotional climate for the children; and they also may be observed to use more complex language or to be more aware of their child's unique characteristics (Stevens, 1978). In programs where parents learn to handle children's needs and behaviors better, the mental health of the family may be improved (Croake & Glover, 1977). The same may be true for parent education that results in "more favorable" parent attitudes. The linkages are indirect in these situations, but children do seem to be helped when their parents are recipients of parent education, even if they themselves are not enrolled in a program or school.

Some *parent* benefits resulting from parent programs have been documented as well (see Table 1). Certainly the family's own development and the support provided to individual mothers and fathers are important factors for the child over the long run. Daycare and nursery-school programs, by definition, are helpful to parents simply by virtue of their assisting in the care of children. Parents' career development has been improved by programs such as Head Start and Follow Through (Gordon et al., 1979; Sigel, Secrist, & Forman, 1972), possibly because parents were provided with free time for making social contacts. In middle-class families, parents have reported that they are better able to manage their time and that they feel a sense of emotional relief when their infants and young children attend a preschool program (Cataldo & Salzer, 1982). Improvements in parents' attitudes toward their children and their effectiveness in managing children's behavior have been associated with those group parent-education programs using specific techniques (Croake & Glover, 1977). Younger parents or those less experienced may particularly profit from parent education (Stevens, 1978), although parents do appear to respond differently to various types of program strategies (Powell, 1978). Satisfaction in marriage and improved family economics also have been associated with successful child care experiences (Belsky & Steinberg, 1978), and improved social relations have been noted that are akin to those experienced in an extended family (Galinsky & Hooks, 1977).

Finally, the *schools* and *agencies* in which children are enrolled tend to benefit from conducting programs for parents, even though there may be some initial costs in time and money (see Table 1). Improvement in the child's achievements does tend to credit the school's activities, the assumption being that they are responsible. If this results in fewer grade retentions and special remedial classes this is also very cost effective over the long run. This has been the case for one special group of early intervention programs (Lazar, Hubbell, Murray, Rosche, & Royce, 1977). Better home-school relationships have been documented, as have improvements in the schools and communities during the Follow Through experience in the early primary years (Gordon et al., 1979). Better adjustment by parents to their child's handicap through more appropriate expectations and planning has also occurred through such programs (Lillie et al., 1977). Children's improved behavior with parents likewise has been seen to occur in the school as well as home setting (Croake & Glover, 1977).

The notion, then, of mutual gains for children, families, and educational programs through the participation of parents is a rather convincing one, possibly for political and social reasons as much as from this research evidence.

The issue of how to ensure or maximize the effectiveness of programs for parents, on the basis of research and experience, has been addressed by Stevens (1978) and others. However, the research base is considered to be very weak (Clarke-Stewart, 1981), primarily because studies typically fail to provide control groups and tend to use unclear evaluation measures. Nevertheless, Stevens (1978), Honig (1975), Goodson & Hess (1978), and others point to particular characteristics of programs that appear to be related to effectiveness, defined socially as well as in terms of documented outcomes. These include flexible structures, sensitive staff members, and responsiveness to parental need.

Current Beliefs about Parent Programs

At this point in the history of school-related programs for parents there is enough accumulated knowledge to form a set of beliefs about the content, structure, and potential outcomes of programs. These beliefs, in turn, serve as guidelines for those who design and implement programs (Cataldo, 1980).

1. One basic belief is that the family is considered to be an important part of early education or treatment programing. Mothers especially are considered to be monitors of the child's growth; the staff, therefore, has to develop some strategies for including, teaching, or counseling the mother of the child in the program. The father also may be involved in family-oriented programs.
2. A related belief is that cross-communication between staff and family is expected to result in greater support for the program and more carry-over of particular learning techniques from center to home.
3. Involving parents throughout the entire preschool period is expected to increase and extend the program benefits beyond the time the child is actually enrolled. This is thought to result in continued advantages among program children over nonprogram children on measures such as achievement, intelligence, and social-emotional well-being.
4. The triangular relationship involving the parent, child, and professional is believed to serve as a supportive system wherein each assists the other to the child's ultimate benefit. That is, where the relationships work well there are informational, educational interactions that help children to proceed more adequately through developmental stages.
5. A related belief is that the professional is an accessible and positive resource for parents. His or her training and expertise can be tapped by the family so that the parenting experience remains beneficial to the child.
6. In terms of the program's structure, it is believed by many practitioners

that a multidisciplinary team staff approach ensures that the program will take account of more of the child's and family's needs than might otherwise be the case. This is especially true for the very early infant and toddler years and the child from a high-risk family, where medical, social, and mental health professionals can help the educator to manage a multifaceted and comprehensive program.

7. In terms of strategies there appears to be a strong faith in the use of both demonstration and discussion in working with families. Whether parents are group members or have individual conferences, a great deal of information and support seems to be transmitted appropriately through these two methods.

8. The structure of the program has to reflect a balance between fixed procedures that guide the participants and flexibility that enables particular mothers, fathers, children, and staff members to expand on their strengths and attend to their needs.

THE TRIAD: CHILD, FAMILY, AND PROFESSIONALS

In children's early years of life and of schooling, the interactions between significant adults who teach and care for them are important. Each person in this triangle of relationships, including the child, has an effect upon the other. When the child, parent, and school or program staff person are able to communicate with, teach, and support one another, then it is expected that the child's development and the well-being of the family and school will all be enhanced. In other words, each element of the triangle has the potential to influence the other positively. This is the hope of most authorities who work to create and implement programs. In a sense, the child-parent-professional triad is a theoretical model of mutual interaction, one in which each can gain information and support from the others and give some in return. The exchanges then create a system that aids the child's development because it eases problems, adds opportunities, enhances learning, and builds supporting links between helping adults and children's developmental and personal needs.

Emerging theory about these relationships has only recently been described (Bronfenbrenner, 1979; Cataldo, 1980; Cochran & Brassard, 1979; Gray & Wandersman, 1980). In the next generation of primarily school-based parent programs, important aspects of family, school, and child relationship should become more clearly articulated. At this point, however, there are tentative theoretical statements that can be made about parents in relation to programs and about professional-parent interaction. There are also some important continuing questions concerning the relationship between the educational establishment and the family and child.

Parents and Programs

Programs attempt to educate and support, yet the information and attitudes that come from various activities may or may not be received by family members and integrated into family life. There are several factors influencing the family's receptivity. Some of these are parental attitudes and value systems, the general life situations of families, parents' feelings about the particular child, and the nature of the program itself. These affective and social states and the relevance of the particular programs to families will affect the parents' and children's interest and acceptance of the program's content and underlying philosophy. Some parents, for example, have strong prejudices about the child's toilet training or obedience to rules. Other families may be preoccupied with economic problems or they may be concerned about other children in the family. A program that is able to relate to the state of a particular family has a greater potential for maintain-

ing parents' motivation than one that cannot adjust itself to these competing factors.

Parents' needs and interests serve as a foundation for programs. Where the content and style of parent education, involvement, or support fit the existing knowledge and concerns of family members, the program is more likely to be effective. Young parents, middle-class families, and inner-city mothers and fathers all have particular needs that programs can build upon. Where professionals are able to address these interests in a meaningful way, there is a better chance of success and progress for the program. Sometimes a needs assessment takes the form of a questionnaire, but attentive, sensitive staff members who are attuned to individual families also will be able to suggest adjustments in the program to fit these needs. The culture, lifestyle, and existing social supports also influence the parent-program relationship. Families each have a unique identity that is tied to a cultural milieu. The lifestyle developed in a given family has to be treated respectfully, or the program will create stress or be rejected by the parents. In situations where cultural priorities serve as constructive influences on the child or where they are neutral, the program staff will need to hold them in regard. Examples such as religious observances, diet, and certain styles of family interaction and neighborhood activities apply here. Other negative culturally derived child-rearing practices, such as lack of language exchange or extremes of physical discipline, have to be treated cautiously, to bring about changes that are more beneficial to the child.

Physical characteristics of the home and neighborhood also contribute to parents' interest and ability to respond to program ideas and suggestions. In congested or high-crime neighborhoods, for example, parents may need to restrict their children; in crowded homes or buildings there is less tolerance for robust play. Families have to develop appropriate standards for their children in these situations, and professionals will need to be mindful of these constraints. Theories of parent-program relationships also must account for unique family problems and the strengths that influence mothers and fathers. Marital difficulties on the one hand and special family traditions on the other are examples of highly individualistic and variable elements that affect the program, making it more or less difficult to establish a productive working relationship.

Professionals and Programs

On the other side of the family-program relationship, the professional staff person fulfills an oftentimes significant role in relation to parents and children. The program structure and content may be more or less prescribed, but the particular parent educator or coordinator is on the front line of responsibility in any program. He or she represents the school or agency and is accountable for the progress of relationships with mothers and fathers. A theory of these influences has to consider that the competence and sensitivity of the professional (and other program staff members), as expressed in attitudes and behaviors with the family, are qualities that often play a major role in the effectiveness of the program. Yet this is one of the most difficult elements to control in the design of a program. Clear policies, frequent self-examination, and an appropriate sense of respect and humility may serve as safeguards in maintaining the competence and sensitivity of the professional. Parents' own feedback about their educators also helps.

Authority relationships are, theoretically, two-way avenues in the interactions between parents and staff members. That is, mothers and fathers have power and decision-making responsibilities over their own family behaviors, and professionals have similar control over their programs. Yet, programs are full of suggestions, advice, and sometimes pressure for change. The nature of these power relationships among participants is not always clear, yet they will influence the conduct and progress of any program. Especially in relation to schools and with high-risk or problem families, these areas of authority have to be made clear. Similarly, the activities that make up the content and procedures in programs also should be articulated. These specifics will be more or less usable in relation to their match with three elements: the parents' concerns, children's real needs, and the capabilities of particular professionals. One example of a frequently discussed topic is child behavior. In developing material on this topic, then, the programmer would want to account for parents' views of causes of behavior, children's developmental stage with respect to the ability to control behavior, and the educational, medical, psychological, and other background of the professional who would address the subject according to his or her experience.

Continuing Questions

As programs for parents, particularly in educational settings, continue to gain in popularity, several important issues can be expected to emerge. One is the question of the knowledge base to be used by the professional. The child development, early care and early education, and family relations literature is unclear with respect to the subject of effective parenting styles. It may be that some practices are tied to enhanced child development, yet each family has the right and responsibility to raise children in ways those parents deem appropriate. The family's educational mandate is a broader one than that of the schools. Parents have to teach values, living styles, coping skills, expectations, and relationships to other ideals far beyond those that are taught by schools. These lines are more blurred in the early years than at any other time, but the issue is just as relevant then. The continuing challenge to the professional is to find the areas of concern for each family that interface with the goals of parents and professionals, while still serving as the child's advocate in situations where these areas are confused. A related issue concerns the parenting images established by the limited research on child-rearing. The professional has to serve as a liaison between this information and the strengths of individual families. To attempt to reshape homes and parental behaviors without questioning the adequacy or appropriateness of the models used would be to limit rather than expand the options of parents in creating a good home environment.

The multidisciplinary nature of activity in this field, while it is very useful and relevant, also contributes to confusion in the advice offered by professionals, each of whom has a different point of view. Parents and staff members will need to resolve some of these discrepancies and understand the underlying reasons for them. Related to this is the issue of differences in training received by various members of a program staff. Few educators today are skilled in working with parents. It is important to the validity of any program that the limitations of the professional or the minimal experience of staff members be openly expressed. In attempting to make the program as effective as possible, professionals also have to resist pressures to do what is most expedient. Sometimes the responsibility for change is inappropriately placed upon the parent, when it is the staff member whose own ability and development is at issue. Pressures for observable results, therefore, will have to be examined and realistic expectations for each participant clarified. At present, people are often uncertain about what outcomes are expected. With increased experience, our goals for programs will be more clearly established.

Finally, perhaps the most basic continuing question in the child-parent-professional relationship concerns a definition of the realm of early education programs for parents. If the child's education—before, during, and after school—and the expansion of our relationships to parents are both considered to be within the educator's domain, then we will need to examine our roles closely. We all have the child's interests at heart, yet our abilities and dispositions will have to be tempered by concern and careful consideration of our proper sphere of influence in relation to the families we serve. In the years ahead professionals and parents will need to study their places in helping children grow up competent and healthy. In order to avoid the power struggles that can occur among those who care about children, we will require a cooperative and sensitive framework from which to operate our parent-education programs.

PROGRAM SUGGESTIONS

1. Describe the history of parent education as it pertains to programs for young children and families. Ask parents to remember their own impressions of parent groups, the PTA, or similar experiences.
2. Introduce the types of programs, using the material in this chapter. Try to illustrate each approach with an example from the local community.
3. Compare general parent education with one other type of program, using details from this section of the text. Try to bring in some of the materials referred to in these descriptions, and ask parents to check their own libraries for information.
4. Have the parents observe and participate in a preschool program if they have not already done so. Talk about the special value of this kind of parent education.
5. Present Table 1, showing the research findings for parent programs in the early years. Talk about the child, parent, and school benefits, and ask parents to add their own perceptions to each of these.
6. Prepare a brief talk concerning the beliefs about parent programs as these are presented in the text. Which ones seem particularly relevant to your situation?
7. Describe the child-parent-professional triad. In a round-robin discussion ask parents to focus on one set of relationships at a time, adding any personal anecdotes they wish.
8. Talk about the issues presented as Continuing Questions at the end of the chapter. Which seem particularly important for the future?

2

Inside the Family: Relationships and Parenting Skills

What is a family? Definitions tend to include the areas of family membership (kinship), bonds between people, and family functions. Even though a great many skills, interpersonal relationships, and general living styles of families have changed over the years, the basic elements of the family unit appear to have remained the same. The most characteristic family grouping is that of parents and children, related to one another, who live with and take care of each other. These persons remain at the core of any family description, even considering the variations that apply to particular situations. For professionals who work with today's families, membership and definition are less important than other issues such as health and schooling, overall development, and social relationships. In this chapter, some background information on family organization is provided, with the major emphasis on relationships and parenting skills inside the family. The requirements of mothers and fathers in rearing children will be discussed in detail. Social interactions and emotional exchanges among family members also will be described as part of the dynamics of life within the family.

FAMILY ORGANIZATION AND FUNCTION

The nuclear family may continue to serve as an ideal that reflects long-standing traditions, but such a structural grouping is not characteristic of many families. Changing lifestyles, divorce patterns, and other social trends have contributed to alterations of at least the appearance of the family. Authorities such as Keniston (1977) have described the pressures upon this child-rearing unit, but there also appears to be a sufficient degree of flexibility and strength in the majority of today's families, whatever their composition, to make them more capable than is often acknowledged.

Family Types

Where the two-parent, several-children, one-home family does exist, family organization may vary from traditional roles in working, child care, and home maintenance to that involving two careers and shared daycare and housekeeping roles. In either case, the nuclear family continues to provide an ideal. Beyond this core, parents may have social networks with other mothers and fathers who may be friends, neighbors, associates, or actual family members. Some arrangements even vary from year to year within the traditional nuclear grouping.

One type of family that appears to be declining in comparison with others is the extended family, where kin, closely related by blood, are actively involved in daily child rearing and home management and are living with or near parents and children. This network of help and support has been credited with making such families appear to be quite independent and self-reliant, able to find resources within themselves for meeting the needs of their members. Today, families tend to live a great distance from relatives. Even though extended families do exist, their definition as a type of grouping is less common. Nevertheless, some authorities do consider communes of unrelated families, affiliated groups of neighborhood parents and children, daycare associates, and networks of other service providers or friends to be substitutes for actual extended families. Organizations of parents with common interests—such as childbirthing associations, handicapped children's groups, parent-education or neighborhood societies, and even groupings of childless couples—are considered to be a form of extended family that is, in many ways, more appropriate to contemporary living.

The most rapidly increasing type of family today appears to be that of the single parent, father or mother, as head of the household. Whether through divorce, death, economic arrangement, or nonmarried status, parents who rear children without a spouse or partner are members of a larger group than ever before. In terms of parenting skills and relationships, the single mother or father fulfills a complex and often difficult series of roles with respect to children and home maintenance. The work-versus-home dichotomy presents a special challenge for single parents, since responsibilities for nurturance and education of the children are no longer shared.

Along with the increase in single-parent homes, especially those due to divorce, there has been a corresponding rise in reconstituted, blended, or otherwise modified families in which one family unit joins another unit or single person. Children thus may be legally rather than biologically related to parents and to each other. The tasks of child rearing are complicated by newly formed ties and emotional-social exchanges in which each person has to adjust to unfamiliar behaviors and values. Where grandparents are part of the household, the child and mother or father have additional historical traditions with which to deal. The rejoined family also has the opportunity for consciously setting standards and priorities, deliberately assigning roles that appear to influence positively the education and nurturance of the children.

Households in which unrelated children are provided with care are considered by some as another type of family unit. Foster homes, family-style daycare, and some adoptive homes may contain the well-known family constellation of parents and children, but the child may not be a permanent member of the family. These temporary arrangements provide unique challenges for the care and development of children, even though the adults are expected to function for the most part like a typical family. In fact, many children are helped a good deal by spending some time in these settings. Such parents often fulfill a commitment to launching youngsters toward good adoptive homes. They also may be quite professional in their teaching and supporting skills while they also provide loving care. Growing up in these homes is a major experience for a significant number of children, and these families may be as important as their blood relations in helping them to grow up.

Family Functions

Those who have studied the family tend to acknowledge at least four major functions or responsibilities that concern children. First, families must provide care, nurturance, and protection for their children. These obligations begin prior to birth in the form of nutrition, prenatal medical care, and social-economic preparedness for the infants' membership in the family. This physically oriented function is a basic right of the child as citizen; when care and protection cannot be guaranteed, society has an obligation to provide it through various child and family welfare programs.

The child's socialization to the values and roles held by the family is the family's second major purpose. Concepts of rights and responsibilities, cultural standards, and other contributions are expected to be transmitted from society to its youngest citizens by way of families and schools. The attitudes and behaviors of children are assumed, to a large extent, to reflect this process by the time the youngster reaches maturity. Where family-society conflicts in values occur, the socialization of children may be confused, sometimes leading to long-term problems in adjustment.

A third function of the family is to assist and monitor the child's development as a learner, and to provide preparation for schooling. Parents help children in early infancy to acquire a wide variety of skills, abilities, and understandings. Parents inform and guide their young over many years, and even though the nature of the learning changes with each stage, the family can support the child's progress along this broad educational continuum.

The fourth family function that is especially valuable for children as individuals is the support given to each youngster's growth into a well-rounded emotionally healthy person. The acquisition of unique qualities and the development of a distinct personal-social style can not be taken for granted; societies depend upon mentally healthy citizens. The youngster's ultimate contribution to his or her culture may rest, to a certain extent, on such human qualities and on the resulting attitudes that reflect a sense of meaning and purpose within the culture. (See later section on Parenting Skills.)

More detailed discussions regarding the functions of the family would include several other purposes not as directly related to children. Leichter's (1975) book on the family's role as educator includes differing analyses, such as the legal, economic, religious, institutional, structural, and interactional functions of families. Smart and Smart (1976) refer to the reproductive and economic purposes of family units. Their strands of family life include spouses' partnerhood, sibling interactions, domestic chores, health and planning, and managing crises. Bigner (1979) describes the meanings of parenthood within the family that are related to functions such as moral and civic responsibilities, natural life processes, sexual identity, and human and instrumental needs.

In relation to schools, Lightfoot (1978) argues that families' educational functions extend far beyond those of teachers. Parents help their children to learn values, attitudes, and information in keeping with their own heritage, culture, and lifestyle. Katz (1981) has specifically highlighted these differences between parenting and teaching in explaining how families create very personal, emotional, and biased learning experiences. Children are thought to benefit from these different treatments at home and school. In a rather political book concerning fathers, Biller and Meredith (1974) emphasize the differences in how each parent contributes to the child-rearing process. Their view of family roles as determined by a mother-father balance of power is a reminder that family responsibilities to children include more than the mother's monitoring and control. The unit tends to require both adults in order to fulfill its obligations.

PARENTING AS A ROLE

When adults bring children into their dyadic partnership, there are several issues and changes that they encounter. The choice of becoming a family, the process of adjusting to the parenting role, and the complexity of many strands of family life reflect only some of their many new responsibilities.

According to Erikson's (1950) theories, wanting to become a parent is a part of the human maturation process. In his text, Bigner (1979) includes this view as one of three explanations for assuming the parenting role. Erikson's stage of generativity encompasses adults' desires to teach and care for others. Bigner (1979) describes Veevers' social meanings of parenthood as well, where six distinct reasons for having children include moral obligation, civic obligation, acceptance of one's gender, marital satisfaction, maturity and mental health, and natural inclination. Rabin's (1965) four reasons for parenthood fall into other categories. One is fatalism, a view in which people believe they exist in order to have children or to extend the family name. Altruism accounts for affectionate and unselfish reasons for having children. The adult who wants to be needed, who desires a sense of adult fraternity and emotional security from a desired object has narcissistic motivations. And the instrumental explanation describes child rearing as a way of achieving goals, pleasing parents, repairing relationships, obtaining power, and having a second chance to grow up.

On the other hand Smart and Smart's (1976) book contains a discussion of deterrents to reproduction as well as satisfactions that influence the child-rearing decision. Restrictions of freedom, economic expenses, fears regarding the ability to parent well and maintain a marriage, concern with overpopulation and lack of social support, the complications of relationships, and the permanency of this role are all considered to be more or less appropriate reasons for delaying or declining to take on the role of parent. Satisfactions, on the other hand, serve as motivations and rewards for having offspring. The status of the role, fulfillment of family duty, and feelings of immortality, purpose, and pride in bearing young are reasons for becoming a parent. Closer relationships with family members, a richer marital life, enjoyment of the child, appreciation of one's own parents, and personal growth through parenthood are also benefits associated with the role.

Once a man or woman elects to become a parent, or otherwise finds that children are about to become a part of his or her personal life, the process of adapting to the role becomes important. Parent-advice books in large numbers often address these needs for seeking methods of adjusting to and planning for the rearing of children. Certainly, husbands and wives each have a history of their own experiences and a current set of ideas and cultural standards that help to guide them. Authorities in child development, social work, psychology, and health care tend to support the notion of providing parents with information and advice, especially during their initial adjustment to the role. Others feel that parents need a stronger sense of faith in themselves, in their ability to adapt and respond to their baby in their own way. Although all materials published for parents typically contain statements of encouragement in addition to information and advice, Brazelton's (1981) text on the family specifically deals with the adjustment of parent and child to each other. The philosophy is one that attempts to free parents from the pressure of perfection, to acknowledge the role of natural inclinations to nurture, and to examine the child's preparedness to respond to this. Brazelton describes normal frustrations that must occur in order for parents to learn important skills. His view is that the essence of parenting lies in the exchanges between adult and child, rather than the specific actions taken. Living with a range of feelings results in a healthy balance of them, so that success becomes quite special. Brazelton refers to this as a process of adaptation.

Contemporary parents deserve this emphasis on gradual accommodation, physical and emotional, to child rearing. The self-consciousness of mothers and fathers, their recent diligence in developing their own skills and understanding of children's growth and feelings, may create a preoccupation with acquiring competence at the expense of building the emotional bonds and rewards of becoming a parent. Both need emphasis. In addition, parents must nurture their own development and interests. Accounting for these many factors requires sensitivity and comprehensiveness in working with families.

It also may be important to acknowledge the many strands of family life that impinge upon mothers and fathers, aside from their relationships with the child. Indeed, demands upon time and resources made by basic requirements for living may overshadow what takes place during personal interaction. A glance at any text on family life reveals an array of time demands, including domestic chores, economic responsibilities, and family crises. Such concerns were documented recently in preparation for the White House Conference on the Family in 1980, when State Conferences were held to generate and gather ideas and concerns about topics relating to family life. In New York State (Margolin, 1980) these included families and the economy, the workplace, housing and community, child care and growth, health, special needs, schools, ethnic and cultural diversity, changes in family life, and stress and crisis. It is apparent that any of these could create difficulties for mothers and fathers, whether or not they acquire extensive skills in management and child development. Parenting thus has to be viewed within a matrix of concerns about maintaining the family unit, especially those issues related to work and adult relationships; and it must be understood as a lengthy and complicated process that taxes any adult.

PARENTING SKILLS

Given the diversity of tasks facing parents within their families and the need for developing competence in rearing children, the subject of parenting skills becomes very relevant. It is important to identify the areas in which parents can, and probably will, gain expertise as children grow from infancy through middle childhood. (See Chapters 6 and 7 for details on child care and play.)

Overview of Areas of Parenting Skills

There are six basic areas of parenting skills. The two that are most familiar are the provision of basic physical care and protection and the modeling of a healthy family life. These roles in family life have always been viewed as necessary to the welfare of the young, and they will be discussed here in relation to the growth of the infant and young child. In socializing the child, the family interprets and supports cultural values that are expressed in attitudes and behaviors modeled for the children. From the point of view of society, this is an essential role assumed by parents; in the early childhood years such competencies have special features.

The third area of parenting skills, somewhat related to the early socializing function of the family, is the successful management of intrafamily behavior. In the social and behavioral sciences, parent counseling and education have focused upon helping children to learn impulse control and responsible behavior toward others. Establishing rational parent-child relationships in the home is considered basic to supporting the mental health of family members. In developing these skills, families are expected to cope more effectively with conflict situations and handle behavior with added success. Adjustments to the young child are needed because of immaturity in communication, anticipation and control, and the strategies suggested for parents in this section can help them develop useful skills along these lines.

The fourth area of parenting skills is the strong, positive influence upon the young child of consistent, rational, affectionate, parental sensitivity and responsiveness to emotional and social needs. This tends to be associated with children's capacities for relating to others and using their experience in understanding and learning about the world. Parental responsiveness also influences competence and the family's overall effectiveness.

The other two of our six parenting skill areas have received attention only recently. These are parental management of the child's activities and educational needs, and family use of community resources and schools, especially in the capacity of liaison and advocate for the child. In the early childhood years, parents are the primary organizers of the child's time at home. They arrange play opportunities and respond to the child's needs for stimulation and learning, the acquisition of language, the accumulation of information, and the development of achievement motivation. Parents also need to serve as advocates for their young children in the world outside the home. They negotiate for services and manage the child's recreational, child care, and schooling experiences. Such activities have the potential for influencing the child's welfare during and beyond the early years.

In the sections that follow, specific parenting skills will be described in each of the six areas that have been identified. These six areas and their corresponding skills are summarized in Table 2. Awareness of these should be very helpful in understanding how mothers and fathers orchestrate daily life with young children.

Table 2
Parenting Skills in the Family with Young Children

PROVIDING BASIC PHYSICAL CARE AND PROTECTION

Food & shelter	Child care & supervision
Home management & enrichment	Teaching self-care

MODELING A HEALTHY FAMILY LIFE

Positive models	Teaching human relations
Family recreation	Values clarification & decisions

PARENTAL MANAGEMENT OF BEHAVIOR

Balancing needs	Preventing conflict
Realistic limits	Adult supports

SENSITIVE ATTENTION TO EMOTIONAL AND SOCIAL NEEDS

Comfort & regard	Involvement & interest
Problem resolution	Peer friendships

MANAGEMENT OF ACTIVITIES AND EDUCATION

Providing opportunities	Information & skill development
Organizing activity	Play involvement

FAMILY USE OF COMMUNITY RESOURCES AND SCHOOLS

Use of resources	Seeking special services
Program involvement	Home-community support

Providing Basic Physical Care and Protection

Parent competence in the area of child care and protection includes the provision of safe shelter, food, clothing, health care, and alternative child care. It encompasses home management, or the organization, maintenance, and enrichment of the home. In the early years parents also must teach basic self-care skills and safety to their young children as a part of their protective function.

In materials designed to advise parents and child care professionals, specific mention is often made of the potential for family stress to occur in response to many normal needs and behaviors of infants and preschoolers. Young children are physically robust and egocentric in their relations with others. They explore their environment and engage in activities that are age-appropriate but nonetheless tend to disregard considerations of safety, privacy, and property. In order to protect the child's developmental needs for some autonomy, parents are urged to provide guidance and monitor behavior in ways that still permit children to move about and express personal interests and feelings (Church, 1973; Gordon, 1976).

To ease the parents' maintenance responsibilities and allow for children's activities, child-proofing the home and arranging separate children's play spaces is frequently recommended (White, 1975). It is good to provide the means by which children can clean and care for themselves, both in homes (Gordon, 1970) and in children's centers where, for example, self-feeding and independent dressing are encouraged. The constructive use of otherwise tedious care routines is emphasized for early childhood group programs (Fowler, 1980; Willis & Riccuiti, 1975), and this can be applied at home as well. Routines can include some learning and personal growth, such as becoming familiar with labels and food concepts during mealtime conversation, learning how to put toys together during clean-up activities, and examining books or listening to music while resting. Such routines become more satisfying for children and less difficult for adults when care giving includes teaching and enjoyment.

Finding appropriate alternative child care when parents cannot be available is difficult for most families, even when extended-family members and neighbors are used. Play coops, shared home baby-sitters, and professional daycare centers and homes are additional options for the quality care of infants and preschoolers (see Chapter 6). Parents, however, are responsible for the monitoring of these, assuring a healthy and reasonably affectionate and educational experience for the child. To do so often means parents must assume an active role in determining if the care meets the child's needs.

Guidelines for health care in a variety of settings, including food and clothing, are available to parents of young children. Well-baby clinics, hospital prenatal classes, home economics courses, and visiting nurse programs help parents to learn about the child's basic care needs. Books concerned with physical growth and health also may deal with other issues such as the child's environment, parent-child relationships, illness, behavior, and so forth (Brazelton, 1969, 1976; Spock, 1976).

Modeling a Healthy Family Life

The maintenance of a healthy family unit depends partly upon how its members are able to support one another, maintain their values, and cope with stress from inside and outside the unit. Parents shape their children's lives by modeling patterns of affect and behavior for them (Church, 1973). Parents also make decisions about the values they adopt and use with their young. Parents' demonstrations of positive attitudes, their caring and affection, their pursuit of family interests that include children, their consistent rules, their uses of cultural values, and their rational approaches to problems all contribute to a healthy style of living with children.

Modeling is a powerful form of learning for the youngster, who can often be seen following the parent around, observing the details of daily living, and soaking in parents' general attitudes and style. Babies, for example, mirror their parents' moods (Willemsen, 1979); toddlers repeat words and gestures as they learn to talk; and preschoolers reproduce extended patterns of their parents' and siblings' behaviors. Prosocial behavior is learned partly from adult and peer models and partly from their expectations (Mussen & Eisenberg-Berg, 1977). Energetic, encouraging parents who model pleasure in their children, appear to have well-developed, competent preschoolers (White & Watts, 1973).

When young children copy others, duplicating patterns they observe, they are not always able to discriminate the positive from the negative. They may adopt the worst as well as the best of what they experience because they cannot judge the difference. Programs for parents in the early years can often help to emphasize the need for appropriate models of caring, rationality, and mutual respect. How a family's style and support system influence the small child is under examination in recent child-development literature (Cochran & Brassard, 1979). It is clear, however, that the home context provides the child with a set of attitudes and patterns that are carried into school and social life and that influence her or his developmental growth. Emphasizing this skill area in light of these trends may improve children's functioning over the long term.

Morality and responsibility are issues that begin to emerge in young children, even though they are only beginning to understand the perspectives of others. Nevertheless, many foundations of human relations grow from everyday experiences, since even young children have to make adjustments to the feelings and preferences of peers and adults. Sharing, taking turns, using good manners, attending to rules, and being empathic toward others are taught to the young, as are simple chores and helping. Parents thereby develop positive or prosocial patterns in children that help them to behave with kindness and consideration.

Programs and written materials on parent-child relations can help parents to explore and establish value systems as part of their family style. Values clarification programs are widely used by some professionals in helping mothers and fathers establish their priorities for handling conflicts. Recreational and educational centers that include the young child in their family activities also help parents to maintain a healthy family style.

Parental Management of Intrafamily Behavior

In the early years children are just beginning to establish some behavior control and to understand rules to which they must adhere. Overly harsh restriction and punishment do little to help family members if there is no accounting for the young child's often contradictory needs for independence and control, for learning and play. Effective parents appear to recognize that the young child gains from exploring and moving about, from resisting them and "talking back." They maintain some firm rules and institute limits gradually and gently throughout the early years (Brazelton, 1976; Carew, Chan, & Halfar, 1975; Gordon, 1975; White, 1975).

The negative side of parenting (Callahan, 1973), that of enforcing impulse control and developing responsibility, requires that adults have realistic expectations about the child's limited abilities to understand and conform (Caplan & Caplan, 1976). Recognition of these limits has to be integrated into parents' discipline strategies. The uses of freedom of movement and expression, simple presentations of rules, nonpunitive controls, an emphasis on gradual teaching, and some planning for preventing conflict, for example, are all parenting activities that account for the qualities of the young. These methods represent a humanistic, mentally healthy approach to child guidance. The consideration of parents' effects on children as a product of their behavior management is part of this approach. The use of power assertion is considered less desirable than psychological discipline that involves disapproval and explanation. Parenting modes such as firmness plus reasoning appear more effective than permissiveness or authoritarianism.

Other strategies for such behavior control have been described to parents and child professionals. The modification of the environment to make it simplified and child-proofed has already been mentioned (Gordon,

1970). Establishing systems of logical rewards and substitutes is useful in shaping difficult behavior (Dreikurs & Grey, 1970; Patterson & Gullion, 1969), as is the use of praise and an understanding of the dynamics of feeling states in families, which are integral to self-esteem models of child rearing (Babcock & Keepers, 1976). (See Chapter 8 for details.)

In early childhood and daycare programs, behavior management techniques typically emphasize (1) preventive planning for reducing frustration, (2) the use of distraction and substitution, (3) prompt attention to needs, (4) strong positive relationships with children, (5) the use of problem solving and language in resolving conflict, (6) observation in detecting maladaptive patterns, and (7) abundant supervision. Parents who observe or participate in these programs have the opportunity to witness the use of such strategies. Inviting parent observations may result in their acquisition of alternatives in handling behavior.

In families and homes, behavior management also may include the control of difficult adult behaviors related to separation, maltreatment, substance abuse, or mental illness. Sibling problems that the young child cannot begin to understand also may require attention. Such situations become crises when these behaviors reach stressful proportions. The child may be overlooked because parents are emotionally overburdened. Since behavior control is the responsibility of the parent, emotional outlets must be sought that are safe and calming. Discussion, recreation, substitute child care arrangements, and help from physicians, mental health clinics, and family members can be arranged so that parent reactions do not damage children.

Support between adults, shared responsibility for children's activities, and consistent efforts to create positive intrafamily interactions are parenting skills that may prevent or mitigate a crisis. The father's involvement in the care and play of young children has received attention recently (Biller & Meredith, 1974; Lamb, 1976) and needs further emphasis in the family. Parent discussion groups, extended family and neighborhood support systems, children's groups, and books and films on family behavior provide additional resources to parents in developing behavior guidance skills.

Sensitive Attention to Emotional and Social Needs

During the child's early years of life, the comfort, attention, regard, and understanding of parents provides a secure base of support necessary for growth and development. Parental responsivity and involvement with infants and preschoolers is thought to be related to the child's later competence and healthy behavior (Caldwell, 1970; Church, 1973; Gordon, 1975). Some specific positive behaviors that have been recommended to parents include making spontaneous vocalizations to the child, involving youngsters in playful social games, providing physical affection, and completing tasks with the child. Parents are also encouraged to recognize and value individual differences, even in babyhood, and to respond with patience and understanding when the child's temperament and style of behavior seem unique or problematic (Brazelton, 1969). The special qualities of particular children can ultimately be a source of pride to families. Immediate and patient attention by adults to distress in the early years is thought to result in healthy child development, including the establishment of trust, autonomy, and initiative (Dunn, 1977). At the toddler age level, behaviors such as resistance and negativism are seen as necessary, important aspects of personal growth. Parents are advised to balance their own and their child's needs in ways that do not negate the child's developing sense of self (Brazelton, 1976).

In programs designed to improve interaction with the very young child, parents learn to recognize emotional states and respond to the youngster's social needs through their own play involvement and the monitoring of friendships and other social contacts (Cataldo, 1980). The focus in these

efforts is often upon raising the quality of parents' emotional support for the developing child (Huntington, 1979). In group care settings, adults also are encouraged to respond to children's specific needs when they are manifested, thereby ensuring that personalized care is experienced (Beller, 1972).

Such an emphasis on individual emotional and social needs is based on notions of children's rights, which form a well-established philosophy of early child care in groups (Read & Patterson, 1980; Willis & Riccuiti, 1975). Significant adults in the life of the child also should be aware that they influence the child's behavior and development in less direct ways. Parents provide models for the young to imitate, and the appropriateness of these should be considered. For black children, special concerns have been described (Comer & Poussaint, 1975), and parents of any ethnic-cultural group have similar issues with which to deal.

When problems occur in the emotional relations between the parent and young child, spouses or other adults may need to provide relief time, a sympathetic ear, or discussion about the needs of the child. Efforts to resolve problems may require insight and sensitivity. Some guidelines for assessing these are available (Carew, 1980; Powell, 1981). In the extreme, emotional difficulties can lead to abuse, neglect, or other forms of ineffective parenting. Mothers and fathers are advised to seek assistance if they cannot resolve early negative feelings (Kempe & Kempe, 1978).

In being sensitive and understanding of children's needs, adults can increase their competence by observing other children; talking with teachers, physicians, and psychologists; and engaging in discussions with their peer parents who appear able to relate to the child's emotions. Learning to recognize the behaviors that signal emotional and social needs is part of this area of skill. Responding to them requires a positive, understanding attitude. Individual and group counseling programs with professionals who have a knowledge of both adults and young children may provide preventive and therapeutic help to families. Parent books relating to the emotional problems of the early years also can suggest alternatives in child-rearing strategies (Gesell, Ilg, & Ames, 1974; Fraiberg, 1968; LeShan, 1970; Salk & Kramer, 1969).

Management of Activities and Educational Needs

The parent is the primary educator of the child in the years before school (Gordon, 1976; Leichter, 1975). As designer of the home environment, organizer of the child's experiences, and primary source of information and support, the parent serves an essential child-development function (Church, 1973; White, 1975). Early home experiences can have long-term effects upon the child's school-related abilities (Bradley & Caldwell, 1976) and they also may influence the family in many ways. Children who learn to manage their own activities, who occupy themselves with materials and engage in imaginative games, may provide parents with a sense of esteem and success in child rearing. Certainly children's abilities to cope with home and school life may ease pressures on the family (Keniston, 1977).

The roles fulfilled by parents with respect to their children's activities include a wide range of what can be termed "educational" substance. Within the home, it is recommended that parents provide an adequate supply of playthings and encourage their use according to the child's age and stage (Caplan & Caplan, 1976; Sparling & Lewis, 1979). Media coverage of good toys for the young can be found on television and in magazines and newspapers. Experiences outside the home contribute to the child's knowledge and sociability as well (Zigler & Valentine, 1979). Parent involvement in the child's activities includes answering questions, talking about experiences, and helping to solve problems encountered in play. This information is processed by children and used to help them understand and learn from the outside world. Games are often passed on from one parent to another and between peers. Children's interests may be the subject of media specials, entertainment events, and library and museum materials.

In early childhood daycare and education programs, children's developmental needs are used as a focus for planned activities and for play. Adult involvement, support, and communication are part of this picture of experiential, day-to-day learning (Fowler, 1980; Gonzalez-Mena & Widmeyer, 1980; Willis & Riccuiti, 1975). A majority of these practices are generalizable to the home (Cataldo, 1980, 1981; Gordon, 1976).

Concrete suggestions for activities appropriate for parents and their infants and toddlers are available in books and curriculum packages designed specifically for home use (Karnes, 1979; Painter, 1971; Sparling & Lewis, 1979; Stein, 1976; Swan, 1977). In most cases, these suggestions come from research on parent-child interactions, early ability tests, educational settings, and cultural folklore. Materials are used that can be found in homes, and activities are designed to be within the limits of parental skills. Photographs and drawings supplement verbal descriptions of simple games and satisfying interactions. Learning and personal-social development are emphasized. These resources can be included in parent-education and social-support programs, to encourage constructive play activity and to emphasize family support for developmental-educational needs. The materials work well in home visits and training programs for home daycare providers, foster families, and high-risk parents. They are used extensively with young children found to be developmentally delayed, handicapped, or experiencing continuous medical difficulties.

Family Use of Community Resources and Schools

Families with children tend to require services from many community agencies and schools. For the young, dependent child, parental utilization of medical, social, and educational resources can have a significant impact on their development.

In programs designed to provide early education and remediation, parent involvement has been linked to child benefits (Goodson & Hess, 1978). This means that it is important for mothers and fathers not only to obtain services but to participate in them with the child. Single and teenage parents especially appear to require social and educational services throughout the child's early years (Sparling, Lowman, Lewis, & Bartel, 1978). In cases where there are developmental problems or handicaps, the child needs a program of early educational experiences (Tjossem, 1976) and the parent must monitor and advocate for these (Turnbull & Turnbull, 1978).

Social and educational support for the family with young children may well become an established part of educational planning (Bronfenbrenner, 1979; Cataldo, 1980). The helping professional will need to aid parents in negotiating the diverse services available in order to find an appropriate match for the child and the family. This effort becomes an important part of parent competence. During infancy, parents need to maintain consistent relationships with health and well-baby clinics as the child completes immunizations and acquires good eating habits. Later, parents will need to seek out neighborhood playmates, and nursery, Head Start, or church cooperatives for the toddler and preschooler.

A variety of educational and service programs for the young child are now available in most communities. Libraries and recreational centers might conduct parent-child programs. Schools may have facilities and staff available during and after school hours. Community centers might sponsor special events for neighborhood children. Social-work agencies may conduct parenting and home management courses, mental health facilities sometimes offer discussion groups, and stores and businesses may offer skills programs. Parents who successfully participate in these activities help the child and family rather directly and expose themselves to professionals who are alert to potential problems and can make referrals.

When parents use the resources of the community, they are in contact with other representatives of society. Such authority and helping figures play a role in child rearing that is usually complementary to that of the family. Both parents and service providers have a commitment to respecting each others' capabilities and values. If the child is to gain from the involvement of the community, all participants will have to find areas of agreement on which to base their relationship.

In all, these six areas of parenting skills reflect a complex array of tasks and responsibilities for contemporary mothers and fathers. The analysis is also a tribute to families' ability to rear children. The competencies described can also serve as anchors for programs in which one or more skills are the target of attention. Understanding the spectrum in which particular activities are imbedded helps everyone involved to maintain a balanced perspective on the demands facing parents.

FAMILY RELATIONSHIPS

There are several ongoing interpersonal relationships within every family that affect children. Parents interact with each other as well as with their youngsters. Siblings engage each other and the adults. In some respects, politics and power are a part of the family system. Individual temperaments and abilities, external pressures and supports, particular interests and styles all assume some importance during interpersonal exchanges in the home. Many of these topics are discussed in relevant sections of the text. Here, three basic relationships will be examined as they pertain to family life: parent-parent, parent-child, and child-child or sibling interactions. The emphasis is on those family dimensions bearing some similarity to the functions, roles, and skills already described.

Parent-Parent Relations

Inside the family there is often an adult couple (husband and wife) or one parent and another adult who provides companionship and assistance. This team is the organizer and manager of family life; they are the coaches, the decision makers who guide the care, nurturance, and education of the children. As a couple they are more or less in constant communication with one another, maintaining a relationship that is tied to, but also apart from, child rearing. More times than not, the spouses have an interpersonal history, extending from their courtship to the processes of setting up a household, bearing children, and helping them to grow. Their initial enjoyment of a partnership and satisfaction with one another may influence their decision to have children who can be part of an expanded family unit. The stability of the couple, the degree to which their relationship remains intact, may vary for every family. In the ideal situation, husband and wife maintain a semblance of their earlier courtship. Their exclusive love and respect nourish them in the face of child-rearing demands that drain some of their personal resources.

In reality, it is probably true that few couples proceed unscathed through the child-bearing and -rearing years. For increasing numbers of families, divorce and single parenting are more characteristic patterns than that of the stable couple who nurture their marriage as the children grow. For those who successfully navigate the stages and life hurdles that accompany child development, a legacy of interpersonal models may be provided to children. Problem solving, compromise, and commitment may well be the gift provided to youngsters in such environments. For those whose lives include major changes and shifts of feelings, authority, and residence, there may develop an understanding of human needs and frailties. Whatever the path taken by particular couples, children still tend to grow around and within shared adult relationships that dominate the home environment.

There are a variety of parent-parent styles and events that influence children and family life. Three such areas are power relationships, social networks, and stress and change. The identity of American parents has been described by Callahan (1974) as similar across families, reflecting a common effort at competence and helping one another to work together. Sociocultural parenting is as essential a part of the lives of mothers and fathers as is the biological act of producing an infant. Common sets of experiences tie people together, and this is true of parents within and among families. Parents also change in relation to one another and the child. There is a need for mutual support and turn taking within the relationship. The power of parents lies in their commitment to children, their interaction with professionals and other parents, and their ability to obtain resources needed for raising families. Parents' mutual communication, affection, and role taking in relation to children can be expected to influence family life.

Parent power relationships also have been discussed by professionals concerned with internal and external family interaction systems. Often problems between parents in their struggles with one another take the form of real or projected problems in the children. Symptoms of psychopathology are seen or created in the child that have roots in the parents' own difficulties aside from the child. In relationships between homes and schools or other agencies, parent power issues emerge in the success or failure of mothers and fathers to negotiate for services that aid the family. As parents find themselves relying upon various experts, their authority in managing the child's upbringing and education may seldom be recognized. Power relationships with children's grandparents are potential sources of conflict or satisfaction (Callahan, 1974), but they are seldom acknowledged. Fathers also may be neglected, both as resources and role models (Lamb, 1976), and parents' knowledge of and commitment to children's growth and learning too often may be considered irrelevant (Lightfoot, 1978). Each of these relationships can create or resolve problems within the family and between parents and professionals.

What also has been recognized recently is the extent to which parents are aided by a social support network among their friends and relatives

(Bronfenbrenner, 1979; Cochran & Brassard, 1979). These individuals offer parents some emotional and material assistance, controls, and sanctions as well as role models for behavior and child-rearing practices. A social network links parents to a world of peers who subsequently influence both adults and children. Between mother and father a support system also exists, and sometimes persists even after divorce. Such support enables each parent to maintain appropriate child-rearing strategies with children.

Related to personal-social networks is the issue of the parent's own adult development within the couple and family setting. Even though parenting itself creates new opportunities and challenges, it also can interfere with an adult's personal identity, career, recreation, and social relationships. The rights of parents as people are seldom discussed, yet it could be said that parents' own satisfactions are as important as children's needs to receive attention (Galinsky, 1981; Rapoport, Rapoport, & Strelitz, 1980).

A third area of parent-parent relationships within the family is that of stress and/or change. Among major sources of upheaval are personality changes, career changes, divorce, death or illness, marital strife, economic pressure, and difficulties in coping with a variety of demands both within and outside of the family. How mothers and fathers cope with changes and other tension-producing events may vary in each family. While many manage to resolve difficulties by making adjustments in role responsibilities, changing their living style, engaging in counseling or consultation with kin or outsiders or employing more or less patient forebearance, other parents may be unable to ease family stress successfully. Sometimes child maltreatment occurs in relation to stress (Kempe & Kempe, 1978), especially when it is compounded by negative factors outside the family that limit its access to resources. Unresolved stress and conflict between parents also can lead to child psychopathology. Programs that ease family stress, provide health visitors, and educate parents have been recommended.

Other adult relationships may be important. Grandparents, for example, may fulfill a role that influences both parents and children (Neugarten & Weinstein, 1964; Robertson, 1977). Certainly, as mothers continue to join the labor force and as health care improves for the elderly, more grandparents may participate more directly in the family's child-rearing activities.

Parent-Child Relations

Until recently research concerning early parent-child relations has tended to emphasize that certain characteristics of families are related to child success in later schooling and socialization. In one review of cognitive and emotional factors (Hess, Block, Costello, Knowles, & Largay, 1971), parents' demands for independence, warmth, and emotional involvement; moderate restriction and rejection; and discipline accompanied by explanation have been associated with achievement. Expectations, attitudes, and values regarding success also aid cognitive development, as do acceptance and respect, verbal interaction, and the use of some teaching strategies such as suggestions and positive feedback. The study of competent parenting and effective parent-child relations has produced many similar findings which, taken together, have helped to describe the educational roles and skills presented in other sections of this text.

It is important to point out, however, that conceptualizations of these roles should allow for the extensive variability among sociocultural groups, where values and circumstances exert their own influences. Laosa (1982) has argued for sociocultural relativism in exploring the behaviors and attitudes expressed in parent-child relationships. Indeed, the research from which professionals gain notions of these patterns is quite varied in approaches taken. Hess et al. (1971) cite the use of case studies, theory testing, pattern identification, manipulation, and natural or social experiments that examine outcomes, processes, parameters, contexts, and methodology. If each investigation takes a different focus, it is difficult to obtain a wholistic picture that explains family patterns adequately.

From the perspective of the child and the parent, however, little is known about the dynamics of relationships, especially expressions of emotion and the quality of life in the home. In a study of children's perceptions about parenting and family members, Cataldo and Geismar (1983) did find that preschool children recognize and appreciate their parents' relationships with them. Play involvement, shared activities, and specific teachings were described. Positive and negative feelings were associated with events at home and often precipitated by and resolved with specific actions such as physical affection and verbal statements from parents. Such studies of family feelings are important but rare for the early years. More investigation of this arena will be needed, to understand what happens within *and* outside of the attachments and discipline approaches used by parents.

Child-Child Relations

Sibling relationships are, in part, a special case of peer interaction (see Chapter 3) where residence, parenting, and resources form both a common core of experience and a source of difficulty. Hartup (1982) has described these relationships as bridges to peer interaction. Although the exchanges are forced, occur without many social amenities, and include a very wide range of activities, they contain many elements common to other child-child relationships. Such experiences can pave the way for children as they venture forth from the intimate parent-child relationship to that of peer interactions and their attendant challenges and rewards.

Research and discussion on sibling interactions have tended to focus on two primary variables, birth order and sex, as they influence behavior and affect. Sutton-Smith and Rosenberg (1970) describe the sibling romance as one in which roles are fulfilled and power tactics are used in patterns that reflect gender and family position. First-born children tend to exercise power, act as leaders, and achieve economic and other advantages and have some tendency to be anxious and apprehensive, often modeling themselves after their parents. Later-born children seem to be more peer involved, role flexible, and egalitarian and use more reason, appeals, and compromise as interaction tactics. (See Heatherington & Parke, 1975, for more discussion.) Male siblings tend to be more aggressive as compared to female siblings, who seem to be more affiliative. These generalizations, however, are influenced a great deal by the pattern of the sexes at home and the relationships in particular families. For example, there is some evidence that first-born males and second-born females have similar characteristics.

What is interesting and useful in discussions about siblings is the speculation on how development and personality might be affected by these exchanges. Certainly everyone knows about the many difficulties that children and parents experience in relation to sibling jealousies and rivalries, especially in association with parental attention and family resources. But there are a variety of other dimensions of children's interactions in homes.

The power struggles that can be observed between brothers and sisters contain more than confrontations of negative feelings. Children are developing skills in dealing with others and in negotiating for success in obtaining desired events or objects. Strategies used may include attacks, interference, bribes, pleads, reasoning, ignoring, affection, and so forth. Some strategies become entrenched, and patterns of dominance, nurturance, conformity, and autonomy develop that characterize the relationship. These may change over time or may become aspects of each sibling's general social style. In any event, they do provide experience in conflict resolution and some understanding of rights and responsibilities.

Sibling relationships also seem to contribute to each child's emotional development. Since many strong feelings, both positive and negative, are associated with these exchanges, children must learn to differentiate and control their emotions. Siblings experience jealousy and joy, frustration and satisfaction, rejection and acceptance, hate and love. In dealing with these typically very intense affective reactions to situations, the youngster develops coping and defense strategies. These may include the complete range of techniques by which people learn to integrate themselves into the social world in which they live. Some sibling lessons are painful, but most contain a measure of parent monitoring, especially in the form of discipline and protection, and the children's growth is furthered by these emotional events.

Beyond this emotional realm, children appear to learn role expectations from their shifting interactions with brothers and sisters. In addition to patterns related to gender, there are roles such as those of leader-follower, teacher-learner, competitor-conformer, actor-observer, and loner-friend that children may assume during their exchanges. To experiment with these roles within the confines of home and family may promote social skills and understanding.

Somewhat akin to such patterned learning, siblings no doubt function as more extended educators of one another. Leichter (1975) has described these teachings in terms of verbal interaction, guidance, modeling, evaluation, stimulation, instruction, and self-definition. In sharing activities, for example, brothers and sisters may exchange a good deal of information and model techniques for games and other forms of play, hobbies, group sports, autonomous interests, and peer relationships. Much of this education may be informal, but it is likely to be powerful in its cumulative impact upon each sibling. It also seems to be related to prosocial behavior, in that children may model positive exchanges (Mussen & Eisenberg-Berg, 1977).

In a similar view, children's self-concepts and identity may be very much influenced by a peer. Indirectly, the child may assume a role in the family and develop social strategies that reflect other members. In a more direct way, self-esteem, patterns of ability, moral understanding, and traits reflected and labeled by others tend to form one's identity. Siblings may be credited with assaults to esteem, yet it is also possible that their honesty will provide a balance between the child's egocentricity and parents' adoration, leading to a more realistic sense of self.

Balance is also a function of siblings in relation to the adults in the family. Sutton-Smith and Rosenberg (1970) have described how children mediate the effects of parent-child interactions, and Hartup (1982) has elaborated on how the siblings and peer systems are intertwined with those of the family. Parents' authority and standards, at first quite fixed and unquestioned in the child's mind, tend to become less powerful as children notice inconsistencies and challenges when parents deal with a sibling. Some acts are ignored or managed differently; expectations vary. A balance of attention results from the presence of more children. Parents themselves may alter their rearing styles as they learn about their children. These adjustments often ease the strength of attachments and allow the child to gain independence. They also may balance parents' tendencies toward inflexibility or rigid expectations.

Finally, it can be said that siblings may serve as companions and protectors to one another. Smart and Smart (1976) have described the tendency of children to defend each other and care for one another when parents are unavailable. They also may participate as playmates in games involving imagination and physical abilities, thus preventing loneliness and building an experiential base for later mature relationships. Certainly, there are many siblings who maintain long-term friendships with common interests and concerns. Many of the negative aspects of their earlier exchanges become humorous anecdotes or guidelines in the rearing of their own children. Companionships may be strained and varied, but sisters and brothers also may benefit from the sense of family engendered by their close early relationship with one another.

PROGRAM SUGGESTIONS

1. Using parents' suggestions, make a list of the purposes of families. Separate them into realistic and idealistic standards, then describe why they were placed into those categories.
2. What types of families live in your neighborhood? List the members of households and compare them to another person's community.
3. Using the list of parenting skills presented in Table 2, lead a discussion of which competencies were more valued in early generations and which may be viewed as most important in the future.
4. Have parents select their best parenting skill and ask them to explain how they developed their competence.
5. From among acquaintances, identify three satisfied and three unhappily married couples with children. Try to explain the differences between the two groups.
6. Have parents describe their relationships with their own mothers and fathers in the areas of caregiving and personal relationships.
7. Obtain examples of positive and negative sibling interactions in the preschool and primary years, and explain how these are handled by parents.
8. What do children think about themselves as future parents? Report on conversations with several children aged five through eight, and compare their answers.

3

The Child, Family, and Others

The family in which a child grows and learns provides an important system of relationships, but families themselves exist within the broader context of society, where additional persons, places, and events influence their members. Mothers and fathers interact with other parents, and children have peer relationships that help to shape their self-images and social styles. Schools and agencies have formal relationships with family members that include exchanges of attitudes and expectations. The way in which a family and child are influenced by these external variables will differ, but it is important to understand the forces that touch so many child-rearing activities. The focus of this chapter, therefore, is on the child, family, and those others outside of the home as they affect parents and young children.

FAMILIES AND SOCIETY

Community and culture create the experiences and environments in which a family group must function. Education and social class provide some abilities and standards, while values and traditions, networks of friends, work associates, and kin contribute attitudes and social support. They help to form the expectations and perceptions of individuals who, in turn, organize and maintain family life. Governments play a role through the policies and services available or not available to parents and children. Some of these, such as schools and agencies, directly involve family members, while others affect parents' economic and emotional resources.

Socioeconomic Status

Society provides the settings within which family status is determined. Social class, education, and income combine to determine the level and standards of daily life. Lower-class families have fewer possessions, live in poorer neighborhoods, and, in general, tend to have fewer options in work, schooling, and recreation than do middle-class families. Youngsters from the upper class may attend private schools, have a great many secure possessions, live in elaborate homes and neighborhoods, and demonstrate a lifestyle that has many social and personal opportunities not available even to those in the middle class. Such characteristics as social class contribute to the family's goals and activities, creating patterns that children experience as their lifestyle. These include expectations about behavior and schooling as well as hobbies, recreation, and career opportunities. They may vary for individual families, but children within a given social class will have much in common.

Education is part of the family's socioeconomic status. The level of education attained will have a bearing upon employment and competence in negotiating within society for the resources needed by family members. While trends may differ for particular individuals, the skills acquired through education can provide opportunities for upward mobility. More-educated parents may increase their children's opportunities as they themselves gain in ability and competence. Acquired knowledge can be transmitted to youngsters directly and through the improved schooling that accompanies families' greater ability to help with learning and achievement.

The family's income level is a major source of status and is often the resource that most influences other opportunities. Standards of living, the parents' needs and priorities, and general well-being in the family are affected by adequate and stable income. To the extent that society promotes employment and rewards work, it can aid child rearing. In economically unstable periods or in geographical areas where unemployment is high, parents may be unable to provide for their families adequately. Groups within society who tend to suffer difficulties in employment (minorities, women, and youth) are often handicapped in their child-rearing activities. Such failures in supporting the family can depress children's abilities and ambitions and may create negative family situations that generate risks for children. Poverty contributes to a great many social ills, and the effects on the young, such as malnutrition and child abuse, may be difficult to correct.

To a certain extent, geographical region also shapes family life. Urban and rural children, for example, are likely to develop different interests and priorities. Warm or cold climates provide distinct opportunities for recreation and social exchanges. The quality of life in mountainous or farming regions, or in apartments or suburban subdivisions, is reflected in the family's daily activities and value systems.

Society and Expectations

Myths and societal expectations for the family exist in all cultures. One difficult myth is the belief that individuals and families can and should be self-sufficient, independent morally and economically, and personally protected. According to Keniston (1977) such a view makes it difficult to identify and alter the many other forces that impinge upon family life, especially when coupled with the belief that individuals can solve their problems by changing themselves. Keniston argues that families should not be viewed as self-sufficient and solely responsible for their well-being and status. The fabric of society has changed a good deal over the past two decades. As parents' functions and powers have altered, they have increasingly been involved with others, especially in raising children. The pressures and anxieties that are part of recent family life come in part from growing expectations for parental skills at the same time that economic, educational, and health care roles have diminished. Families must depend upon others over whom they have little control. Their lives are affected by policies and agencies that regulate, teach, and care for their children or supply them with resources for these tasks. This creates added stress and reduced satisfaction for parenting.

Expectations for the family are often felt as generalized pressures by parents. As the persons primarily responsible for successful child rearing, mothers and fathers must have sufficient knowledge and skill to fulfill the roles of coordinators of family and work life, cultivators of school and community relationships, caregivers, teachers, and spouses. Today's parents have a great many tasks to organize and manage, but they may not have a clear conception of parenthood itself and their own identity in relation to it. Nevertheless, expectations for perfection may be very strong. Some experts do recognize that the process of adjustment and growth in relation to one's child demonstrates that parenting is not a fixed ideal to be achieved (Brazelton, 1981). Today, pressures are high and global: Parents are expected to be competent in all areas and produce children who are intelligent, sociable, and mentally healthy, regardless of society's difficulties in providing employment, child care, and programs that promote family well-being.

Parents are expected to fulfill a romantic ideal of nurturing, affectionate care giving, yet they also must employ firm discipline and provide moral teachings. They should work to provide for all of their children's material needs yet arrange to be available at home and in school. Parents should enjoy the good life together, yet give children all the attention they require. Parents are encouraged to make use of any services that society has supplied (health care, counseling agencies, parks, and so forth) but supplement these in times of budget cuts. They are to instill positive cultural values even when bombarded with media messages that compromise standards of cooperation and prosocial solutions to conflict. They are expected to be strong and independent yet encourage conformity to officials in schools and government.

The mixed messages in all of these expectations are part of the parenting experience. As mothers and fathers adjust to their roles, their notions of what is expected of them will be colored by their interactions with helping professionals; their experiences with persons in agencies, schools, stores, and the like; and their impressions from books and television. Throughout the early years, parents are developing attitudes and ideals by which they judge their competence as parents. What society appears to expect from them, how persons react to them in public, and their own needs and goals all create a set of expectations that parents use to measure their skills. Often this set is an ideal that cannot be achieved within the constraints that exist within individuals, families, neighborhoods, and the society. Where parents do develop a realistic view of their responsibilities or where improvements are needed because of difficulties with children, then such expectations can provide useful guideposts for child rearing.

PARENTS' PEERS

Parents are members of several groups who have characteristics and needs in common with one another. The peer groups to which mothers and fathers align themselves outside the immediate family tend to provide a great deal of information and reflect some varying attitudes. Their duration does differ; some groups, such as the parents in a child's classroom, may have brief associations, while others, such as neighbors and friends, may exist for long periods of time. Groupings also vary in their degree of support or contradiction of parents' own values and child-rearing methods. Finally, groups may be informally organized or consciously structured to fulfill particular needs, provide resources, or allow families a means for self-expression. What is important is that such groupings be recognized for their potential to lend social support and an interpersonal context in which mothers and fathers develop child-rearing attitudes and skills. They also may supply assistance for some parenting tasks. Unfortunately, peers sometimes provide negative influences that interfere with family functioning and lead to stressful relationships. For all these reasons it is important to look at parents as a peer group.

Common Interests and Needs

All parents have in common their experience with children. Regardless of differences in their styles, concerns, and commitments, mothers and fathers all know the difficulties and satisfactions in caring for infants and young children. From pregnancy through the periods of coping and learning new child-rearing skills, parents share some strong feelings and highly significant events. The common characteristics of children during each stage of growth and the reactions of family members are unifying experiences among parents. The tension and humor, the successful and frustrating practices, form an emotional basis for sharing. For the most part, parents relish discussions about their children, although their tolerance for one another's pride, complaints, and challenges may vary. Some prefer to express themselves with family members or school personnel rather than engage in a dialogue with friends and acquaintances. But each usually wants to know the views of their peers about raising and managing children for the society they all face.

An area of child rearing in which parents show strong interest very early in their children's lives is their health, nutrition, and safety (Sparling et al., 1978). Because there are a great many medical and health problems, parents are often overwhelmed by the care of newborns and the physical progress of toddlers. Even preschoolers may demonstrate poor eating and toileting habits or recklessness in physical activities. Parents need to obtain information about such matters. They need to know about age-related expectations and methods of dealing with health requirements. They are interested in unusual signs of either slow or very rapid growth and may need advice and alternatives in helping the child in either situation.

Another major area of interest for parents is their children's social and emotional well-being. Most parents want very much for their youngsters to be happy and well adjusted, able to play with and enjoy other children, and cooperate in demonstrating good manners and respect toward adults. Yet in the early childhood years children's personalities are in early formative stages and their ability to use language and to understand social rules is rather limited. It is difficult to determine a child's state of mental health, other than looking at obvious and often temporary mood states. Parents tend to worry either too much or too little about family mental health. Sometimes children's patterns of aggression, withdrawal, tension, or loneliness are symptoms of school or family difficulties rather than psychopathology in the child.

Nevertheless, children's behavior and feelings tend to be priority concerns of parents, and they are likely to feel concerned about more than one issue at any given time. The need for suggestions and for assurance that they or the children will successfully resolve the matter is very strong. Parents want to believe that their ideals will eventually be achieved, either through their own efforts, the help of others, or from the child's own progress toward maturity. Their need for confidence and/or for guidance may express itself in discussion, complaints, requests for advice, or other behaviors with peers and family members. On occasion, professionals in schools and child care centers can direct parents to groups of their peers or to individual parents likely to be of assistance to them. Even with support or intervention, however, parents may be quite resistant to change. Most mothers and fathers believe their goals and methods are the most appropriate. Suggestions provided to families are usually filtered through parents' own beliefs in managing their youngsters. Most peers recognize and respect the fact that each parent has these uniquenesses even though they may share the same views of children and society.

Parents tend to be very interested in a third aspect of their young child's upbringing, and that is the area of learning. Even though families differ in their ideas about children's abilities and knowledge, most want to see evidence of increased capability and acquired learning as the child grows. Some parents define themselves as teachers of their young, and they enthusiastically engage in efforts to expand skills and understanding as they begin to emerge in their children. Others feel that love and acceptance should be provided and that children will learn what they need to, as their activities require. Some parents are unable to focus on learning because there are too many family matters that require their energies, while still others trust to the later years for children to engage in formal learning. But the majority of parents still wish for their children to be skilled and knowledgeable, competent in using and gaining new learning. What parents often need in this area are resources that help them to monitor or become involved in teaching their children. They want to see their offspring as capable of the typical demands of schools and may show interest in working with school representatives to assure that their youngsters perform well. Within the peer group, parents can often take note of the ways in which others encourage learning and reward children's success. Books and educational playthings may be recommended; programs in the community may be supported by groups of families.

A broad area of need and interest for parents in relation to children is the desire for more time with the family. Especially in the case of working parents, it may be difficult if not impossible for parents to spend time engaged in any activities with their children. Where time is available, parents may want to raise the quality of their activities and relationship with the youngster. The need for this important ingredient in family life may be frustrated by inflexible working hours or a variety of pressures. Parents can sometimes support each other's need for time with children. Family events, shows, outings, recreational activities, and even quiet games may be substituted for other experiences that do not include children. Sometimes parents learn from their peers ways in which to enjoy such family times, or they may gain ideas for organizing them. Mothers and fathers can provide direct help as well by sharing housekeeping and child care responsibilities so that a spouse can participate in an activity with the child.

Parents' Own Development

The process of adult development is seldom considered by those who work with children, but mothers and fathers have rights and priorities for their own growth and maintenance, at the same time that they are concerned with their children. It is probably quite common for parents to neglect their own development while their children are young. They may sacrifice hobbies and social engagements and even bemoan this aspect of parenting with their peers. Others may turn their energies toward new projects and exchanges with additional sets of peers from the families of their children's playmates.

Adult development includes relationships with spouses, friends, and one's own parents, as well as with growing children. It occurs at home, at the workplace, and in the neighborhood. It involves skills, attitudes, knowledge, and feelings. Adults also are changing over the child-rearing period. Physical changes may be seen in reduced good health and in increase or reduction in exercise or sports or changes in the intensity of these activities. Career changes may occur at several points, perhaps in relation to financial and child care needs or because parents' perceptions of their work value and future goals have altered. These may be accompanied by changes in residence, with the upheaval in lifestyle and friendships that accompanies such moves. Parents may witness the deaths of their own mothers and fathers or other adults close to them. These tend to affect feelings about one's self and family, perhaps resulting in altered lifestyles. All of these shifts in adults' lives are likely to create the need for adjustments that involve children and peers. The peer group may be important in stabilizing feelings and relationships and in helping parents cope with their own developmental changes.

Discussions about parents as people can be found in a variety of texts concerning their development and relationships. Rapoport, Rapoport, and Strelitz (1980) have taken the position that a framework is needed for understanding contemporary parenting. Their review of the literature in this field has led to several propositions: Parents are people engaged in their own personal development; parenting is one of several roads to self-fulfillment; parents' and children's needs do not always coincide; families vary in goals and structure; parenting consists of a wide range of tasks; others fulfill some parenting functions; parents' outside lives require attention; there is no "right" style of parenting; some parenting skills are learned; parents develop from their experiences; parenting creates some life opportunities; and children can and should reciprocate in family life. In terms of the relationship between parenting and adult development, these propositions form a useful philosophical base.

The notion of developmental stages in parenting is helpful in understanding families. Galinsky (1981) has described nine stages seen in parents, which accompany the child development process. During pregnancy, parents attempt to form images of their new roles; the infant-nurturing stage includes adjustments and attachments; the authority stage deals with rules for toddlers; the interpretive stage includes preschool and school-age children, involving parents examining their effectiveness; the interdependent period runs through the children's teen years and necessitates new solutions; and the departure stage is one of taking stock. Transformations and growth are seen to be a part of these experiences, and variations are to be expected, especially with several children at different ages. The stage concept is seen as useful, however, in helping parents to understand their own development.

Parents' Networks

Parents' social environment of friends, neighbors, and family members has been discussed by Bronfenbrenner (1979) and Cochran and Brassard (1979). Concern with these networks of persons who interact with mothers and fathers is also reflected in family-centered projects such as Family Focus (Weissbourd & Musick, 1981). The child's experiences within the home include the personal and material environment provided by adults who may have a weak or strong external network to aid them. The child is the ultimate beneficiary of such support, but parents also gain from relationships with others. In the view of Cochran and his associates, the parents' personal network may supply the home with material and emotional assistance, stimulation, access to resources, and caregiving models. These enable parents to engage better in activities with children that enhance their development, and they also may directly affect children's perceptions, skills, and behaviors such as independence, self-concept, and involvement in learning tasks. Networks may be influenced by key members who are very important to parents, by individual parents and how they create and maintain networks, and by larger institutions such as schools, which may foster or inhibit these ties.

Networks of peer relationships among parents are a form of mini-society. Friends and relatives who live nearby, who are available over long periods of time, who have skills that can be borrowed, and who are emotionally supportive of the parent may contribute significantly to the quality of family life and ultimately to the child. Other types of peer experiences reflect a less permanent set of ties but may provide important feedback for parents. Childbirth classes, support groups in intensive care or regular pediatric units, home visiting programs, health care groups, daycare centers and preschool parent coops, school PTA's, neighborhood clubs, YWCA programs, community center special-interest groups, hobby programs, and other such alliances can offer social associations for parents.

Networks of friends and relatives also can create difficulties for parents. Inconsistent child-rearing practices, goal confusion, power struggles, poor social skills, and personal insecurities all can be worsened through these relationships. Parents may not be able to cope with challenges to their newly emerging skills and knowledge. They may become frustrated with different values or attempt inappropriate new ideas that do not fit their family context. In parent groups those members who are admired may be emulated by others who judge themselves in comparison. While these may lead to positive changes, they also may cause parents to become negative about their own child-rearing styles or doubtful of their strengths. Cultural and ethnic characteristics may be strengthened in groups of parents, even though they may interfere with practices that better prepare the children for school or peer relationships. While these difficulties may occur, parent networks are nevertheless valuable to the socialization of children and the development of families.

CHILDREN'S PEERS

The peer groups in which children participate comprise an important part of their social networks. Friendships and group experiences in the infant and early childhood years seem to be desired by children, needed by parents, and valued by many professionals. As child care programs continue to be necessary for working families it is expected that children will spend longer periods of time with youngsters of their own age. There has not been a great deal of research on the characteristics of peer relationships in the earliest years, but reviews of the literature are available in some recent texts (Osofsky, 1979). A major focus has been on prosocial or kind behaviors.

Overall, peers are seen as necessary for the child's growth and development, in part because these relationships differ from those with parents and enhance complex social skills (Hartup, 1982). Even though there may be negative modeling and conflict, peers contribute to children's socialization (Rubin & Ross, 1982). Patterns of acceptance, conformity, and dominance are present in peer groups, just as they are in the larger society. Moral development is also an important feature of the peer experience in that children model and reinforce behavior and provide a forum in which notions of right and wrong progress from concrete, family-centered criteria to those in which approval and rule conformity are used to judge good or appropriate acts (Mussen & Eisenberg-Berg, 1977).

To illuminate some of the dynamics of peer relationships and the influence of these "others" upon children and families, the characteristics, expected benefits, and potential problems of the peer group will be discussed. These are summarized in Table 3. Details of the literature can be

Table 3
Characteristics of Children's Peer Relationships

GENERAL FEATURES

Mutual interests and similarities, or complementary characteristics
Relative equality in power or level of the relationship
Mutual exchanges, mostly positive, with conflicts resolved
Influenced by circumstances and interpersonal characteristics

EXPECTED BENEFITS

Gains in independence from parents and home-family situations
Socialization growth in identity of self, roles, games, negotiation
Friendship skills of involvement, acceptance, sensitivity, and problem-solving
Cognitive development in relation to toys, ideas, communication
Behavioral models that teach personal-social strategies
Moral development, especially for rules and standards, social approval, and
    equality
Cultural values related to the peer group and larger society
Sense of community or connectedness with others

POTENTIAL PROBLEMS

Divergence from the family, including contradictory attitudes and behaviors
Patterns of dominance and submission in some relationships
Conflict and aggression, with related feelings of jealousy or frustration
Social pressure for conformity or rebellion
Popularity hierarchy, with related problems in rejection and self-esteem
Inappropriate social models for relationships, achievement, and behavior
Lack of adult skill in problem prevention, limit setting, or supervision

found in the sources just cited, and these will provide the basis for the
following discussion.

Characteristics of Peer Relationships

One special feature of peer relationships that is not always appreciated
by parents and teachers alike is that children seem to be interested in peers
at a very early age. Even in the first year of life babies look at and reach for
one another, imitate one another's behaviors, show interest in the same toys
and activities, and generally display positive emotional responses from one
child to another. Supervised and well-organized peer experiences at this age
may not be widely available, but model programs have demonstrated that
infant groups can be successfully established with small numbers of chil-

dren, trained staff, appropriate toys, and conscious adult encouragement (Cataldo, 1983). In some cultures, children are raised predominantly in groups of peers from infancy through the school years, with good results. Peer relationships also are seen as egalitarian in nature, unlike the uneven power that exists between an adult and child. Youngsters of similar ages tend to have many skills and interests in common. Since they are functioning at relatively comparable levels, their interactions appear to be equivalent in affect, power, and style. The give and take that flavors relationships among equals enables a peer to learn many basic competencies that cannot be practiced with parents and family members.

Activities with playmates are characterized as well by their reciprocity or mutual exchange of behaviors. Peers tend to imitate and duplicate one another's acts, including vocalization, uses of toys, expressions of emotions, and participation in play. This reciprocity can serve to teach and reinforce, to enhance the child's social repertoire, and to demonstrate a variety of problem-solving behaviors.

Peer relationships seem to be quite influenced by the immediate situation in which the peer activities take place, a point that should be especially interesting to parents and teachers. For younger children especially, the particular toys available, the tendency to cluster in small groups around materials, the experience and familiarity with the peer group, and the activities that are ongoing all may influence the amount and characteristics of peer exchanges. Group size and the skills of the supervising adult also may assume roles in promoting positive and productive peer relationships.

Finally, peer friendships seem to develop out of children's perceptions that they and their peers are similar, having common interests and complementary characteristics (Rubin, 1980; Rubin & Ross, 1982). The maintenance of the relationship may require communication, shared activity, the exploration of differences, conflict resolution, positive exchanges, and self-disclosure. All of these features characterize real friendships at either child or adult levels.

Expected Benefits of Peer Relationships

Although there may be little documentation as yet of the specific benefits young children derive from peer exchanges and friendships, several important contributions to development can be described. One such benefit is the child's exposure to the larger social world outside the family. Peer experiences are a part of every culture and as such appear to be both natural and necessary for children and societies. Just as the family is needed to provide nurturance, to teach social patterns in a small group, and to serve as a base of acceptance that is both a refuge and a launching pad, so experiences outside this unit are required as introductions to the larger society. In a sense, families are not enough; children must gain skills and understanding beyond the home setting as part of their overall socialization.

An important reason for the use of play groups and nursery schools that is expressed by parents of young children is to help the child gain independence from their intimate relationships with mothers and fathers. A gradual reduction in dependence upon parents for meeting their needs promotes self-reliance and prevents difficulties such as separation anxiety and poor adjustment to school. The peer playmates with whom children become engaged ease the transition from home to center. Their activities are self-sustaining with minimal adult intervention, so the child can gain the sense of confidence that accompanies the assumption of responsibility for one's own care, activities, and belongings.

Peers are seen by Hartup (1982) as providing the opportunity for children to exercise advanced and complex social skills that cannot be learned or practiced at home. Self-assertion, role rehearsals, sexual identity, and peer games can be rehearsed with children of similar age, whereas these are not as appropriate in the parent-child relationship. The skills of friendship (Rubin, 1980) include the ability to enter a group of peers, to be attentive and helpful, to manage conflicts successfully, to be tactful or sensitive, and to learn by experience how to interact positively. The socialization of children to their peer culture is needed in order for them to take their place in the society outside of home and family. Experiences with peers help to shape these social skills for both the child's present and future.

Cognitive development appears to be enhanced within the play of children. Exploration, discovery, modeled learning styles, communication, and curiosity about new ideas can be found within the activities children share with one another. This intellectual education may be informal and sporadic, but there is some evidence that cognitive development is enhanced as children use toys and materials together. Indeed, the alert observer in any preschool or first grade is likely to find that shared peer learning experiences occur with a good deal of frequency. Children tend to provoke each other's curiosity and stimulate ideas. One youngster's comment or interest in an activity encourages others to attempt the same and compare the results. Intellectual learning becomes a part of daily play and interpersonal exchanges with peers.

It has long been recognized that children model a variety of sociable or unsociable behaviors for one another. These provide alternatives that children can examine and use. Since personality development consists, in part, of a style for expressing feelings and interacting with children and adults, individual youngsters are incorporating such models into their behavioral repertoire. Methods of self-expression, make-believe problem solving, uses of materials, and so forth, are selected by the child and practiced within the peer group. Some become a part of an interpersonal style while others are discarded. In the early years some adult supervision and mediation may be required in helping children to understand the behaviors they experience and rehearse. Negative, hurtful, destructive, and inappropriate models need to be seen as such, and for this adults are valuable. Nevertheless, peer behaviors are demonstrated almost constantly for the child's observation and incorporation, and a good many of these are useful and necessary.

Moral development is enhanced by peers. To help children progress from egocentric, authority-bound, concrete notions of good and bad, the peer group is needed as a source of alternative standards. Theories of moral growth described by several authorities (e.g., Mussen & Eisenberg-Berg, 1977) propose that peers introduce children to different sets of rules. Approval, rules, and standards based on equality are presented that tend to be broader than those expressed within the family. Cultural values are transmitted. The child struggles with these concepts, and observers discipline and praise. The peer group provides ample opportunity for the testing of newer ideals and the exercise of confirming or negating behaviors. This long-term development of mature morality thus appears to require experiences with others outside the home, and, even though negative acts are attempted, the process of error and correction eventually facilitates growth.

The peer group can offer a regular, ongoing set of interpersonal experiences to children and a sense of belonging to a community apart from the family. In this regard, peers may help children to feel secure in a world of confusion and changes, even in their own abilities and interests. A stable group of playmates provides a structure in which the child learns and develops. Personal relationships, games, and routines are somewhat predictable and thus may help youngsters to see themselves as members of a broader society. Where there are difficulties at home, the child's playmates can offer some reassurance.

Finally, for many children, peer experiences lead to extended friendships, with their accompanying familiarity and shared activities, feelings, values, fantasies, and expectations. Growing up with friends may support children's personal growth in many ways, enabling them to establish relationships that may last throughout their childhood. Friendships are humanizing experiences, promoting a sense of self and acceptance of the give and take inherent in most interpersonal exchanges. Personal relationships also help individuals to cope with difficulties and deal with challenges. They provide some satisfactions and enhance esteem, making success more meaningful and failure more tolerable.

Potential Problems in Peer Relationships

No parent or teacher is unaware of the hazards involved in children's relationships and play activities with their peers. The negative reputation of "peer pressure" attests to the frequency with which it is viewed as something to be condemned and avoided. Even when the benefits of playmates can be appreciated, there is still the concern that peers can be harmful to the child's personality and behavior. Perhaps some of the negative experiences can be mediated, or they may be short-lived, but many adults worry about permanent pollution of the child's social skills and self-esteem.

To a certain extent, the potential problems in peer relationships outside the family are part of the same process by which benefits can be accrued. That is, children are influenced by peers in directions that often contradict or at least diverge from those of the family. These very differences create a state of imbalance between what the child learns within and outside the home. The process of adjusting to differences, to changing expectations and behaviors, even if they are eventually positive, is a difficult one that is often accompanied by distress and disruption. Sometimes parents are bewildered and distraught at the new trends they see, especially when the child seems to disregard their standards. Teachers also may worry when a previously cooperative youngster appears to be adopting the behaviors of more difficult peers. However, since there are many such shifts to be expected in the dynamics of peer relationships, it may be more appropriate to adopt a process-oriented view of children and peers; that is, it may be possible to examine problem areas for their potential contributions to positive change. Perhaps adult mediation and discipline can then focus on ways of helping children gain deeper understanding about the benefits and pitfalls of associations with their friends and about what is good and bad in their values and behavior.

One rather intrinsic difficulty in the peer group is the creation of patterns of dominance, of leading and following, as opposed to the ideal of shared or alternated power and influence. Often dominance is accompanied by aggression or social pressure to maintain or enhance the activities of the children high on this characteristic. Those who already display a good deal of reticence or dependence may be unable to turn aside from the pressure to accept another's bossiness. Such assertiveness is often disruptive and can damage confidence. Related to dominance is the problem of conflict among peers. Whether fueled by jealousy, frustration, or competition, conflict can be expected to occur in every child's experiences with peers. Often the children are able to negotiate and resolve their differences, while in other situations the friendship may be ended.

Another problem in such groups is the potential for the growth of a hierarchy of popularity and sociability. In such situations children who gain the interest and affection of their peers will have a great many relationships from which to choose, while those less outwardly sociable are likely to feel isolated and discouraged. The loneliness of youngsters whose behaviors are well within the norm but who are not selected as friends can result in personal problems that are hard to resolve. Peers tend to be quite insensitive to the feelings of children who fail to acquire playmates, and adults may have to work very hard to create alternative peer experiences for such youngsters.

As has already been mentioned, peers also are likely to model inappropriate behaviors for one another. These may range widely from disruptive or damaging acts to those that fail to meet adults' standards of acceptability regardless of their inherent wrongfulness. Discipline and moral teachings are often used to discourage this type of peer pollution; however, some experiments with modeled acts are to be expected in every child. For those who are compelled by a preoccupation with peers' naughtiness, it may be difficult for adults to shift attention to positive models. They are likely to remove the peer or punish the offending participant. In either case such behavior models will continue to be available during the child's growing years, and adults will have to compete to gain conformity to their own standards.

A final area for potential problems with peer relationships is the lack of skill and understanding in some adults who are responsible for children. Improper or harsh handling of peer conflict and contagious misbehavior can reinforce rather than reduce it. Failure to set appropriate limits and to plan for preventive strategies may promote negative patterns that are very difficult to discourage later. Inadequate materials and restricted play opportunities can lead to frustration and aggression in children. Insensitivity to children's needs as individuals within a peer group can create resentment and hostility that fuel conflict and competition. Effective management of the peer group not only discourages many difficulties but contributes to prosocial behaviors such as cooperative play, affectionate concern for others, and a desire for friendly and generous exchanges.

GRANDPARENTS

Although one or more grandparents sometimes live within the family, contributing to its structure, in most instances these extended-family members function as significant adults outside of the smaller unit of children and parents. The roles of grandparents in relation to children vary a great deal from family to family and culture to culture. Neugarten and

Weinstein (1964) found that the primary significance of the role of grand-parenthood for grandparents could be classified into one of five categories: providing a source of biological renewal and/or biological continuity with the future; providing emotional self-fulfillment; serving as teacher or re-source person to the child; providing a sense of vicarious achievement through the child; or having little effect on their lives because of a feeling of remoteness from their grandchildren. Interactional styles include the for-mal, playful, parent-surrogate, authoritarian, and distant-figure forms of involvement. The effects of grandparents on grandchildren (Robertson, 1977) include providing role models, modulating family life, and contribut-ing to growth and to child-rearing practices. On the less positive side, grandparents may be relatively indifferent to or impatient with their grand-children. Conflicts with parents, demands upon parents' time, domination of a parent, and usurping the parenting role also may occur.

The role of the grandparent upon the child and family may depend upon many factors and may take several forms. Interpersonal dynamics among all family members may determine the extent to which grandparents can be supportive, and these may change as children develop and families

mature. Attitudes and rearing patterns previously experienced by the parent may reflect the grandparents' styles or may differ greatly from them. Networks that include siblings and cousins may enhance or reduce the grandparents' roles in the family. As the number of working parents grows, especially mothers, grandparents may be needed to provide more child care and guidance as an adjunct parent. Such services may need to be rewarded by family members, who might be expected to offer emotional or financial support or, at the minimum, demonstrate appreciation and respect for such help. When families are able to manage successfully the contributions of grandparents, children may be provided with an added measure of learning and social skills during their early years. This can happen to a certain extent even when grandparents live far away. Letters, telephone calls, visits, and photographs can help to maintain the family's emotional ties.

SCHOOLS AND FAMILIES

A discussion of ways in which others outside the home can influence children and families must certainly include the school as a formidable force in their lives. While specific information about children's education, personality, and behavior is presented in other chapters, this section deals with school environments, activities, and personnel as part of the "other" experiences of family members. Schools, for example, have characteristics that are experienced by youngsters and dealt with by parents, such as scheduled activities oriented toward acquiring and using information and skills. Social relationships in school are somewhat structured and limited; behavioral standards are firmly applied. Materials and opportunities reflect particular educational goals. Instructional procedures are prescribed, and teacher-child-parent relationships are generally formal. The family's experiences with schools are in many ways unique among external relationships. No other agency or representative of society has such extensive contact with the child and family. It is useful, therefore, to examine some features of the school experience during the nursery and early primary years.

Schools and Society

Throughout the history of public education, schools have assumed key roles in the learning and socialization of children. As compulsory schooling has ensured a broad and long-term exposure to classrooms, expectations of schools appear to have expanded. In their chapter on school experiences in relation to the developing child, Blank and Klig (1982) point out the discrepancy between the extensive demands upon schools to teach literacy, socialization, job skills, and personal well-being and the limited means for accomplishing them. This imbalance contributes to dissatisfaction and conflict regarding the responsibilities of schools as imposed by the larger society.

Differences in culture and social-class variables also create difficulties related to schools and society's values and expectations. While there appears to be a good deal of home-school continuity, such as in the relationship between parents' intellectual stimulation and children's school achievement, there is a discontinuity in the experiences of nonmainstream children who attend schools reflecting the dominant culture. There are varying amounts of overlap in the skills and behaviors expected by adults in each of these environments. Some families indoctrinate children into the content and process of school culture to the extent that they provide a path of continuity that supports the child's socialization and achievement.

Schools also reflect society in their own microsystem of relationships and structures. Even nursery schools and daycare centers contain the elements of an organized social unit. Parents and children encounter a set of rules, personnel, procedures, and so forth that represent a small system to which they must adjust. In large schools this institutionalized microsociety presents a formidable face to the public it serves, and families must negotiate its requirements and characteristics. Children experience many of the inner dynamics of this unit. The relationships among teachers, helpers, and administrators; the physical setting and resources made available; and the ongoing activities of this minisystem are part of the children's daily routines. For nonmainstream or minority families, the school society may represent a major obstacle to success. Lightfoot's (1978) text on this subject describes the difficulties sometimes experienced by cultural groups in schools that fail to account for the histories and priorities of their families.

School Settings

The physical characteristics and organization of schools also are important. Some are small and comfortably furnished, while others are large and institutional. Some administrators may be remote and out of touch with individual families or teachers, while others may function as director-teachers who are aware of every youngster's personal background and needs. Classrooms may be organized to promote self-learning and peer interaction, or they may reflect the teacher's use of adult-oriented teaching. Materials may be abundant or limited in availability and usefulness as learning aids. Depending on the experiences that families have on either side of such continua, the school can serve as a rich or deprived environment for them. Certainly young children who spend a major portion of the day in a room will feel some positive or negative emotional effect from their surroundings.

Most early childhood and many elementary texts provide suggestions for organizing centers and classrooms. Infant and preschool programs are seen as requiring spatial arrangements that permit children to explore, interact, and pursue learning tasks with a good deal of movement and choice. There are interest centers in which materials are arranged by theme: blocks, table games, artwork, and music areas, for example. Many kindergarten classrooms resemble the preschool in using open arrangements of space and materials that encourage small-group activities in various areas of the room. In some primary classrooms teachers have retained the notion of flexible space and independent learning areas, while others rely upon rows or clusters of desks that enable the children to follow large-group lessons conducted by the teachers. Decorations and curiosity corners may still be used to create cheerful and usable space for some independent activity.

Within these various physical settings there is an interpersonal organization as well. A network of supervisors, teachers, assistants, office, and building maintenance workers exists in schools and child care centers. These

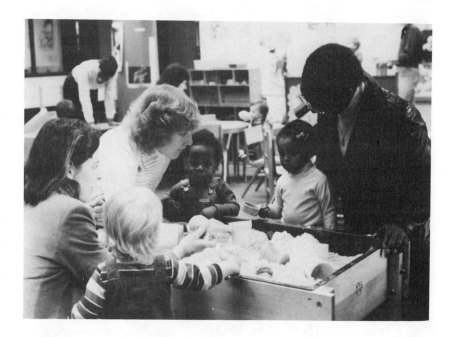

working relationships include both affective and organizational elements that sometimes affect families. In some settings, the social atmosphere is one of cooperation and concern, of high positive regard for children, parents, and teachers. In other situations there may be a good deal of stress and conflict or rigid lines of authority among staff members, resulting in more negativism toward family members. Since early childhood programs are characterized by small adult-child ratios, most staff members function in teams of two or three. Interpersonal relationships within these groups are likely to be reflected in the kinds of experiences children and parents encounter.

Teachers and Child Care Providers

Certainly the primary adults in the child's classroom contribute significantly to the family's experiences. In their discussion of schools as related to child development, Heatherington and Parke (1975) emphasize the importance of the teachers' interactions, behavioral standards, expectations, discipline, motivation, modeling, use of peers, and organization of the room for

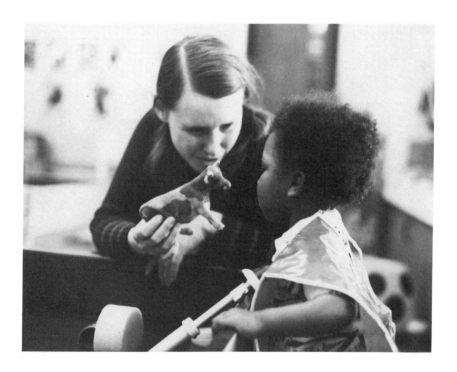

children. These are seen as potential shapers of the youngsters' learning and personal-social skills. Blank and Klig (1982) also point to the ways in which teachers provide for children's needs and manage their academic learning. They cite Rutter's emphasis on teachers' lessons, standards, responsivity, motivations, continuity, and support from administrators as determinants of the quality of children's school experiences. In their texts on parent-teacher relationships, Berger (1981) and Nedler and McAfee (1979) describe the teachers' roles in establishing and maintaining positive and productive relationships with family members, including the provision of information and support as well as ensuring adequate communication and special assistance for any problem areas. Traditional early childhood education has always placed great importance upon the human relationships established and modeled within the classroom among peers and between children and adults (Read & Patterson, 1980). Even during infancy, the role of the primary teacher-caregiver is considered to be significant in the children's learning and well-being (Honig & Lally, 1981).

Thus, teachers and those assistants who function in this role along with them are expected to recognize and act upon their potential for giving help beyond academics. There appear to be four major categories for describing these effects: providing for children's needs, managing behavior and discipline, arranging for academic progress and learning, and dealing with home-school relationships. Effectiveness and responsiveness are likely to mean that families' experiences with teachers and child care providers will be positive and supportive of the child and family.

School Activities

The curriculum of planned learning activities, enrichment experiences, and social activities with peers all comprise children's daily school activities. Once again, they may encounter a well-implemented and organized curriculum that is broadly based, sequential, and relevant to the interests of children and families. On the other hand, there may be very little in the way of curriculum planning. This may be the case in child care programs where staff members have little training in early childhood education or in schools where there are minimal resources and support for teachers in curriculum planning. On occasion, the educational program may reflect rigidly organized or inappropriate content, such as an overemphasis on basic skills prior to children's readiness for them or a single focus on one aspect of learning, such as reading, to the exclusion of others that build reasoning skills or promote physical health.

After-school activities also differ in availability and scope. Some buildings contain recreational facilities that can be used by school teams and groups, or by adults and neighborhood associations. Optional sports or creative activities may be available to young children later in the day. These enrichments are important to families, especially when they promote interest in music, art, sports, reading, and hobbies. They enlarge the scope of the school's curriculum, using children's own preferences, and make the school or child care center a more friendly neighborhood resource.

Formal meetings of parents and teachers have been a traditional part of the school year, and they continue to assume an important role in home-school relationships. Conferences focus on the child but provide an opportunity for communicating about many social or program-related matters. The goals of most meetings are to discuss progress, problems, and plans for the child. Optimally, early childhood and primary teachers schedule a minimum of two sessions per year, either following preliminary and final achievement tests or when reports are completed that require parents' signatures. Teachers and program staff tend to vary in their abilities to conduct conferences that are informative, productive, and sensitive to the needs of participants. Regardless of skill, it is important that attention be given to conference preparation, the meeting itself, and follow-up activities.

When preparing for a session with parents, professionals need to bring together all available information about the child and examine this data carefully for patterns that indicate strengths and needs. Narrative observations, work samples, activity records, formal test results, and developmental checklists are used to describe the child's progress, behavior, and general personal-social growth. When there is confusion about the child's functioning, when parents have expressed concern, or if there are indications of developmental delays or problems, the teacher or caregiver should discuss the information with a supervisor or director. Such conferences will require a great deal more skill, since more complex problems need to be resolved. Parents and teachers both need support in managing these matters and minimizing some of the stresses and conflicts that can result.

During the conference itself, professionals are responsible for greeting and orienting the parent. Since schools and centers are the hosts, they are expected to arrange scheduling, rooms, refreshments, and sometimes child care. A pleasant, positive tone to the meeting is helpful in easing parents' concerns about receiving what is often quite revealing information about their child. Most mothers and fathers expect some good news and bad news at teacher conferences, and they often are open to suggestions about their own child rearing or management of learning, play, or discipline. For both parents and teachers, however, it is a strain as well as an opportunity. Honesty with tact, specific examples, and clear observations are important. Opinion should be given only when it is relevant to facts or when it is necessary to make a judgment or speculation. Professionals provide better information when they use their past experiences or borrow suggestions from others who have had success in handling a parallel situation. The content of the meeting can vary, depending upon the interests of participants and the child's progress. Questions and concerns can open the discussion. The goals of parents and teachers, some specific curriculum or child-management strategies, test and checklist results, informal observations of the child, and plans for the succeeding months all should be included. Anecdotes that reflect the child's special nature or interaction style are enjoyable for opening or closing the conference.

Following the meeting, the professional is responsible for carrying out any plans discussed, acquiring new information desired, or contacting additional professionals. Records of the parents' concerns or suggestions and the teacher's recommendations are important to keep and use. Follow-up discussions with supervisors and continued observations of the child also should be done. Often, both parent and professional feel a renewed sense of commitment to the child and the program, and they may begin to make changes in their methods of working with the child. All these are important results of conferences with family members.

Peer experiences may be major or minor parts of a child's school activities. Children may learn with and from their playmates for the major portion of the day. Their small-group activities may contain a great deal of verbal exchange and discussion of ideas, and their play may include concepts that further extend their learning. Where peer interactions are reserved for playtimes, children will have fewer opportunities to experiment with and share the information that has been presented or made available. Peer tutoring may be used for remedial work, for helping to socialize new children into the classroom, or where particular youngsters display unusual abilities that can be shared with classmates.

PROGRAM SUGGESTIONS

1. Ask parents to describe what they think society expects of a model "parent of the year." Put these characteristics and behaviors in order of perceived importance.
2. Who are parents' favorite peers? Who do they talk to about their children? What are the satisfactions and frustrations in these relationships?
3. Lead a discussion of how parents maintain their own interests while raising children. Include ways in which parenthood might contribute to or detract from personal development.

4. Use Table 3 for a debate on the pros and cons of peers in the child's growth, development, and socialization. What can be added to the table, from the parent's point of view?
5. Create a list of recommendations for avoiding potential problems in peer relationships or for turning these into learning experiences.
6. How are grandparents viewed by children? Interview kindergarten and early-primary youngsters about these family members, their roles and feelings, and their reactions to them.
7. Locate a number of families who use grandparents for child care. Create a list of the ways in which their arrangements are successful or problematic.
8. Ask parents to describe the child's center, classroom setting, and teacher or care giver. Include a discussion of what the child might find similar or different from the home.

4

Models of Parent Education and Child Rearing

When professionals attempt to provide assistance and advice to parents, it is important that they use a framework of philosophy, method, and content that serves as an anchor for their recommendations. Often a model is developed that incorporates all of these elements and may include a curriculum sequence or a handbook that presents central concepts and encourages parents' skill development. Other kinds of advice are less structured but fall under a general point of view about children and parents from which suggestions are made. Since the programs and consumer materials offer a great deal of conflicting advice, it may be helpful to know how they relate to one another. In this chapter, we will describe a variety of these materials, which fall into two basic types: single-author media-based child-rearing approaches, and professional model programs of parent education. Both types should provide enough information from which teachers and other programers can select to develop their own models.

APPROACHES TO CHILD REARING FOR PARENTS

The large number of sources of recommendations about how parents can achieve effectiveness in dealing with children reflect the tendency of each source to adopt a single perspective. This makes it difficult to analyze or compare philosophies and methods. The approaches taken in media materials on child rearing are all somewhat unique, but they often overlap in their emphasis upon many points, such as communication, rational discipline, and consideration of children's and parents' needs. To highlight distinct features of a particular approach does not mean that similarities or underlying themes go unrecognized, but rather that the primary characteristic of each warrants focus. The approaches presented here fall into groups with several general orientations in common. Some view parenting as a process of acquiring and applying information in a personal and rather informal manner, to be determined by particular families. A second theme highlights parents' needs for dealing with the behaviors of children, while a third group focuses on the parenting function of guiding the development of a healthy personality. A fourth general orientation takes account of children's development, learning, and overall competence. Each of these general views of the parenting process is reflected in several approaches to child rearing, which we will now discuss. Table 4 provides a summary listing and authors whose work is representative of the approach. References in the bibliography will allow the reader to locate resources for the further study of each.

Information for Parents

Child Study Information.   The history of parent education as a deliberate effort to inform and advise families began during the child-study movement of the late 1920s (Cataldo, 1980; Croake & Glover, 1977). The emphasis on disseminating knowledge of child development and behavior was strongly related to the growth of nursery schools for the young. As parents became aware of the activities and skills of professionals they began to show a desire for access to such resources to use in their own child rearing. Professionals' involvement in early childhood programs was motivated partly by an interest in aiding parents as they observed or "studied" their children. The acquisition of information by direct contact or through written materials represents an early and traditional method of improving parents' knowledge, and hence skills, in child rearing. More recently, Dodson (1970) reflects this same approach, as do Caplan and Caplan (1976).

Rather than develop scripts or systems, these authorities present a wide range of concepts and strategies that are recommended by child psychologists and educators. They include topics such as milestones of growth, responding to emotional needs, attending to learning, managing special situations, discipline, communication, love, social relationships, play, and so forth, all of which are very useful in the early and middle childhood years. Overall, the approach emphasizes the acquisition of information that parents can apply to their own situations. The value of observing children, planning for changes, and being responsible for family life are all implied in the activities suggested. So also are the abilities of mothers and fathers to translate information about children into appropriate parenting skills. These texts focus as well on enjoying children in their various stages of growth, through learning about them and sharing their activities.

Health and Nutrition Information.   The writings of the pediatrician Benjamin Spock are well known to families and those concerned with the

Table 4
References for Various Child-Rearing Approaches for Parents

INFORMATION APPROACHES

Child study information:	Caplan & Caplan (1976), Dodson (1970)
Health and nutrition:	Spock (1976)
Theory information:	Brooks (1981), Mead (1976), Rutherford & Edgar (1979)
Special family situations:	Brutten et al. (1973), Crow (1978), Kempe & Kempe (1978), Gardner (1977)

BEHAVIOR-ORIENTED APPROACHES

Problem solving:	T. Gordon (1970)
Behavior control:	Becker (1971), Patterson & Gullion (1969), Wesley (1971)
Logical consequences:	Dreikurs & Grey (1970), Dreikurs & Soltz (1964)
Limit setting:	Dreikurs & Grey (1970), Ginott (1968)
Assertiveness:	Bakker & Bakker-Rabdau (1973), Kiley (1978), Westin (1981)

PERSONALITY & MENTAL HEALTH APPROACHES

Personal support:	Elkind (1981), Fraiberg (1968), LeShan (1970), Salk & Kramer (1969)
Communication:	Dinkmeyer & McKay (1976), Ginott (1968)
Values/moral development:	Mussen & Eisenberg-Berg (1977), Simon et al. (1972).
Acceptance & esteem:	Babcock & Keepers (1976), Briggs (1975)
Mutual adaptation:	Brazelton (1969, 1976, 1981), Church (1973), LeShan (1970)

DEVELOPMENTAL APPROACHES

Play participation:	Adcock & Segal (1979), Caplan & Caplan (1973), Kennedy Foundation (1977), Sutton-Smith & Sutton-Smith (1974), Wolfgang (1977)
Developmental guidance:	Elkind (1978), Gesell et al. (1974)
Developmental curriculum:	Gordon (1970), Karnes (1979), Koch (1976), Painter (1971), Sparling & Lewis (1979), Stein (1976), Watrin & Furfey (1978), White (1975)
Parent-family development:	Galinsky (1981)

care of very young children. Recently many more such texts have become available, yet Spock's revised *Infant and Child Care* (1976) continues to serve as a major reference for parents in managing the infant's and young child's health and related activities. It covers topics such as feeding, bathing, illness, toilet training, immunizations, first aid, and clothing. A good deal of the information and advice is neutral in tone, using concrete descriptions of the child's state and physical needs. Nonetheless, it also includes child-rearing advice related to managing these tasks and balancing them within the family unit. An attitude of attention to needs and personal nurturance is conveyed that some interpret as child-centered or indulgent.

Health books also are available that describe pregnancy, childbirth, and breast feeding. These are similar in their accent upon the value of health and well-being as basic to good parenting. Parents of all kinds rely upon these sources of information to help them care for children.

Theory Information. While concepts dealing with personality as well as developmental progress are discussed in books such as Caplan and Caplan's (1976) guide and Dodson's (1970) text, a definite theoretical approach to child rearing can be seen in Mead's (1976) paperback on the subject. Here the parent is provided with thorough descriptions of theories of maturation, socialization, cognition, behavior management, and psychoanalysis as these relate to child rearing. Parents are encouraged to use this information on personality development to create their own approach to the guidance of behavior and to experiment with the methods and consequences of one approach or the other. This spirit of eclecticism is seldom found in parent-oriented materials, since most authors present only their own points of view. Parents may appreciate knowing something about the variety of ways in which personality is thought to develop, particularly since these represent some speculation and judgment rather than scientific fact. Later chapters of the book present an overview of such theories as they may relate to the early years. Texts for teachers and parents by Brooks (1981) and Rutherford and Edgar (1979) also contain descriptions of theories and systems related to child rearing.

Behavior-Oriented Approaches

Special Family Situations. Numerous books directed at both parents and professionals have been written which deal with a wide range of special family situations (Brutten, Richardson & Mangel, 1973; Crow, 1978; Kempe & Kempe, 1978; Gardner, 1977). These authors cover topics dealing with children at risk, coping with divorce, and situations of child abuse in the home.

Problem Solving. One of the most familiar phrases associated with child-rearing advice is *Parent Effectiveness Training* (PET). The PET methods described by Gordon (1970) may be characterized in several ways, but the approach seems generally to emphasize strategies for solving problems that occur between parents and children, particularly child behavior that parents view as difficult. Decoding the child's needs and problems by observing and listening, accepting feelings, avoiding provocations, changing the environment, using motivation and thought rather than power assertion, and finding "no-lose" solutions are all designed to prevent and resolve conflict. Parents are seen as capable of reasoned, democratic authority that accounts for the needs and priorities of all family members. The positive emphasis on seeking solutions and on working cooperatively on interpersonal relationships that satisfy parents and children appears to be a useful way in which to view parental handling of problem behavior. The approach also emphasizes clear communication of feelings and avoidance of messages that block understanding. Gordon's text has been adopted for use by teachers, and many mental health agencies have found it helpful to conduct PET courses for parents, particularly of children in the middle-childhood and adolescent years. For young children, the concepts of tuning in to problems and feelings and altering the environment to maximize youngsters' independence are consistent with traditional early childhood philosophy and are effective for child rearing.

Behavior Management and Control. The control of behavior through its straightforward shaping and reinforcement to fit desired standards has been emphasized in psychology by B. F. Skinner (1953) and in parenting by Becker (1971), Patterson and Gullion (1969), and Wesley (1971). What is also called *applied behavior analysis* focuses on a system of establishing criteria for acceptable behavior and rewarding children contingently for demonstrating desired patterns. At the same time those behaviors that are deemed inappropriate are extinguished through punishment or other means. This approach requires learning some techniques for carrying out procedures and finding meaningful reinforcers. Once a behavior is deemed unacceptable parents attempt to determine how it is triggered and what rewards can be used in stimulating approved alternatives. Parents are expected to concentrate on the specifics of the behavior and the situation, rather than on the broader functions of child rearing and interpersonal relationships. In cases of persistent behavioral difficulties this approach may be useful in helping parents to cope and to establish skills for handling later problems. In early childhood, it has been helpful in reducing resistance to limits such as in the area of attention getting or destructiveness, and in developing success in toilet training and other kinds of required conformity to standards.

Logical Consequences of Behavior.   Another approach to handling misbehavior and encouraging cooperation with established rules and procedures is that of applying logical consequences to children's undesirable behavior. That is, whatever consequences might be likely to result from a youngster's behavior are allowed, within safe limits, to occur, or they are engineered. These natural effects are logically tied to the behavior, and their occurrence is viewed in this way by the offender. Thus, the child is discouraged from repeating acts that produce negative consequences, but without the emotional side-effects that are associated with punishment and with more obvious parental control.

Rudolf Dreikurs is best known for this logical consequences system. Among his books, the Dreikurs and Grey (1970) and Dreikurs and Soltz (1964) texts outline principles and uses of this approach and tie them to personality development and the need to reflect the real social order with which youngsters must deal outside of the family. Logical consequences are expected to reduce the incidence of attention getting, power struggles, and revenge and the use of disability as ultimate goals of children's behavior. Specific daily situations of conflict are described that can be managed by parents, allowing children to experience consequences. Also emphasized are the importance of firmness, respect, cooperation, independence, consistency, reason, and the family council meeting in which all members can express their feelings and needs. The usefulness of these methods extends to a wide range of ages. Parents can help to teach children about the effects of their behavior and can sometimes remain a step removed from the role of disciplinarian.

Limit Setting.   While the words *discipline* and *behavior management* tend to produce both positive and negative responses in an audience, the term *limit setting* represents a somewhat neutral approach to the same subject. The child's behavior is managed by defining boundaries of what is acceptable and unacceptable and by communicating this clearly to the child. In the early years such an approach is very consistent with traditional early-childhood practice where teachers monitor behavior through a system of rules and expectations. What is particularly appealing in this approach is the accent on learning for children. The teaching of appropriate standards, of what the youngster should do or is expected to do, is an extension of the education process. Limit setting has been described within other approaches; for example, Dreikurs and Grey's (1970) book includes limit setting as important to their definitions of discipline. Ginott (1968) in discussing some concepts of Fritz Redl, presents the notion of zones in helping youngsters understand behavioral borders. The green zone is approved and encouraged behavior; the red is intolerable and dangerous to others' health and welfare. The yellow zone includes tolerated behavior that is judged according to circumstances. This approach, then, emphasizes thoughtful, planned, value-defined, and practical aspects of managing behavior.

Assertiveness.   What is sometimes referred to as *protective parenting* (Kiley, 1978) is the application of human territoriality concepts in helping parents to assert their rights as family members with their own needs and priorities (Bakker & Bakker-Rabdau, 1973). In this approach, children's behavior is seen as sometimes constituting a violation of a parent's psychological space or private domain. Assertiveness skills include management of one's territory, defense of it, acquiring new areas, and bargaining or problem solving in cases of conflict. For parents, children's behaviors may serve as weapons that require parental defenses. Irritations are analyzed and desires expressed in an effort to locate and resolve problems. What may be useful in this approach, even for parents of young children, is the sense of strength parents gain in facing their youngsters' crying, tantrums, or outbursts, and the value of parents' limit setting to protect their own developmental and personal needs. For mothers and fathers who have difficulty maintaining limits and who tend to overindulge their youngsters, such an approach could help them and their children to learn greater respect for the rights and needs of others. Westin's (1981) "take-charge" discipline has a similar theme tied to the view that parents need to reassert their authority using traditional values.

Personality and Mental Health Approaches

Personal Support.   Parental understanding and nurturance that support individual differences, encourage independence, and promote emotional health constitute this approach to raising children, who, it is hoped, will reflect the best in human nature. Salk and Kramer (1969) and other writers such as Fraiberg (1968) and LeShan (1970) emphasize commonsense, naturalistic parenting that encourages children's personal growth. Like the informational approaches, specific scripts and methods are avoided, while enhancement of the child's gradual unfolding and emerging interests in others is encouraged. Children's increasing abilities and personality characteristics are described and the "magic" of this process is emphasized. Parents are considered to be fully capable of accepting and guiding, loving and enjoying the youngsters' progress to maturity. Problems are mostly viewed as transitions and stages that are expected and managed best with understanding and support. Indeed, as Elkind (1981) has argued, many of the stresses felt by children represent recent trends toward pushing children too quickly through the stages of childhood and emphasizing achievement over personal well-being. This approach to children, then, is a personal and affectionate one in which parent-child bonds are seen as the essential resources that help families to cope and children to grow. It is very useful for parents who may not feel confident in their roles and whose capacities to nurture need to be supported.

Interpersonal Communication. The communication between and among family members is a pivotal feature of child-rearing skills and family relationships in this approach. Open exchanges of feelings and expectations are seen as forming the basis for understanding children's behavior, needs, and growth toward maturity. Cooperation and encouragement, listening and expressing ideas, and, in general, using language as the primary medium for positive relationships are all emphasized. The STEP program (Dinkmeyer & McKay, 1976) uses communication for its central theme, along with the concept of logical consequences. Ginott's (1968) book emphasizes ways in which parents can use "childrenese" to talk with youngsters so that their feelings are expressed more clearly. As these patterns of communication are established, parents are better able to guide their children toward more independence and responsibility while reducing the frequency of self-defeating or ineffective patterns of interaction. Praise and responsibility and the communication of love and personal availability to children are encouraged as part of the approach. While verbal expressions and discussion may not be considered useful for younger children, the communicative strategies can be adapted to the earlier years. The sense of family interaction is certainly valuable for parents making use of this material at any stage of growth.

Values and Morality. Familes have long been considered to be primarily responsible for teaching children the values and standards held by the larger society. In this approach, parents are encouraged to use values as a major child-rearing strategy. Simon, Leland, Howe, and Kinschenbaum (1972) describe the process of clarifying values in order to focus on the ideas and beliefs held by people. Such values are seen as indicators of goals, aspirations, attitudes, interests, feelings, beliefs, activities, and problems. In helping children to develop values parents use examples, persuasion, limits, feelings, rules, cultural models, and guilt. Decisions about behaviors and personal goals are seen as made more appropriately when guided by values. This is moral training in some respects, but it also is a way to help children to understand and cope with their social world. An emphasis on prosocial, morally positive feelings and acts is described by Mussen and Eisenberg-Berg (1977), whose text includes theories of morality and research suggesting parenting activities that promote caring. This is a different type of work but can be related to the values approach. The values approach may become more useful as children acquire reasoning skills later in the early childhood years and during primary school, but parental support for positive relations with others is important even in the toddler stage.

Acceptance and Esteem. To support fully the development of children's personalities, this approach emphasizes the importance of parental expressions of acceptance and regard for children and the conscious promotion of self-esteem. The "I'm O.K." emphasis of transactional analysis (Babcock & Keepers, 1976) and the direct encouragement of esteem (Briggs, 1975) are considered essential in developing self-confidence and self-worth in children. These positive feelings aid the youngster's behavior and success. If they feel adequate and valued, nourished and loved, they are provided with the emotional strength needed for personal relationships and achievement. Feelings of value contribute to cooperation, conflict resolution, intelligence, and creativity in youngsters. Thus, the parents' responsibility lies in helping children to build self-esteem through their acceptance and the communication of love. In the early childhood years such an approach may be particularly valuable for the child's emerging sense of self and first attempts at independence and competence. Parents may profit from this emphasis in balancing the family's experiences with their children's normal but taxing behaviors and their interests in others outside the home.

Adaptation and Mutuality. The mutuality and correspondence of child development with parenting behaviors are described in a variety of materials dealing with parenting. The emphasis in these resources is upon the process of adapting to the child. As the youngster moves along a developmental continuum and expresses a variety of individual differences, parents must make adjustments in their own child-rearing activities. Both the adults and their offspring have somewhat unique sets of needs and motivations, constraints and obstacles. Each brings something to the relationship, and each is required to make some adjustments. Good family relationships are based upon making allowances for and respecting the other's characteristics and changes. Brazelton's (1969, 1976, 1981) books for parents reflect this view of personal interactions and adaptations as important features of the parenting process. Helping mothers and fathers to deal with their uncertainties and to trust their abilities to grow and change with their children is also reflected in books by Church (1973) and LeShan (1970). These authorities all argue for less parental guilt and more common sense—a more "natural" approach to parenthood and the qualities of children. During infancy and early childhood, this approach may be quite helpful to parents in their adjustment to the realities of the role and their efforts to coordinate their own needs with those of all other family members.

Child Development

The last four approaches in this section reflect a general orientation toward child or family development. Parenting is seen as providing opportunities for protecting and enhancing play, learning, and development; parents are encouraged to fulfill such a role as a major feature of their child-rearing style.

Play Participation. As the persons responsible for maintaining or encouraging play opportunities, including toys, games, play groups, and so forth, parents in this approach are helped to understand and facilitate play activities for their children. Play is viewed as a medium by which the development of personal, physical, and intellectual growth is supported. Through play activities, children gain information and skills, experiment with concepts and relationships, rehearse roles and situations, and develop a sense of mastery and competence. Many materials for parents include chapters on play. A book by the Caplans on *The Power of Play* (1973)

describes a broad range of activities and benefits. Parent-child play is the central theme of a series of books from Nova University (Adcock & Segal, 1979) and others (Sutton-Smith & Sutton-Smith, 1974; Wolfgang, 1977). It is also the focus of a program from the Kennedy Foundation (1977) for families of handicapped children, called "Let's Play to Grow." In the early childhood years such an emphasis on play can assure that children have these experiences as babies, preschoolers, and gradeschoolers. In the later years play is often the focal point for constructive peer relationships and a way in which families can plan recreational times together.

Developmental Guidance. The work of the Gesell Institute for several decades has provided information and guidance to parents about the unfolding or maturation of the child from infancy through the preschool period. Typical behaviors, abilities, interests, and differences are described in order to provide parents with appropriate expectations and responses to the child. Development is viewed as a series of cycles reflected in characteristic ages and stages. The revised text by Gesell et al. (1974) and a similar book that proceeds through adolescence by Elkind (1978) both give parents detailed descriptions of the personal-social growth they will observe. This approach is an informational one, based upon the child-study movement of the 1930s, but it also can be characterized as guidance-centered or focused on children's stepwise progression through a predictable sequence of developmental markers. Such guidance is intended to aid parents in noting their children's special traits and taking account of their social needs and abilities. It is information that also can be used to monitor progress and detect unusual characteristics that might indicate difficulty in growing up or in relating to peers and adults.

Developmental Curriculum. Similar to the guidance provided in the preceding approach, this type of parenting resource also catalogs child development sequences. The emphasis here, however, is upon ways in which skills and understanding can be enhanced at each stage. The intent is to maximize the child's achievement at and between milestones. To help their children to learn and grow fully at each stage and to move smoothly from simpler to more complex stages, parents are encouraged to provide children with experiences that match and extend new skills. The "curriculum" of suggested activities is tied to the child's movement along the developmental continuum. Because intellectual competence is increasingly viewed as central to children's well-being and success in school, early learning is the theme of many recent publications for parents. Books and kits by Gordon (1970), Karnes (1979), Koch (1976), Painter (1971), Sparling and Lewis (1979), Stein (1976), Watrin and Furfey (1978), and White (1975) all provide parents with sets of activities that constitute a developmental curriculum. Parents are the child's teachers in this approach. As such the playful use of learning games, language, books, and projects are important parenting skills. Since young children tend to spend a good deal of time with their parents, this approach is very appealing during the infant-through-kindergarten years. It is basic, as well, to group child care and early education programs, where learning experiences are planned on the basis of child development sequences.

Parent-Family Development. Just as children's development is central to parenting effectiveness, so also is the adult development of the parent. The sociology of parenthood, as described in several texts, and the Eriksonian notion of stages of men and women served as the backdrop for Galinsky's (1981) book dealing with the stages of parenthood. The material she presents serves as an approach to child rearing because it helps parents to understand the differences in their feelings and priorities as they move from the imminent arrival of a baby to the departure of children from the home. At each of six stages there are skills gained, obstacles overcome, relationships adjusted, new priorities set, and consolidations evaluated. Images of one's effectiveness, of children's characteristics, and of options and identities all vary in accordance with the child's developmental progress and the parent's own growth. Such challenges and satisfactions affect parents as people, determining their directions and needs. An understanding of this approach, where parents are viewed as developing in stages that parallel those of their children, may contribute a good deal to parents' abilities to rear children well and enjoy the family experience. It is useful throughout the childhood years.

MODELS OF PARENT-EDUCATION PROGRAMS

Programs of parent education for the early years have recently been designed to address the needs of children, families, and schools. Unlike the parent-directed approaches described in the previous section, these professional programs were created within agencies or schools to enhance child development and family-child relationships for particular populations of parents or those with problems. Such programs serve as useful models for professionals who are planning similar activities. The type of program selected may reflect one or more of the primary goals of parent education, including general information dissemination, educational skill training, problem prevention, counseling and rehabilitation, special education, or social support for parents. In this section, several models will be described briefly in each of these categories. Some projects still exist; others were temporary demonstrations. Resources by the authors or program sponsors will be found in the bibliography.

General Information and Involvement

The most traditional type of parent-education program provides information that helps parents to care for, manage, and teach children. In many cases the program is administered by schools, child care, or early education programs in an effort to maintain parent involvement in the child's education at home and school.

Head Start's Exploring Parenting. This program was designed as a guide for Head Start staff in conducting parent meetings to supplement the children's educational experiences (Zigler & Valentine, 1979). The overall purpose of the materials is to acquaint parents with concepts about child development, learning, and relationships, to make them more aware of their own skills, to enhance these, and to expand their choices in dealing with their children. Skills in parenting are thought to improve with added information and through sharing with peers. As adult learners, parents are viewed as responsible and self-directed, determining for themselves what they need to learn, based upon their interests, needs, and experiences. Stated goals include recognizing parents' educational roles, responding to needs, observing and looking for reasons, teaching values, and reducing stress. Parents are asked to get to know themselves better, understand the child, and use knowledge in making decisions. Twenty group sessions deal with problems, play, art, fears, anger, love, discipline, coping, safety, and other issues. Since the program uses a modest reading level, the materials are well suited for most types of parents and communities.

Brookline Project. The public school officials in this Massachusetts community developed a parent resource project for families with young children (White, 1969). The program attempts to provide educational and health care services prior to the school years. Parents are encouraged to participate in developmental screening programs, acquire and apply information on development and learning, attend children's playgroups, and interact with other families. There is an emphasis on individualized, as-needed services to parents and children. Levels of programing are varied to ascertain the effects of such contacts. It is hoped that the program will help families to enhance their children's development, resulting in greater school competence over the long term.

Footsteps. The U.S. Department of Education has funded a media program that is designed to support new and prospective parents in their efforts to understand child growth and development and to underscore the value of the parenting role. Thirty video programs and a curriculum guide can be rented or purchased. The topics deal with identity and individuality, attachment, discipline, play, social skills, feelings, competence, values, schools, peers, siblings, developmental tasks, and so forth. In each program segment, the theme is explored with a fictional family living in various settings and diverse situations. The program appears to have the potential for utilizing television as a medium of parenting support. A given community can elect to make use of this promising resource, especially if coordinated by schools or social service agencies.

*EPIC.** A program that has been developed in Buffalo, New York, called Effective Parenting Information for Children, is designed to provide information and peer contact to parents of elementary- and secondary-school children. The project began as a cooperative venture guided by civic leaders and helping professionals. It aims to provide coordinated child curriculum, parenting workshops, and teacher education that focuses on positive behavior, personal support, and responsibility as deterrents to a variety of social ills. Topics include values and decision making, managing feelings, communication, friendships, positive child rearing, and a range of subjects that emphasize the importance of helping children and parents to be helpful and responsible. A parent handbook is used to facilitate discussion among parents in meetings held at schools and community centers and led by teams of trained volunteers. The children's curriculum is used by teachers as part of the regular academic program in the public schools.

Educational Skills Training

The teaching of specific skills to parents differs from providing them with information that can be adapted by a family or integrated within the family. Skills training is focused and limited. The program staff usually determine the methods, and the parent/learner is expected to demonstrate observable abilities.

Verbal Interaction Project. The goals of this project (Levenstein, 1977) target the parent skills of providing language stimulation during toy-focused interactions with children. Trained home visitors demonstrate activities to parents and help them to repeat and practice them. Books and toys

*For further information contact: EPIC, 1300 Elmwood Ave., Buffalo, New York, 14222.

are used in the modeling of language and social exchange that are expected to enhance the child's development and cognitive growth. While there is some counseling and peer support in the relationship between mothers and toy demonstrators, the emphasis is upon participation of the parent in the child's learning in ways that are specifically modeled by staff. The successful mother is able to continue such activities and extend them to other developmental tasks.

The Portage Project. A program of curriculum activities geared to assess child development milestones characterizes the Portage materials (Bluma, Shearer, Frohman & Hilliard, 1976). They were designed for use in the home when a staff member pinpoints the child's needs. A card file of suggestions is used for those abilities the child should be achieving at a particular age. All areas of development are included, and parents are expected to carry out the activities they are taught. While the skills emphasized are broader than those in the Levenstein program, the focus also is upon specified activities that parents use with children. The materials were published by the Portage, Wisconsin schools, in part to provide early intervention for youngsters who appear delayed in developmental progress.

Florida Parent-Education Program. This program emphasizes the training of parents in playing educational games with children that enhance their mastery of sensorimotor and manipulative skills. (See Gordon, Guinaugh and Jester, 1977). Home visits by parent educators are the framework for demonstrating how to help the child complete specific tasks. A game format is used, and families are encouraged to enjoy these activities with their children. The tasks outlined for the youngsters are viewed as helpful in developing understanding that is expressed in physical competence and enjoyable problem-solving games. Parents who are able to engage their children in such a manner are seen as more likely to nurture intellectual growth, so that the broader skill instruction children receive is thought to translate into enhanced cognitive performance. Gordon et al. (1977) developed this program, and their curriculum materials are published parent resources.

Problem Prevention

Some parent-education programs are designed to reduce the incidence of problems that interfere with children's developmental progress. Families considered high risk for such difficulties are recruited for these programs. Two such groups are low-income, poorly educated families and teenage, single mothers. Three such programs will be discussed here.

Badger's Teen Program.   This program was developed in a Cincinnati hospital with the goal of helping adolescent mothers to develop their parenting competence (Badger, 1977). Such families are seen as high risk because of the teenager's lack of skills associated with mothering of an infant, who also may be in need of help. Group instruction is used to provide peer contact and support as well as shared information. Child development and learning are the focus of activities the mothers observe and practice with their babies. Over a period of weeks, the curriculum deals with topics in child care and nurturance using such methods as films, toy workshops, demonstrations with children, visitors, lectures, and so forth. The sessions developed by Badger are organized and relevant to many needed parenting competencies at the same time that they are made appealing to this youthful population. Teaching includes demonstration and repetition, positive reinforcement, group pressure, education in child development, and learning.

Abcedarian Project.   The Frank Porter Graham Child Development Center at the University of North Carolina at Chapel Hill was developed as a means of reducing environmental contributions to mental retardation. Ramey, Holmberg, Sparling and Collier (1977) have designed research and curriculum to demonstrate the value of child-centered early education, family support, and nutritional supplements. Teaching-learning activities are used by professionals and parents in a game format that resembles typical parent-child interaction and is based on broad definitions of competence and interpersonal skill. Parents are given individualized contacts with staff, and use of the curriculum materials is encouraged. The program is thus child and education oriented, with a strong emphasis on contributing to the child's developmental progress, both directly in small daycare groups and indirectly through family education and support.

Hi-Scope Programs.   These programs in Ypsilanti, Michigan focus on helping children from low-income families to achieve optimal cognitive development. Weber, Foster and Weikart's view (1978) of such growth is based on Piagetian theory and reflected in the program's emphasis upon creating educational environments that are responsive to the child's own efforts to learn. Parents are seen as teachers in the sense that they are responsible for providing opportunities for their children's own learning activities, and they serve as primary sources of stimulation and reinforcement. Home visitors discuss the importance of this role and encourage mothers to support learning within the framework of their own child-rearing goals. They help mothers to interpret the child's behavior as it relates to developmental need and to solve problems that interfere with effective and healthy rearing. The model is an open one, with respect to parenting activities, but firm in its commitment to improve parents' support for the child's growth.

Counseling and Rehabilitation

In cases where parents have been unable to provide adequate child rearing for their children it may be necessary to implement a program of counseling or rehabilitation. Such efforts are designed to remediate parenting skills and rebuild positive parent-child relationships.

Bromwich's Interaction Program. The broad goals of this program, begun at UCLA, are to build mutually satisfying relationships between mothers and infants by helping mothers enjoy their children, respond sensitively to them, and support their developmental progress and personal well-being (see Bromwich, 1981). Mothers' feelings of adequacy and skill in managing play, learning activities, and personal needs are considered essential to the parenting process. Observable behaviors of mothers are scored on a scale that gives descriptions that are tailored to the goals. The clinically oriented intervention includes strategies such as listening, observing, commenting positively, discussing, asking, modeling, experimenting, and encouraging. The modes most effective for each individual parent-child difficulty are used, once the problem areas are identified. The model implemented for the UCLA population of at-risk families (case referrals from pediatric clinics) emphasizes parent-child interaction through infant curriculum, parent therapy, or parent-education approaches. The counseling and guidance procedures, while anchored to a scale used in the program, reflect the belief that both children and their parents contribute to problems and resolutions.

The Mothers' Project. This Chicago-based program (Weissbourd & Musick, 1981) was created to provide psychiatric rehabilitation for mentally ill mothers of young children. A therapeutic nursery for the preschoolers and clinical efforts to improve the mother-child relationship are included with therapy, social events, and a course in child development. The program focuses on the conflicts felt by these mothers with respect to the care of their youngsters and their difficulties with differentiated social relationships, such that a child is viewed only as a reflection of the mother. Within an emotional support system, the mothers are helped to learn care skills and general competence in child rearing. Education in parenting is thus complementary to psychotherapy and a means by which it is given relevance and confirmation. Mothers work in the nursery as they are able, and there is a group lunchtime where nurturance is encouraged and monitored and the parent-child bond receives attention. This clinical-educational model appears to be useful for a variety of families in which parenting difficulties appear to need remediation.

The Milwaukee Project.   Although children's improved developmental studies (IQ and school success) was the original focus of this program, maternal rehabilitation also has been an important component. Heber and Garber (1975) developed a program of "radical" intervention for families with retarded mothers who are likely to produce children with the same delays in development. Mothers are taught skills for employment, home-making, and child rearing, in an effort to improve children's home environments. Basic education and job training also are provided, while children receive an intensive learning program from infancy to first grade. Cognitive, language, and social goals are emphasized, and paraprofessional teachers used. Mother-child interactions also receive attention in that parents are expected to demonstrate more complex, higher-level interactions with their children, particularly in relation to language use and problem solving. The mothers' rehabilitation emphasizes overall increases in parent effectiveness and stimulation of the child's growing intellectual skills.

Special Education

Some important parent-education models have been developed for families in which children are handicapped by medical or physical problems. These tend to be designed for the purposes of supporting the parents in coping with the family's emotional trauma and for the educational and handling requirements of the child. Many such programs are conducted under the Handicapped Children's Early Education Programs, where over 100 specific projects have been implemented. Most of these have comprehensive parent involvement and counseling programs that are conducted parallel to the children's services.

Project Edge.   This program at the University of Minnesota (Rynders & Horrobin, 1975) has used maternal tutoring that concentrates on children's communicative abilities. Down's syndrome infants were enrolled, but mothers were the target of training until the child was of preschool age. Sensorimotor activities are combined with language stimulation into a series of lessons where mothers are expected to provide direct modeling, instruction, and praise as teaching strategies. This structure is used to guide mothers' activities yet allow room for individual styles. Siblings are involved, and an effort is made to provide extra services such as counseling and respite care. A mobile unit serves as a transition from home to shcool and expands the space available for families and staff. While some parents may not respond well to the tutoring-lesson format, this model demonstrates the importance of parents' roles in helping their handicapped youngsters prior to and during the preschool experience.

*Cantalician Family-Infant Program.** This model, located in Buffalo, New York, focuses on the entire family as well as the handicapped child. An individual curriculum is created after each youngster is administered a detailed assessment battery. Diagnosed needs serve as starting points for demonstrating to parents a variety of activities and handling techniques for their particular child. The trio of teacher, parent, and child decide jointly upon the goals and content of the work sessions, and a curriculum resource file is made available to them. Parent meetings and individual counseling sessions are designed to provide emotional and social support as the children's handicaps are clarified. Home visits and satellite programs extend the services to other families. Fathers attend on a regular basis, and parents select their involvement sessions from the program schedule. The skills of parents are enhanced through the use of educational resources, while peer-group meetings are used to air concerns and future plans for the children.

Play-to-Grow. A program quite suitable for older children, this was developed by the Kennedy Foundation in Washington, D.C. (1977) to help families experience the physical and emotional satisfaction of play and shared understanding with handicapped children. Books and guides can be used individually or in groups to suggest types of play and recreation. Involvement and attention to the child, affection and enjoyment, as well as specific skill demonstrations are emphasized. Parents teach, model, provide hints, join, and share success as their children try new physical exercises and sports activities. The program provides a structure of support in that guide-sheets, charts, posters, certificates, and clubs are used. Thirty-hour segments are rewarded as successes in parent-child play. The model can fulfill a very important role in helping families accept and enjoy their handicapped child, even in the face of the many difficulties and disappointments they also experience.

---

*For further information contact: Cantalician Center for Learning, 3233 Main St., Buffalo, New York, 14214.

Social Support For Parents

One final type of parent program that may be organized by professionals is that of the parent-interest group. Many such leagues and clubs are developed and maintained by parents themselves; examples include childbirth training programs, nursing clubs, and single-parent associations. Others are generated initially by professionals or supported by them, yet parents themselves assume major responsibilities for the groups' purposes and functions.

Family Focus. This community-based program was developed in Michigan by Weissbourd (1983) and associates to serve the family as a whole. There is a meeting place where activities are scheduled for parents and children and where there are drop-in, as-needed services available without regard to qualifications of any kind. Family advocacy and peer relationships are a central theme, and parents are viewed as people who can establish and maintain their own mutual-aid networks. Child care is used to provide developmental information and to model positive relationships. Parent-child activities are conducted to create an environment of satisfaction and esteem. Professional staff are available to provide resources and guidance to the family, both within their home situations and in relation to agencies with which parents must negotiate.

Parent-Child Centers. While these programs are conducted by professionals, the emphasis is upon providing a broad range of services, education in child development, knowledge of community resources, and parental competence within the format of peer discussion groups and a parent-child laboratory. The New Orleans center (Andrews, Blumenthal, Bache & Weiner, 1975) uses paraprofessional staff to help parents fulfill an active role in arranging their child's learning environment. Methods include modeling, role playing, and group discussion, as well as teaching and demonstration. Day-to-day suggestions are supplied. Thus, parents are regularly involved with peers, staff, and children.

The Birmingham center emphasizes mothers' daily activities, use of information, and expanded social skills as well. Mothers handle the children's learning under staff supervision, while they also assume varying roles with their peers. Mothers' involvements outside the home also are encouraged. In the Houston center (Johnson, Kahn & Leler, 1976) home visits are used to help Mexican-American families to become more skilled in English, while the child's home environment is improved and mothers gain teaching skills. Group meetings deal with home management and community issues.

These parent-child centers can be seen as focused on both children and on parents as adult members of a peer group. Families are expected to benefit as a whole from increased social contacts and program resources. (See Beller, 1979, for a longer discussion.)

Children's Coops. The history of parent-run play groups extends to the early child-study movement, but it is probably characteristic of many cultures in one form or another. The coop generally contains professionals as supervisors and liaisons, or it employs parents who themselves have teaching credentials. Mothers serve as the primary staff members for the children, arranging their play and learning experiences along the lines of a traditional nursery school. The process of planning and conducting such programs generates extended peer contact for parents. Discussions about children's behavior, growth, and learning occur regularly. In some situations the coop may provide an extended family experience for both parents and children where strong friendships are similar to kinship ties. What is interesting about this model of parent education is the potential for a great deal of peer education around the children's program. Where professionals are able to provide extra resources and guidance, the model may serve as an effective form of parent education.

PROGRAM SUGGESTIONS

1. Have parents describe the sources and usefulness of the child-rearing information they have acquired on their own.
2. Compare the behavior approaches to each other. Construct a framework for integrating these into a single approach to child behavior, using parents' suggestions.
3. Examine how the personality and mental health approaches reflect the process of parenting in basic ways, and indicate how they are of value in particular families.
4. Ask parents to describe their own philosophies and approaches to child rearing. Use their statements to construct a group point of view.
5. How do the developmental approaches relate to schools? Ask teachers and parents to identify the overlap between their roles in these approaches.
6. Use Table 4 to create a library for parents. Use donated books and photocopied chapters where possible, and collect free parent brochures where available.

7. Have parents select four model programs. Study them and consider whether one or more could be used by the group.

8. Have a helping professional visit the program to discuss parent-education efforts in agencies concerned with problem prevention, intervention, special education, or social support.

5

The Conduct
of Programs with Parents

When parents and professionals come together in the context of a planned parent-education program, many organizational and social factors are involved. The program itself is designed and launched. Participants' needs and concerns are determined. Difficulties are noted that require attention. In working with family members, the professional will assume the responsibility for coordinating activities and dealing with people. Some management tasks have been described in preceding chapters, as have the many approaches taken in parent education and alternative models of child rearing. In these next sections, the focus will be on administrative procedures and interpersonal behaviors of which professionals will need to take account, and on the parallel responsibilities of parents as members of programs and heads of families. Strategies and outcomes of different program formats also will be discussed, including groups, home visiting, classroom participation, and parent support.

PROGRAMING PROCEDURES

Once a decision has been made to design and implement a parent-education program, the major challenge is to develop one that is manageable, responsive, and successful. Criteria for effectiveness are usually based upon specific goals with a particular population of families, using a given set of resources. Goals may be oriented toward processes and/or products; that is, success could be defined in terms of ongoing parent involvement processes or as particular outcomes, such as increases in adult knowledge or changes in child behavior. The administrative procedures described here can serve as general guides for the implementation of any program, once the particular philosophy, goals, and target population are identified.

Establishing Purposes and Selecting a Model

There are two overall, broad goals of most parent-education programs: (1) to ensure or enhance adequate child development, learning, and personal-social growth; and (2) to build parent-family skills, understanding, confidence, and support. Often these two types of goals are interwoven in the structure of the program, but they are not always carefully articulated to parents and professionals. Within these two overall themes, at least eight subordinate program objectives can be identified for use:

1. To inform, advise, or guide parents about child development, learning, and socialization. A wide range of topics can be included under this heading.
2. To involve parents in children's learning and school experiences, or in the conduct of school-related projects. Classroom visits and meetings and social and fundraising projects are part of these goals.
3. To teach specific skills to parents, especially in the areas of child learning and behavioral management. A variety of "curriculum" and child-rearing approaches may be adopted in meeting this goal.
4. To prevent problems in child development or family relations. High-risk families are often the focus of this goal. However, broadly conceived prevention programs with normal populations of parents and children appear to be on the increase, partly in response to the acknowledgment that most families need help at varying stages of children's growth and development.
5. To provide intervention, counseling, or rehabilitation in families where there are known problems in child development or family relations. The originating problems identified here are often sociocultural or mental-health related and show effects on children's school success and emotional or physical well-being.
6. To assist parents in rearing and educating children who have developmental problems or handicapping conditions. Programs with these goals typically focus on high-risk or handicapped youngsters whose needs present special problems to families.
7. To provide social supports to parents in the general community. This goal focuses on the need of all families for external societal supports such as information resources and a sense of regard for the parenting role.
8. To encourage and facilitate parent-promoted self-help and special-interest groups. School and agency professionals can assume a key role in aiding parents' involvement in these programs so that networks of supportive friendships can be maintained among families in the community.

Once the program planners have identified and rank-ordered the objectives they wish to adopt, a program framework or model can be selected. In Chapter 4 of this text, a large number of child-rearing approaches and model education programs were described. These fall into several categories that can be fitted to the goals just outlined. For example, if general parent information and advisement is the focus of the program, a good deal of content and some methods can be borrowed from child-rearing materials in the area of child study, health and nutrition, and developmental theory. If the overriding goal is to prevent problems expected to occur in a particular group of families, other appropriate strategies could be developed. Child-rearing approaches for use in such programs could also include any of those in the categories of child-family development, mental health and personality development, behavior management, and parent information. The needs and preferences of those attending a parent-education program, the skills of the staff, and resources available to the school or agency will help to determine the particular content areas selected. This same procedure can be used for the other program goals described, using the details in Chapter 4.

Selecting and Training the Staff

Teachers, social workers, guidance counselors, psychologists, and even trained laypersons have served as staff members in the many parent-education program models described here. Experience in working with families and children is important, particularly familiarity with the population being served. Staff members who themselves have participated in parenting children have unique understanding and can often share anecdotes with others. However, the qualities and skills of those who work with parents are likely to be the most critical components of the program, following its goals and structure. The following two lists show a variety of qualities and skills that seem to be important for parent-education staff members to possess. The skills described can be incorporated into a training program along with the training topics listed in the third list.

IMPORTANT STAFF QUALITIES

1. *Friendly and positive*: creates a pleasant and comfortable social atmosphere and demonstrates an outgoing interactive style that helps parents feel welcome
2. *Supportive and sincere*: demonstrates acceptance and honest respect for parents in the tasks they face in child rearing and the goals they pursue for their families
3. *Informed and aware*: understands issues and styles in parenting and in

child development, care, and learning, and is well acquainted with program goals and content

4. *Organized and flexible*: is able to function in a careful, organized manner, but is also flexible enough to make changes in response to program or family needs

5. *Courteous and tactful*: handles difficult situations with some openness, but assumes a courteous manner and a tactful approach to problems involving parents or other staff

6. *Empathic and sensitive*: demonstrates the ability to recognize and appreciate the perspectives, concerns, and feelings of others in a somewhat personal way

7. *Objective and professional*: maintains the status of staff member in terms of relationships with clients, with attention and concern for all parents

8. *Energetic and resourceful*: can employ a variety of strategies to maintain the interest and involvement of parents and staff in the program

IMPORTANT STAFF SKILLS

1. *Realistic expectations*: sets goals for parents that are relevant to their concerns and reflective of the program's focus but also are realistic and can be achieved to some degree

2. *Planning skills*: develops plans for the majority of meetings with parents so that content, strategies, and resources are clearly thought out and relevant to program goals

3. *Democratic leadership skills*: shares his/her leadership with participating mothers and fathers in recognition of the unique abilities and experiences they contribute to the learning process

4. *Attentive to parents*: can recognize and deal with parent's needs for self-confidence, some control over children, and understanding of the child's role in family relationships

5. *Facilitative skills*: is able to stimulate a dialogue with parents and encourage their active participation with others

6. *Protective and responsive*: is able to protect parents from criticism, overwhelming feelings, or discussion that may damage self-esteem or overly challenge family standards

7. *Positive modeling*: demonstrates appropriate behavior and discussion that is sensitive and consistent with program goals

8. *Consistency*: keeps program goals in focus, maintains efforts to recruit parents into the program, and in general attempts to keep the momentum of the program at a comfortable pace

9. *Maintains self-awareness*: recognizes own impact on family members

and seeks assistance, in a confidential manner, for any interpersonal difficulties

10. *Coordination skills*: works effectively with a variety of professionals and families to keep the program functioning smoothly

TRAINING TOPICS

1. *Program goals, population, methods*: This includes information about how program effectiveness is determined; the special strengths, needs, and characteristics of the population to be involved; and a thorough understanding of how program techniques are expected to accomplish goals.

2. *Group or interview skills*: The management of groups of individuals requires an understanding of the dynamics of groups and the uses of discussion. To work with individual parents, the staff member needs to develop some counseling and interview skills as well.

3. *Ethnic-cultural diversity*: No matter how homogeneous a group of parents may seem to be, there are varying cultural, familial, and ethnic standards of which staff members should be informed. This includes special resources as well as special needs.

4. *Communication skills*: The process of ongoing adult communication needs to be understood by teachers and others who usually work only with children. Staff training in adult relationships is likely to add greatly to the success of the program.

5. *Public relations and recruitment*: The staff may assume a pivotal position in helping others to understand the program. As staff experiences accumulate it may be important to involve them in any efforts to publicize the program.

6 *Needs assessment and evaluation*: If the program is expected to meet the needs of participants and to ascertain its effectiveness in meeting its goals, the staff will need technical assistance in conducting these assessments.

7. *Sensitivity training*: Work with parents has a strong affective base. The staff will need to expand their abilities to recognize and deal with the emotions of participating parents.

8. *The content areas*: The actual content of the program, from the perspective of the parents and staff, may consist of the topics included in the core chapters of this text. These will form an important part of the staff's training, serving as a focal point for many concepts and controversies. Each staff member should develop a good deal of knowledge in the following content areas when working with parents of preschool and early-elementary-age children:
   a. The history of parent education

b. Family relationships
c. The family in society
d. Models of parent education and child rearing
e. Child care and problems
f. Child play
g. Child behavior
h. Feelings and personality in children
i. Education in the family

Parent Recruitment and Involvement

The initial recruitment of parents for organized educational programs is the responsibility of professionals and sometimes other parents. These beginning efforts involve extensions out into homes and the community to make contact and provide information. As parents respond, their participation can take many different forms, most of which involve reciprocal exchanges between families and professionals. To gain parent support at the outset, however, the staff will need to arrange for personal contacts and the dissemination of information about the program.

Newsletters. Many agencies and schools use newsletters to communicate with clients and families about their activities. Announcements in this format might include an overview of goals, some content, and expected outcomes. The staff might be introduced, along with an invitation to make personal contact for further details. Brochures can be attached as well.

Posted Announcements. Written notices and posters can be very effective as program announcements, if they are placed in locations likely to be visited by prospective families. Very brief phrases can highlight the program's special features, along with dates, times, and telephone contacts for more specific information. Photographs that call attention to children or families might make such posters appear more friendly and inviting.

Personal Contact. Many types of parent-education programs require that staff members make personal face-to-face and telephone contact with parents. Home-visiting and parent-support models, in particular, depend upon personal relationships that have to be established and nurtured. Group and school participation programs also will gain from personal invitations and discussions that demonstrate to parents the staff's regard for their programs and the families who attend them.

Public Relations and Promotions. In large agencies and school systems it may be important to promote the program in the media in order to reach a wide range of families and supporters. These efforts may take the form of community awareness broadcasts and newspaper stories. To the extent that a program relies upon external funding, such efforts can be very effective in maintaining enrollment and building a supportive constituency.

Parent Networks.   Parents themselves are the most essential program builders, and their social networks are an important source of new families. Recruitment efforts that put mothers and fathers in contact with one another often add warmth and stability to the program. Social networks also are valuable in spreading the effect of parent education beyond the confines of the school or agency and into homes and neighborhoods where parents frequently meet.

Referrals.   Participation in specific family programs often is encouraged by helping professionals in health care, social work, education, and mental health. Such individuals also may be consulted about program goals and content. This last suggested recruitment method can be tapped in order to build an awareness of the program in the professional community. Brochures and personal descriptions can be effective, particularly when this information comes from those with firsthand experience in the program.

Once parents take the first step by accepting the program's invitation to join, it becomes important for staff members to maintain their involvement over time. The following suggestions will offer some options, but parents themselves may develop additional ideas as the program matures. Many of these activities can be conducted by either parents or staff members, or both. In either situation, the resources of many people are likely to make the effort more successful than when it is organized only by a single professional.

Program Open House.   This activity often serves as an orientation or program presentation at which all family members are welcome. The materials and facilities of the program are usually available for inspection, and the staff members serve as hosts for the occasion.

Parent Meetings.   A more structured format is the parent meeting, at which the program can be presented in the context of other business of the school or agency. Outside speakers and media presentations may be made. Parents may have the opportunity to meet other families at the same time, for brief social exchanges. In group program models, these meetings are scheduled regularly.

Parent Advisory Groups.   In many programs, an advisory board is organized, to deal with issues that require thoughtful parent input. This group may assist in setting program goals, determining effectiveness, handling public relations, and managing funding efforts.

Social Fund Raisers.   The format of these activities may vary widely, from spaghetti dinners, book or bake sales, and flea market fundraisers to club activities designed to support the program. Their primary goals include opportunities for parents to become acquainted with one another in an informal, enjoyable situation and to raise funds for particular projects in a sociable atmosphere.

Children's Events.   Art and craft shows, music and drama presentations, photo exhibitions, field trips, sporting events, and fairs that include children, their products, and interests are generally enjoyed by all family members and staff. The focus on the children builds family relationships at the same time that it contributes to family fun and program support.

Work Projects.   School- and agency-sponsored activities may include those that require parent contributions of work time in the program. Such work projects may focus on building or repairing children's materials and playthings or beautifying the physical facility in some way such as with a garden, a painting, or a clean-up activity.

Child-Helping Projects.   Some parent-participation programs focus upon assisting children in their activities. Play, reading, music, or physical education may be enhanced by parents working with youngsters in small groups on a regular basis under the supervision of teachers or child care professionals. Such parent involvement is common in the preschool.

The Parent Place.   A small area of the school or agency may be devoted to parents' own use among their peers. A parent library, bulletin board, or snack area may be used for this kind of continued involvement. Such a setting offers parents social and informational exchanges on a range of matters that interest families.

Health Screening Programs.   Many agencies are able to transport their screening programs to schools or other centers where parents can bring their children. Speech and hearing, developmental progress, vision, lead poisoning, and other tests of children's well-being can be conducted.

Home-School Visits.   Many programs encourage exchange visits between homes and the program setting. Parents are expected to visit the child's classroom, for example, while teachers or care givers make a brief visit to the youngster's home. Of course, some programs focus exclusively on home visits.

Conferences and Interviews. While regular one-to-one meetings between parents and staff members are necessary in the parent-support and -counseling models, they also are used in other types of programs. Needs, concerns, information, advice, and feedback can be discussed privately, and new suggestions developed for both parents and staff. Such exchanges can be very important indicators of program progress or problems.

Parent Perspectives and Roles

Every family is different; every parent is unique. These statements hold true regardless of the parent's skills, knowledge, and preferences, which also vary in each family situation. There are, nevertheless, some common themes to be found across any parent population, especially in daily responsibilities and child-rearing concerns. Virtually all parents want their children to grow up well, to get along, to be reasonably successful as they become adults. Parents who become involved in educational programs may be especially concerned and self-conscious, or they may be recognized as needing resources by others.

The perspectives, needs, and cultural-familial diversity of parents are important for program staff members to begin to understand. Parents have a wide scope of responsibility for children that extends across days and years. Their relationships are emotional rather than objective or distant. Their standards of behavior and care are influenced by their own history and culture. Their views of development and learning are gained from observation and experience more often than by college texts. Their preferences reflect an attempt to balance a variety of roles and needs within their own family unit. Of necessity, parents will need to adapt anything they learn in a program. Some messages and goals will be received and welcome. Others will be challenged, discarded, or ignored. Parents are expected to use their judgment in helping children to grow up. That same skill will influence the program's effectiveness and perhaps its very organization.

The needs of children are often the ultimate focus of a parent-education program, yet parents' views must be part of the learning process because they also affect the children's experiences. Parents' attitudes and priorities tend to form a protective ring around the child in the home. The staff member who can attend to these more elusive but powerful program intermediaries is likely to be more successful in assisting both the adults and the children involved.

Expectations about the outcomes of a program are also important to consider. Although the staff will want to promote the program and focus on its potential for success, there must be a realistic and relevant set of goals to consider. Parents have a right and a responsibility to know about these in order to consider or reject them. To the extent that expectations can be identified and discussed, it is important to do so. Program goals and anticipated outcomes can serve as starting points.

The roles to be assumed by parents also can be discussed. There are usually several in each program, ranging from that of a program advisor who contributes suggestions and feedback, to that of learner and recipient of services. Parents also may function as group members, project supervisors, counselors, and hosts in the home or center. If the family has agreed to participate in the program, they are likely to remain involved in their respective roles. The staff members will need to recognize these positions and how they relate to the structure of the program. Regardless of the specific role, however, parents should be active contributors to the educational process. Even in relatively passive group-member roles, parents have the responsibility for expressing their needs, priorities, concerns, information, and feedback. Their views about the impact of the program on the family, agency or school, and community will contribute to its effectiveness.

Program Rapport and Respect

It is the responsibility of the program staff to establish rapport between themselves and family members and to facilitate mutual respect among all participants. Rapport is developed through a friendly, outgoing attitude that is expressed to parents. Openness in communication, where parents' views are facilitated and appreciated, helps to maintain this atmosphere. Since confidentiality is necessary in parent-education programs because personal information is shared, the staff must explain some ground rules of privacy. It is important to reflect fairness and equal treatment for families in discussions where everyone's contributions are sought. Rapport also is maintained by staff members' understanding and concern, shown by remembering people and events and by sensing feelings and responding sympathetically to them.

Respect is as necessary among participating families as is rapport between parents and staff. Respect is encouraged through attentiveness and politeness in discussions, and through calm reactions and acceptance of a variety of feelings. The professionals should help parents to notice the concerns of others, to take such needs seriously, and to try to understand different goals and constraints. It is also important to look for the positives, the strengths and value, of each family in the program, because they can often be used by parents to deal with many areas of need. Respect also can be furthered by the staff's acknowledgment of their own lack of expertise and experience in many child-rearing matters. This is a field in which conflicting advice, evidence, and experience abound. Open admission of one's limitations will not interfere with professionality but can contribute to mutual respect and regard in the difficult areas of parenting. Finally, respect is often engendered by experience and natural wisdom, by humor and irony. Those who enjoy working with parents may find some of these qualities emerging as they gain in experience and understanding.

Program Progress and Evaluation

The impact of parent-education programs is seldom measured carefully unless a research component or grant regulations make evaluation a necessity. In Chapter 1 of this text, program effectiveness was discussed in the context of the history and development of such programs. In general, parent education is thought to result in gains in children's development; improved home environments, including parenting behaviors; a greater sense of satisfaction for parents in their child-rearing responsibilities; and benefits to schools and centers where children and parents are in attendance. These types of consequences have been documented by procedures such as child pre- and posttests; achievement test scores; analyses of physical environments and of adult-child interactions; questionnaires; rating scales; and data on attendance, participation, and so forth. Statements and testimonials from parents also have been used.

To determine program progress and evaluate effectiveness, it is important to begin with program goals. These help to keep an evaluation on target and focused, but it is often the case that unforseen benefits or side-effects become increasingly valued as a program matures, making goals only a part of the overall picture of impact. Those who develop and administer the program should discuss the matter of evaluation at length and determine what criteria would best reflect success. If this is done at an early stage, program activities can focus on outcomes. If evaluation criteria and procedures are established at a later point, it may be possible to include a variety of program effects identified by staff and parents. In either situation, the observations and concerns of participants can be expected to provide many ideas for documenting progress and success, and these should be actively solicited.

Once some criteria are established, some or all of the following different methods can be used to evaluate the program.

Record Keeping by Staff. It is often valuable in a program to have ongoing records of the actual proceedings, whether these are group meetings, home visits, interviews, or a variety of agency and school-related activities. The records kept by the staff can describe attendance figures, topics of interest, problems experienced, unusual interactions, and so forth. Such records can give a very useful overview of the program and can highlight a variety of possible effects, especially when they are examined in large numbers. If goals and methods change, this information can provide comparative evidence.

Self-Evaluation by Staff. The key figures in any parent-education program are the staff. Their skills and understanding and their use of content and procedures may determine the program's degree of progress and ultimate success. While regular supervision of the staff is integral to some model programs, in others this effort must come from staff members themselves. Self-evaluation can be done formally, using a checklist that reflects the program's orientation, or it can be done more casually, through reflection and consultation with other staff members. It should focus, however, upon the parents and the program, rather than attempt to challenge the staff member. Since the focus of evaluation includes program progress and outcomes, staff evaluations should examine consequences thought to be associated with staff attitudes and behavior. Consideration also should be given to the appropriateness of the roles and responsibilities assigned to the staff. A profile of the strengths and problems of individuals also can be useful.

Structured Observations by Staff. Casual observations of the program can provide useful information about its functioning; however, formalized and systematic observations of parents, children, and staff members also can be carried out as part of the evaluation process. Descriptions of specific behavior and conversation, of activities and social exchanges can be placed on a form and checked at various times by either staff members or outside observers. These can be analyzed for possible program effects, especially changes and increases from the early weeks to the program's completion. Observations of both group and individuals' behavior, done in home and program settings, may be carried out. Patterns showing how parents use information and skills will be valuable evidence of the program's effectiveness.

Ratings by Staff or Parents. Rating scales allow people to compare themselves on particular characteristics or to rank-order descriptions of behavior and attitudes. Such ratings help when used early and later in the program, because they can identify perceived changes that might have occurred from the parents' participation. Differences in knowledge of and attitudes toward the children, for example, may be reported by parents on ratings of themselves. Staff members might rate the parents on their involvement in the program and with one another, although these items would have to be described as objectively as possible in order to acquire realistic responses. Even though there is a tendency for people to rate themselves positively, many such scales can still detect changes in first and second assessments. Often there are frank and honest responses that do reveal program impacts.

Parent Report Forms.   Parents also can provide useful evaluation information through self-reports, especially when they are organized as forms that can be quickly filled out on a regular basis. Reactions to the program, changes observed in the home or in relation to children, feelings about parenting, information gained, and activities that were carried out are all important kinds of information to obtain. Forms should be simple to use and their value stressed. If parents fail to use them, the staff will need to redesign the forms and the procedures so that data can be collected in a systematic way. Reactions to the program can be counted, categorized, and placed on charts or tables to help the staff analyze patterns that indicate problems and successes.

Parent Interviews.   Structured interviews between parents and an outside program reviewer may produce additional evaluation information. When the focus is on program goals, content, procedures, and so forth, parents may be able to describe complex results, such as shifts in perception and attitudes, altered patterns of behavior, new interests and activities, and feelings about the role of the program in child and family relationships. The questions asked of each parent are usually organized on a printed form, but interviewers are expected to exercise their judgment and make any needed changes that lead to accurate and detailed responses. Standard interview practices also are used to make the person comfortable and assure them that answers will be treated confidentially. Those conducting the interview should be relatively objective about the program so that parents' ambivalent or negative responses as well as their complimentary reactions can be solicited and recorded.

Questionnaires.   A formal questionnaire with multiple-choice response options is a typical evaluation tool for many parent programs. Items often describe knowledge of child development, attitudes about children and family life, perceptions about the program, and methods of child rearing. For research or evaluation purposes, the same instrument is usually given at the beginning and end of the program. The changes occurring between pre- and posttreatment assessments are attributed to the parent education that was experienced. As a measure of success, such questionnaires can be quite useful, but they are dependent upon parents' skills in handling them. Program-derived questionnaires also may be difficult to create, and the use of other instruments may mean that specific program goals are not included in the evaluation. Nevertheless, questionnaires or surveys are relatively objective and can be sources of significant information on program outcomes.

Child Assessments. In programs where child development is the primary target of parent education, assessments of children's gains and achievements may provide critical information. There is a wide variety of developmental measures that focus on intellectual, physical, and language growth and on school achievement in children. Few, however, are available for assessing their personal-social functioning, which is often central to the parenting process. Nevertheless, positive changes in children's tested abilities is considered to be strong evidence of the effectiveness of parent education, particularly for families considered to be at high-risk for delays or other problems in children. Since the instruments are usually standardized and formally presented, change scores are seen as objective evidence, especially if these remain consistent over time.

External Reviews. An external evaluation of the program may include one or more of the methods described in this section; however, a professional who has little initial knowledge of the program can be asked to examine its structure and effects. The process generally involves the reading of program materials, meetings with staff and parent participants, observing meetings or visiting sessions, and examining any other collected data. These are compared with the program itself over time and with other similar programs. Strengths and needs are identified in the context of progress and success in fulfilling goals and requirements.

Impact Study. Sometimes it is important to determine the impact of the program upon other segments of the community as well as upon participants themselves. A program, for example, might generate interest in similar projects, influence professional groups, provide assistance to the community, or support publication and media events. It might stimulate the growth of parent networks or develop a sense of support among families. These impacts may be quite difficult to ascertain but also may have far-reaching positive consequences. Methods differ in conducting an impact study, but often an outside evaluator with skills in the field can work with staff and parents to find evidence of such broad effects.

PROGRAM FORMATS

The organizational structure of a parent-education program influences the roles assumed by parents and professionals. Group programs that take place in schools or agencies are conducted quite differently from those using home visiting, parent counseling, and classroom participation. Each type also employs somewhat distinct program strategies, expects particular outcomes, and uses varied educational resources. In this section, the four most common formats for parent education will be examined, with particular emphasis upon administrative matters considered to be important for those actually conducting the programs. These four formats and their corresponding resources, role expectations, methods, and outcomes are summarized in Table 5.

Group Programs

Parent education that is carried out in group meetings is the most familiar format used by schools and agencies. Indeed, the parent-education movement can be said to have begun with the child-study groups of the 1930s, where mothers attended weekly sessions about child development and behavior. More recently, group programs have been used for informational sessions, formal training meetings, workshops, discussions, and even group counseling that deals with specific issues common to many parents. Primary resources used in groups for mothers and fathers include articles, manuals and books, films or videotapes, talks by known authorities or helping professionals, and discussions by other parents whose experiences provide a framework for understanding and action. The school or agency generally provides space and materials for the group meetings, which may be ongoing or periodic.

The Professionals' Roles.   In group programs the roles of the professionals center on administrative responsibilities, but they also include the handling of social relationships, such as using group dynamics or providing brief individual counseling. The group's initial establishment is most often the first administrative item of business for the professional. This may include the recruitment or registering of parents; arrangements for meeting times and locations; and even the planning of topics, resources, and speakers. Evaluations of the parents' responses and the program content and methods also may be an administrative responsibility of the group leader.

A second major role of professionals in group programs is that of actually conducting meetings. Where specific guidelines or manuals are used, the sessions can be rather structured and focused. Often the leader has

Table 5
Parent-Education Program Formats

Program Format	Primary Resources	Professional Roles	Parent Roles	Distinct Methods	Expected Outcomes
GROUP MEETINGS	a. Media: written materials, films	a. Recruitment, scheduling, planning, evaluation	a. Attend, be receptive, share ideas & concerns	a. Meeting content or topics	a. Increased information, expanded skills
	b. Expert consultants	b. Group leader, guide, problem solver	b. Become involved, contribute suggestions	b. Parents' own ideas, skills, and needs	b. Adjustments in attitudes and expectations
	c. Parents' own ideas	c. Neutral relationships, facilitator, orchestrator	c. Bring ideas & concerns from and to the home	c. Social support and reference group	c. Strengthening of parent social networks
HOME VISITING	a. Home visits, telephone contact	a. Establish a personal relationship with parent & child	a. Hostess to visitor, receptive to program goals	a. Demonstration of activities with child in home setting	a. Child-centered parent learning
	b. Packaged playthings & notes	b. Inform, guide, teach, consult	b. Try new activities & methods	b. Use of private relationship with parent	b. Sense of school/agency support
	c. Supervisory framework	c. Plan for & record visits & home changes	c. Extend learning to others	c. Specific family needs determine goals	c. Documented changes in home setting and relationships

110

CLASSROOM PARTICIPATION	a. Classroom materials	a. Plan activities & schedule visits	a. Helper & resource to school or agency	a. Work with children in school or agency setting	a. Extra help provided to school or agency
	b. Parent-teacher meeting	b. Teach parents about methods & materials	b. Child guide, teacher, & supporter	b. Information & training sessions for parents	b. Builds parent-child understanding & communication
	c. Adult-child interaction	c. Help children to work with parents	c. Learner of new methods & content	c. Clear definitions of parent tasks re: child learning	c. Parent learns about classrooms, materials, & other children
PARENT COUNSELING	a. Regular discussion with trained professional	a. Help parent understand goals & methods	a. Try to understand own attitudes & skills	a. Feelings & attitudes openly discussed	a. Increase in adult development
	b. Parents' own skills & understanding	b. Maintain records of sessions	b. Attempt new responses to child & family	b. Alternative strategies explored	b. Satisfaction with parenting activities
	c. Articles or books made available	c. Serve as liaison between parent & others	c. Integrate new understanding with family goals	c. Parent supported in facing own style	c. Problem resolutions re: parent & child relationships

had some training in using the program materials. Many groups are less organized in that topics may be selected as the members choose or as the professionals determine are relevant. In these cases, skills in managing groups of people may be critical. The leader has to stimulate and guide discussion, deal with disagreements or irrelevant conversation, and maintain a sense of group coherence.

Such responsibilities are strongly related to a third role, which is to provide a neutral affective zone. That is, the professional remains somewhat apart from the group and the individual members, seldom developing any personal relationships. The task is to facilitate and orchestrate, to keep the group functioning smoothly without becoming involved as a member. Advice and suggestions generally come from other parents unless the leader is an experienced helping professional.

The Parents' Roles.   In group programs, the roles of parents can be described as those of receptive participants, involved contributors, and home liaisons. When mothers and fathers attend group sessions, they are expected to listen and participate by giving attention to the material and sharing their reactions. Discussions include dealing with ideas and concerns. That is, parents are to make the effort to understand the program topics and to be receptive to the information under discussion. The second, related role, of becoming a contributor to the group, means to suggest ideas and strategies and to offer discussion and advice to other members. Of course, each parent's degree of involvement will vary, so a good leader attempts to balance the contributions of very active or very passive members. Indeed, particular mothers and fathers will react to and use the program's content differently. It is expected, however, that parents also will assume the third role in this regard, which consists of bringing ideas and concerns to and from home and program. In this way, the family can integrate new information and suggestions into the home situation and, in turn, contribute home-tested ideas to the program.

Distinct Methods.   There are several distinct methods used in group programs in providing information and building understanding. The content of the meetings is particularly important as a stimulant for discussion, but the topics themselves, presented meaningfully, are expected to educate parents. To the extent that this content deals with children's needs and family dynamics it will be relatively effective. Of course, care must be taken to avoid duplicating information or skills parents have already acquired and to avoid using concepts above or beneath parents' abilities to understand. A second method is the use of group members' suggestions, ideas, and concerns. Parents are often able to transmit skills and understanding to one another or to build on their peers' strengths and needs, when these are discussed in the group. Finally, group programs often provide an organized social support for parents in which they can function as peers to others who are experiencing the same parenting joys and difficulties. This reference group can help parents to test out their attitudes and understanding within a highly relevant social framework.

Expected Outcomes.   The expected outcomes of group parent education center upon increased information, adjustments in attitudes about children and learning, and the strengthening of parents' social networks. Gains in information are expressed goals of the other program types as well; however, this is quite central to groups. Adjustments in the ways in which parents perceive their children are similarly important for groups, especially since parents are exposed to the reactions of their peers. Other parents' styles and ideas provide a sounding board that can reinforce or alter an individual family's methods of raising children. Social networks are related to this. Mothers and fathers may continue to seek out group members after the program has ended. Such relationships extend the family outward into the larger society, and this can help children by increasing their models and their resources.

Home Visiting Programs

For many populations of parents, home visiting programs are both effective and cost-beneficial. Where schools and agencies have limited space or large geographic regions to serve, if children are very young or have medical or social difficulties, and when changes in home settings are sought, then home visiting formats are appropriate for parent education. The primary resources used focus on the home setting itself, where visits and telephone contact bring the professional to the home rather than the parent to the agency or school. Program activities are carried out using materials brought in and typically used with the mother and child by a trained visitor.

The Professionals' Roles.   In home visiting formats, the professionals' roles emphasize personal relationships, direct teaching, and record keeping that links the home to the program. A home visitor is trained in the program's content and methods, is given a caseload of families, and then coordinates the program on a one-to-one basis with each parent-child pair. A critical role is that of establishing a personal relationship with each parent-child pair, most often the mother and her infant or young child. This relationship is the foundation upon which the educational program is contructed. The professional (sometimes a trained paraprofessional with a similar cultural background) must listen briefly to the parent's concerns at each visit and be sensitive to the emotional ties between the mother and child.

A second role involves the teaching activity planned for the session. Age-appropriate play materials are used with the child, to demonstrate how learning is a part of the activity and to explain the value of working with the child. In addition to this teaching-guiding role, the professional is also responsible for reporting to a supervisor. Plans and records of each visit are communicated, and the parent's progress in working effectively with the child is discussed.

The Parent's Roles.   In home visiting programs, parents' roles include serving as hosts to the professional, trying new activities and methods of working with the child, and extending new skills and information to other children and family members. In a sense, the mother's or father's involvement in the program is very personal. Certainly, fulfilling the role of host requires that home and family be open to the perceptions and teachings of others who bear no long-term relationship to the family. The receptivity of the parents is also reflected in their very obvious learner role, where demonstrations of particular activities are observed and tried. The professional's suggestions cannot be easily ignored or rejected when these persons are physically present in the home for regular periods of time. While the extension of new learning to others may not be apparent during the program itself, it is considered an important parental role. Younger siblings, spouses, and others involved in the child's care often receive generalized program benefits because parents describe, demonstrate, or use their new skills even when the home visitor has departed. A particular game with a new toy, for example, may be practiced with many others, once it has been mastered under the professional's guidance, and this means that the program is extended to nonparticipants.

Distinct Methods. Some distinct methods used in home visiting parent-education programs also reflect its personalized approach. Toys and learning materials are demonstrated with the child during each session so that the parent's learning is made concrete and is directly applied to interactions with children. Establishing a personal and private relationship between the parent and the professional is a second important method in which attitudes, knowledge, and skills can be examined and improved within a framework of mutual respect and acceptance. Particular needs unique to each parent-child pair are examined in the home visiting program and used to establish goals directly relevant to that family. This last method ensures that the program fits the family, even within the structure provided by preset schedules of visits and sequences of content. Home visiting programs therefore remain relatively flexible and family centered, yet may be quite focused in the education provided to the family.

Expected Outcomes. The expected outcomes of home visiting parent-education programs center on changes in parents and homes. The skills and understanding acquired by parents tend to be very reflective of the child's emerging needs for learning and guidance. Some of these developmental requirements, such as language expansion, may continue to be relevant to the child's growth even after the program has ended. A sense of support from the sponsoring school or agency is often an additional positive outcome, in that mothers and fathers are aware of the sponsor's interest in a successful and enjoyable child-rearing experience. The "somebody cares" attitude can help otherwise socially isolated families to feel more important. Documented changes in home settings and in relationships between parents and children are also to be expected. Immediate program effects such as these are important signs of program success, even when longer-term changes are the ultimate criteria requiring substantiation.

Classroom Participation Programs

Parent-education programs that include parent assistance in the classroom or other agency facility have some special strengths and problems. Their task involvement provides a framework around which parents can observe, interact, and even teach their child and her or his peers. Staff and parents may work side by side for periods of time, so that each becomes familiar with the style of the other. Classroom or agency materials and resources are used and, in early childhood, these aids to learning and child development are play centered and successful for adults. Meetings and discussion between parents and teachers also occur, in formal ways while preparing for work with the children, and in informal ways when responding to events as they occur in the classroom. Adult-child interaction is a third primary resource for parent learning. While working with the children, the mother or father has to communicate, monitor activities, deal with problems, and teach those methods and content that are part of the activity. Where projects are completed with other parents outside the classroom, the children's needs are still of concern; however, parents interactions with different families may take the place of teacher-parent exchanges. The focus on children is nevertheless a central theme in classroom participation.

The Professionals' Roles. In these types of programs, the professionals' roles include managerial and teaching tasks. Teachers or parent coordinators plan activities for parents, schedule their visits, and organize any other procedures, such as providing coffee or a break time or arranging additional resources needed for an activity. Two teaching tasks are also part of the professionals' roles. One involves teaching parents how to use particular methods and materials. This may be done by verbal explanation or demonstration. Parents also may initiate other activities, such as holiday projects or themes related to their own interests, and these are often completed with minimal teacher involvement. Such enthusiastic parent participation can provide enriching experiences for children that teachers may not have been able to consider. Another teaching role involves helping children to work with parents. When teachers begin to share classroom activities with others, children often need guidance and rules of procedure that reduce confusion about who is in charge or who can be expected to help with problems.

The Parents' Roles. In classroom participation programs, parents' roles center on the assistance provided to children and schools and on the acquisition of new skills and learning. The parent becomes a school or agency helper, a resource for the staff who is able to strengthen the children's programs by providing extra attention, assistance, and sometimes new experiences. Participating mothers and fathers are also guides, teachers, and supporters of their own children and other youngsters in the group. In working with the children, parents deal with behavior, learning, and social relationships. Often, there is a good deal of affection shown because the children know this is someone's parent who is available to them, someone noticeably pleased to be there as a helper. The parent also assumes the role of learner in the classroom. Since many materials are unfamiliar and the teacher-parent relationship is still somewhat unformed, the mother or father functions as a learner under the teacher's guidance. In a sense, this role is quite disparate from that of a guide to the children, or authority figure in the home. Sometimes it is an uncomfortable position, and parents may need some moral support when assuming these roles in the program.

Distinct Methods.   In classroom participation programs there are several distinct methods used, the most important of which is the use of small groups or individual work with children within the classroom setting. Here the agency or school serves as a host to the family, opening its facilities and materials to them. The method relies to some extent on a second technique, that of information-training sessions for parents, to prepare them for such work. Even with preparation, the parent's own attitudes and skills will contribute to the success of the program. If the classroom activities are unsuitable for parents, if the adults do not work well together, and if the child cannot handle the situation, then these methods may not be effective for parent education. A third strategy may provide some help. Classroom participation programs often provide clear definitions of the parents' tasks in relation to children and teachers. There may be a checklist of selected projects, or parents may deal with a coordinator who helps to explain program expectations and options. In small programs, parents may participate informally, with teachers and administrators providing help and support where needed.

Expected Outcomes.   The expected outcomes of these programs include benefits to parents, children, and schools or agencies. Extra assistance and enrichment are provided, which contribute to program quality. Parents acquire new information about classrooms, the teaching-learning process, the peer group, educational toys and materials, and child management. Children and families are helped as well. Parent-child relationships may improve with greater understanding of the child's out-of-home experiences and more opportunities to discuss these. Indeed, from the early days of parent coops, participation in the child's nursery school has been a major early childhood education theme. Since the programs are not compulsory, parents are responsible for selecting and monitoring these experiences. This tends to make them more open to participation, except in the case of daycare. Working families present a special case, but they can be encouraged to experience the child's classroom, even if the resulting program is less extensive than when parents are available for parts of the day.

Parent Counseling Programs

Parent education also can be accomplished within a counseling framework. In many cases, such one-to-one or small-group discussions with a trained professional are needed to enable parents to learn about the child's developmental and educational needs. When parents or children come from special situations, counseling programs can provide highly personalized assistance. Discussions about sensitive issues or very specific needs can usually be handled only by an experienced counselor. Such regular exchanges are a primary resource of these program types. Another is the parent's own perceptions, concerns, abilities, knowledge, and so forth. That is, parents bring these with them as sources of content for their discussions. Articles and books also may be used to help parents learn about the child's general development or specific problem and about options in child rearing, guidance, and education that parents may want to try.

The Professionals' Roles.   The roles of the professional in such programs include direct work with the parent, record keeping, and liaison activities between the family and the school or agency. The staff member attempts to help mothers and fathers to understand children, to teach and guide them effectively, and to deal with the goals and methods used by the program. This direct work with individuals or small, homogeneous groups of parents is unique to parent counseling formats. The professional is responsible for maintaining records of assessments, evidence of progress, and any important interactions with staff or family members. Liaisons with other programs also may be important. The professional may receive or send a referral or may help the family to deal with classroom teachers, daycare staff, or physicians and psychologists from other agencies.

The Parents' Roles.   In counseling types of parent education, parents' roles are rather simply stated but very far reaching in their consequences, when the program is successful. One task is for parents to understand their own attitudes and feelings about their children, especially as they relate to helping their offspring to become more competent. Mothers and fathers are expected to attempt some new activities and responses to children and family members. This is often a difficult task because new behaviors are initially uncomfortable and it takes time before they become part of familiar routines. New learning and attitudes also have to be integrated into family goals and culture. This usually requires some adjustments between the professionals' approach and the parents' own value systems, most of which have to be identified by mothers and fathers themselves.

Distinct Methods. Some distinct methods used in this format have already been mentioned. Discussions of attitudes and feelings occur on a regular basis between the professional and the parent. These provide important insights and help to relieve tension. Alternative child-rearing strategies are explored, including adjustments that make new methods effective for particular parents and children. Parents also receive emotional and social support, regardless of how successful they are in gaining skills and understanding. Such personal support is basic to the counseling process and quite unique to these programs.

Expected Outcomes. The expected outcomes of counseling parent-education programs may be more difficult to assess than in the other formats. Certainly, the parents' own development receives attention, and they are expected to grow as people and as mothers and fathers. Satisfaction with the parenting role is also considered to be important. Greater enjoyment of children and appreciation of their competence make parents feel more successful and valued. Many problems also can be resolved through counseling programs. Parent-child relationships present difficulties, and obstacles exist in every family. Opportunities to work with professionals on some of these are rare for mothers and fathers. Success is expected not only from direct treatment but from the sense of caring and self-confidence gained in a counseling relationship.

PROBLEMS IN PROGRAMS

Parent-education programs are not always appropriate or successful. There may be conflicts over methods and content. Enthusiasm may be replaced by boredom or resistance. Resources may become unavailable and support withdrawn. Those planning to design and conduct programs should know about problems that can seriously undermine success. In this section, a variety of known difficulties will be discussed so that administrators can be alert for them in their own programs. Each will have to be treated in relation to the particular program and staff involved, but it is hoped that awareness of these potentials will aid in their resolution.

Initial Recruitment Problems

To launch a parent-education program successfully requires resources, staff commitment, and some good luck. Parents may not understand the goals or may have had negative experiences related to working with professionals. The needs of families may not be clear, or families may not see the value of giving them some attention. Fear of change, perceived value differences, hectic schedules, lack of transportation, or any number of other difficulties may contribute to poor recruitment results. These may change with alterations in approaches to enrolling parents. Personal contact, peer recruitment, and unique program incentives may be tried. Contacts with other professionals also can be expected to produce some new ideas and recruitment suggestions. Nevertheless, the rate of participation expected in the program should reflect the availability and constraints of families.

Conflicts in Views and Values

As long as families are different, parents' own standards, values, and viewpoints about children also will differ. Conflicts are to be expected, and the staff should be prepared to deal with them. In extreme cases, value conflicts may undermine the program, especially when expressed frequently and intensely. If a particular program model is adopted, the implied values can be discussed with relative neutrality. Parents can be free to accept or reject some content and strategies, and staff members may be able to manage these conflicts to the benefit of all. It should be remembered that professionals also disagree about child development and parenting. Parents are entitled to the same questioning and challenge, provided the program does not suffer from conflict that is overly disruptive or cannot be used to focus discussion.

Inadequate Staff Training and Skill

When professionals have little experience in working with adults or with particular types of families, there are likely to be problems in understanding. These may lead to confusion, bias, conflict, insensitivity, poor communication, inadequate record keeping, and even crises with individual mothers or fathers. Many programs are undertaken by concerned teachers, supervisors, social workers, nurses, and psychologists. Often there are no real training opportunities unless a model is purchased that includes inservice sessions. Small, carefully developed programs that reflect the skills of staff members would be more likely to succeed than those that require abilities not demonstrated by the professionals. Advisory boards and consultations with other programs can help to alleviate some inadequacies if professionals can rely upon their assistance. Self-training by the staff also would contribute to reducing problems of this type.

Loss of Parent Interest

Many parent-education programs experience decreases in the involvement of mothers and fathers over time. Attrition rates are high, even when program incentives and rewards appear strong. Sometimes parents simply are too busy to fit another appointment into their family schedule. The program content may not fit their pressing needs, or the time and location may not be convenient. Other parents attending may not appear friendly, or the staff member could be perceived as only minimally effective. Parent enthusiasm at the outset may be unrealistically high, in which case there is often a later sense of disillusionment. The program content, even if relevant, may be poorly presented. When parents seem to lose interest, the staff may need to create morale-building experiences. Special events, visitors, a radical change in approach, new members, and so forth may add spice to the program and rekindle interest. Goals and content also may need to be reevaluated and additional resources used that relate more effectively to parents' needs.

Privacy Concerns

When parents are discussing their families, they are revealing a good deal of sensitive information about themselves, their children and spouses, and sometimes about their experiences with teachers and agency staff members. They need to be assured that such conversations will be kept in strict confidence, not only by the professional but by other involved parents. Even when the issue of privacy is resolved, many mothers and fathers are reluctant to reveal too much about themselves. It is sometimes possible to deal rather effectively with child and parenting topics without delving very deeply into the lives of individual families. This is especially true for group meetings and classroom participation types of programs. In counseling and home visiting, more personal discussion may take place, but the staff in these cases is usually trained to deal with concerns about confidentiality. When violations of the privacy rule do occur, they should probably be discussed openly. Gossip may be overly important to some parents, and their lack of sensitivity to members' feelings will require some staff attention. On the other hand, it is expected that parents will discuss the comments of their peers in a rather general way with others, in part because new ideas and suggestions are being examined by them as changes are considered. Guidelines agreed upon by the participating parents can be established early in the program, to prevent privacy problems from occurring.

Group Management Problems

In any group meeting there are interpersonal dynamics that influence the attitudes and participation of members. This is especially true of groups of parents, whose needs and feelings may be quite strong and very individual. It is common for a parent educator to have to deal with a variety of responses to groups that can be problematic. These include individuals who may monopolize the conversation, disagree with other's beliefs, challenge the group leader, divert the discussion, form competitive liaisons with other parents, refuse to participate, or become dependent upon the leader. It takes some degree of talent and skill to manage groups where these dynamics occur on a regular basis. Sometimes parents withdraw from programs because they feel uncomfortable with such interpersonal dynamics. Certainly, staff training can reduce such problems. Supervision for the professionals also may be needed, to help them to cope with these difficulties.

School or Agency Disruption

On occasion, a parent-education program places overly taxing demands upon sponsoring schools or agencies. Resources such as staff, secretary, and telephone services; building space; and financing may be usurped to such an extent that the host reacts negatively to the program. In schools there may be disruptions to teachers and children's curriculum; and in health, social, or child care agencies there may be confusion about referrals or program content that leads to staff conflicts. Certainly, the professionals can schedule regular progress reports for sponsors and arrange for information or feedback sessions. Sensitivity to emerging problems also may lead to resolutions that prevent difficulties along these lines. It is important to maintain close ties among the staff of the parent-education program and the sponsoring school or agency so that communication is ongoing and productive.

Lack of Follow-Through

Parent-education programs vary considerably in their scope and duration. Unfortunately, most are short-lived efforts spanning several weeks or months. Even though it could be argued that parents are unwilling or unable to make longer-term commitments, the tendency toward brief program periods seldom allows for gradual family change. Often the program ends just as mothers and fathers are beginning to respond effectively to their children's affective and educational needs. It may very well be the case that this lack of follow-through limits the program's potential to aid children and families. In cases where the program population includes high-risk or handicapped children, teenage mothers, or parents with special problems, it is important to maintain established ties with the family throughout the early childhood years. As their youngsters grow and change, parents require new information and skills that program staff can locate. Follow-through efforts are important for many other families, even if the long-term contact is minimal. In a sense, such continuity expresses the school or agency's commitment to those who have participated in programs they established.

PROGRAM SUGGESTIONS

1. Following a discussion with parents about their needs and interests, add three sub-objectives under each of the eight program purposes described in the text.
2. Using the lists of staff qualities and skills, prepare a draft evaluation form for use by parents and staff members. Rate yourself, then ask a few parents and a co-worker to rate you as a potential or actual parent educator.
3. Select and use four methods of parent recruitment and involvement that have not been attempted previously. Report on the results.
4. In a round-robin format, ask parents to identify what makes them feel comfortable and respected, or ill-at-ease and not valued by professionals.
5. Select three types of parent evaluation and use them to examine what parents and children may be learning and experiencing as program participants.
6. Using Table 5 as a framework, examine a recently published model or approach to working with parents of young children. Determine its type and describe its features according to the items in the table.
7. Talk to parents and staff members about their roles and expectations in parent education. Make a list of these and locate their place in Table 5.
8. Take three problems identified in the text that you or others have indicated can be expected to occur. List the methods parents and staff could use to prevent these from disrupting the program.

PART II

Content Areas for Parent-Education Programs

6

Child Care: Activities, Developmental Issues, and Problems

A major portion of family life concerns care for children. Particularly in the early years, care-giving routines and other child-related activities occupy a large percentage of parents' time and energy. For the children themselves, care and play provide the framework for a great many of their daily experiences. Care-giving routines, especially, serve as organizers of the day, thereby ensuring that children have regular contact with adults in ways where their needs are given personal attention.

In this chapter, child care will be discussed in terms of activities occurring in homes, schools, and supplementary care settings. Problems during developmental transitions and crises will be examined as part of overall care-giving responsibilities. In the following chapter, children's play will be discussed as a medium for learning and personal-social growth.

CHILD CARE WITHIN THE FAMILY AND CENTER

The feelings of security generated by good care giving are familiar to almost every adult. Being nurtured within a safe and healthy environment gives a sense of emotional and physical well-being. There is a great deal to be said for the care of children, and one tribute to its value may be a description of the many responsibilities involved. These care-giving responsibilities are listed in the upper part of Table 6 and will be discussed in detail in this section. Also in the table are the developmental issues and problems that are the responsibilities of parents and will be discussed later in this chapter.

Safety and Shelter

A protected and comfortable home with minimal opportunity for harm or fear is a basic right of children. Safety and shelter are first and foremost

Table 6
The Child Care Responsibilities of Parents

CARE GIVING
Provide shelter and safe surroundings
Provide food and manage nutrition
Ensure health and physical fitness
Teach care of self and belongings
Teach self-protection
Provide a special place in the family

DEVELOPMENT
Provide opportunities for and manage play
Deal with behavior toward self and others
Help with feelings and support personal growth
Encourage learning and monitor education

PROBLEMS
Help with developmental transitions
Detect and manage problems
Deal with crises
Protect children's rights

adult responsibilities in any child care setting. A protective environment free of risks and hazards requires some organization and supervision. Dangers must be minimized and the setting kept sufficiently clean to promote good health. Hazards must be assessed regularly, for infants and preschoolers especially. Electrical wires and outlets, chemicals, medicines and sprays, sharp tools, and flammable items need to be out of reach and securely stored. Furniture and toys should not have sharp edges, small loose parts, or slippery surfaces, or be likely to tip or collapse. First-aid materials and procedures should be accessible for emergencies such as fire and other accidents. Children's areas must be protected from extremes in temperature and from hazards such as traffic, animals, and so forth. The environment should be monitored continuously during these early years while children are gradually taught how to avoid and handle difficulties in homes and centers.

Supervision is also important in assuring children's safety. Parents and staff members often understand the need to be constantly alert with infants and toddlers, to monitor closely the activities of preschoolers, and to check frequently on school-age youngsters whose independence and judgment are still immature. Supervision tends to involve some mediation or intervention in addition to observation, and adults should anticipate the need to get involved and to follow through, being certain their actions are effective in minimizing risks. Supervision is a preventive procedure that reduces the odds for accident and injury. It also teaches children to be aware of any dangers to their safety through observing adults helping them and adjusting their behavior according to the restrictions placed upon them.

When accidents do occur, many parents and teachers have only minimal knowledge of how to deal with them. First-aid handbooks and training would ease many fears about the correct handling of an injury. A text by Green (1977) lists the following incidents requiring some adult knowledge: bites; bleeding; bone breaks; breathing difficulties; burns; chest injuries; choking; digestive problems; drowning; ear, eye, and nose injuries; falls; fevers; flying objects; parasites; poisons; punctures; rashes; and seizures. Every home and center should have at least some information for these emergencies, as well as posted phone numbers and procedures to follow when there is a situation requiring first aid. In many communities, telephone listings can be obtained from Red Cross and other health care agencies.

Food and Nutrition

Children's diets have come to be viewed as important contributors to their learning and well-being. More and more adults have expressed their concern over chemical additives, food preparation procedures, and allergic reactions to particular food substances. Salt and sugar contained in baby foods are thought to be unnecessary and detrimental. Toddlers are encouraged to feed themselves a variety of nutritious snacks. Preschoolers often participate in the cleaning and cooking of diverse foods in order to expand their eating interests and develop scientific concepts about chemical changes such as occur with heat or cold. Grade-school youngsters may be consciously steered away from "junk foods" by using curriculum such as food fairs, farm trips, and home economics classes. The area of nutrition is one where parent and teacher concerns often overlap, and children may develop good eating habits if these are emphasized in both settings. Library books, films, gardening experiences, grocery store studies, and similar activities can help as well.

Health and Fitness

Care of the body includes safety and nutrition, but it is also important that youngsters are provided with adequate health care and at least minimal amounts of exercise. Preventive health includes immunizations; health screenings for vision, hearing, teeth, and overall growth; medical examinations and routine check-ups and for illness; and maintenance of the child's general physical and mental health. Exercise is important as well in promoting fitness in physical activities and sports. Infants can exercise during play with adults or when alone, using a cradle gym or other toys. Toddlers need a good deal of time reaching, crawling, walking, climbing, and pushing or pulling toys attached to sticks or strings. Preschoolers need little encouragement to run, climb, or ride bikes, while school-aged children can extend their activities to include swimming, ball playing, and a variety of gymnastic and sports-oriented games. Physical stamina and fitness promote good health, and this includes mental health and social skills in the form of reduced stress and enjoyable interactions with others.

Self-Care

Children gradually learn to assume many of the care functions handled by adults early in their lives. Feeding, washing, toileting, dressing, and grooming skills are acquired throughout the preschool period. Safety, nutrition, and fitness also are learned, and by the elementary years children are

able to negotiate their neighborhoods and care for themselves and their belongings remarkably well. Parents and child care professionals teach these concepts and skills through demonstration, explanation, and limit setting. The children's independence and pride are almost as satisfying as the conserved time and energy parents gain as rewards from teaching self-care. One difficulty sometimes associated with such instruction is that of unrealistic expectations for conformity. Children achieve these skills very gradually, with experience. Often they themselves are motivated toward independence and want to begin caring for themselves with less adult assistance. The line between too many and too few freedoms or demands is a difficult one for adults to draw, who have to keep children safe and healthy but also encourage their independence. Discussions with other parents and professionals and observations of other children similar in age can provide some guidance.

Self-Protection

Protection of children against maltreatment, abduction, or assault is a vital responsibility of adults. The vigilance of parents and teachers regarding these serious crimes is part of daily child care, and a network of helping professionals and child advocates also may be available to provide information and services that help to prevent these problems. There may be some precautions, however, that parents can teach to children directly that may aid them when a vigilant adult is not present. Youngsters also can learn to report any activities that are suggestive of maltreatment.

Young children have fewer options in protecting themselves than older youngsters whose physical and mental skills enable them to perceive more dangers and report more details. Preschoolers, however, are able to abide by some clear rules, are less likely to be unsupervised outside of the home, and may be more direct in responding emotionally to a situation. These characteristics protect them slightly, offset some developmental limitations, and bolster the guidelines that may be useful in working with the young. Six areas can be suggested: setting rules of behavior, observing dangers, thinking ahead, avoiding potential problems, resisting advances, and reporting the incident. Rules will vary by neighborhood, but parents can set limits about remaining near responsible adults, not wandering beyond certain boundaries, coming when called, not changing plans without telling a parent, and waiting in a particular place when being picked up. Observation of dangers includes noticing any threatening situation involving others or self, such as unexpected gifts, candy bribes, or an overly solicitous adult. These can be handled with storybooks, filmstrips, or puppet role play when the child spots a danger to self or another and avoids or resists it. Thinking ahead includes some reasoning about the possible consequences or meaning of an action. For example, the child is asked to consider what might happen if she wanders away and cannot be located, or if something happens that seems wrong or suspicious even when others say it is acceptable.

In avoiding potential problems, the child is encouraged to check with parents on where to play, whom to visit, what situations in the neighborhood to avoid, and how to decide if something is right or wrong. Resisting difficult situations also should be encouraged, even if children also are taught to be polite and respectful to adults. Learning to say no, to refuse, and to react to some threats can help children to gain confidence in their own rights. Discussion and modeling, using dolls and even some television programs, can demonstrate that parents will support the child's refusal to go along with something they feel is wrong, immoral, or a real violation of themselves. These incidents should be discriminated from those that are reasonable forms of discipline. Finally, children can be encouraged to report confidentially anything they feel is hurtful or disliked. Parents can listen, gently probe for more information, observe for themselves, or explain that the child's concern was appropriate but the situation was innocent, if this is found to be the case. Nonverbal communication is also important. If children's behavior is unusual, withdrawn, or stressed, or if there are nightmares or suspicious pretend play with dolls, parents should look for the reasons why.

The Child's Special Place in the Family

A final concern in the area of care giving within the family and center is the amount of time and energy given lovingly by adults on behalf of children. Care routines; play; and interactions around learning, behavior, and personal-social growth all use varying amounts of adult resources. To rear a child at home or in centers and schools requires a commitment to the child as a person who belongs, who has a special place, and who makes some special contributions to the group. Children have rights of many kinds, just as parents and families have their needs and priorities, but one very important one is to be valued by the people who are providing care. The child's place in the home or center—how he is regarded by the family or group—is often expressed through daily care. Babies may be cheerfully diapered and fed specially prepared homemade foods. A toddler may be provided with some cabinet space containing safe kitchen objects to play with and taken for brief walks around the block. Older youngsters are helped to care for their toys and are coached in joining a family ball game. These are examples of ways in which care communicates value and respect. Even if a tired or frustrated adult has a lapse in patience and attention, the love expressed through good care lets young children know that they hold an important place in one's life. In a sense, this kind of expression of value is one of the most traditional in defining good parenting and should continue to be viewed this way.

SUPPLEMENTARY CHILD CARE

Daycare for children of working, student, or disabled parents can take the form of group programs in centers, family care in a home setting, or private care arrangements using babysitters or relatives in the child's own home. To a certain extent, nursery schools, kindergartens, and play groups or coops also fulfill the child care needs of families. Such care alternatives are necessary family supports. Without good care, the children of working parents may fail to develop the competence and well-being needed to grow well. Daycare should approximate good home care and nurturance. A major responsibility of the family in need of supplementary care is the management of these arrangements. Management includes searching for and selecting a daycare program or provider, helping the child and other family members to make adjustments, monitoring the quality and effectiveness of the arrangement, and providing the resources and support for continuing the experience as long as it is needed. To fill these roles, parents must become both informed consumers and child advocates, while they also must deal with the emotional and managerial requirements that are part of the supplementary care experience.

Daycare Services

The history of daycare has been one fraught with political-cultural issues that have overshadowed family and child needs for positive and developmentally useful experiences. Up to the present time, daycare for the young has not been viewed as acceptable by a large segment of American society. Unlike clearly educational or intervention programs for infants and preschool children that have demonstrated value, those described principally as providing daycare services have had a problematic history. They have been plagued by difficulties with funding, staff training, and regulations, all of which can lower the quality of care giving. When this happens, only minimal consideration may be given to promoting children's development in the areas of play, language, personality, intelligence, and peer relationships.

While the social and monetary support for daycare is an issue that relates to quality, it may be useful to make families aware of the benefits and tradeoffs that seem to be part of the picture. Research and reviews of the impact of daycare have established the presence of some positive effects and the absence of some expected negative effects. Daycare, for example, had previously been equated with maternal deprivation or a disturbance of the primary bond between mother and child. Reviews of many studies now conclude that this does not occur (Belsky & Steinberg, 1978; Kilmer, 1979) and that children continue to regard their parents as their primary providers. In terms of child development, daycare has been examined in relation to children's social adjustment, intellectual and language skills, and other indicators of growth. In general there seems to be a consensus that the degree of benefit to many children is a function of caregiver skills and program priorities (Carew, 1980; Fowler, 1978), staff qualifications, group size, and staff-child ratios (Roupp et al., 1979) and the stability of the child's family (Golden, Rosenbluth, Gross, Policare, Freeman, & Brownlee, 1978).

The composite view attained by this research and review process can be described in the following way. Children who benefit from daycare programs are likely to attend small centers, with an adequate number of continuous and qualified staff who are able to guide them in adjustment, language and intellectual growth. They may also be found in daycare homes where the adults provide a similar learning environment. If the child's family is poor or there is an unstable home situation, the child is likely to benefit even from an average program. Middle-class children appear to require high quality programs to demonstrate gains in development. If the daycare situation includes early education or intervention there are likely to be long-term benefits in later status in school (Brown, 1978; Lazar et al., 1977). If parents are involved in the program it contributes more to the child (Fowler, 1978; Goodson & Hess, 1978). In programs focusing on infants and toddlers, few differences in daily activities can be expected between home-reared and daycare children (Carew, 1980; Kagan et al., 1978; Stevens, 1982), although a skillful adult and small groups appear to be needed in either environment. Peer relationships among daycare children have been found to be generally positive and consistent with the socialization of American children (Belsky & Steinberg, 1978).

Families as a whole may be assisted by daycare programs beyond the time made available for parents to work or attend school. Increases in employment, improved family relationships, information concerning children, and the development of social networks among parents have been associated with early childhood programs (Belsky & Steinberg, 1978; Cataldo & Salzer, 1982; Cochran & Brassard, 1979; Galinsky & Hooks, 1977; Zigler & Valentine, 1979). Daycare fulfills a role in child protection as well, if used in treatment programs aimed at both child and parent (Kempe & Kempe, 1978) and as a means of early detection of abuse, neglect, family dysfunction, or stress that impact on children.

Parents who wish to make arrangements for supplementary care but have mixed feelings about it may need some reassurance and guidance from professionals. It is hoped that the preceding summary may be of some assistance.

Selecting Care Arrangements

Once a decision is made, the process of choosing child care becomes a major parent responsibility. Several recent guides have been prepared specifically for parents. Auerbach (1981), Clarke-Stewart (1982), and the Day Care Division of the U.S. Department of Health and Human Services (USDHHS), have each published inexpensive paperback books for families. They describe some pros and cons of daycare, types of arrangements, relationships with care providers, some problems to expect, and personal-environmental features to examine. Checklists included in the texts cover a wide variety of items for parents to assess when they visit a home or center. The physical environment is described in terms of safety, cleanliness, nutrition, and space. Playthings for physical, intellectual, and imaginative play are included, as is the general atmosphere of the setting. Observations of the adults and children include the adults' personal qualities; responses to children; behavioral guidance; involvement in care, play, and learning activities; and relationships with parents. All of these are important since they represent major areas of competence in the care giver and program. The children who are present also may be observed in terms of their numbers, their ages in relation to the child being enrolled, and their general attitudes and moods. They should be talkative, involved in play, and interested in learning activities.

Other considerations are important as well, and these include expense, convenience, parents' own goals, and the child's temperament. A neighborhood center with established friendships and a stable staff may be preferred over one with excellent resources but far from home with no familiar faces; hence the selection process is really a juggling act for families. The initial choice may be based upon factors different from those later considered important, as families gain experience in assessing child care arrangements.

Visits to at least two prospective centers or homes, observations of the environment, interviews with staff members, and discussions with family members and friends are needed, regardless of the type of program being considered. Parents should probably trust their feelings about what they see; however, no center or home is perfect. The pattern of strengths and needs that emerges can help to clarify what it is that parents prefer for their children. Once there is strong assurance that basic good care is being provided, families can examine the various ways in which one program or another meets children's educational, developmental, personal, and social needs. All are essential, but there is often a good deal of variety in how these are satisfied. A minimum standard should be applied, nevertheless, and parents can expect their children to learn through play, games, special activities, and from other children. The child should feel valued and satisfied, and be able to handle peers and adults most of the time.

Family Needs and Concerns

Once parents become informed about the potential benefits and risks of daycare, determine the quality and convenience criteria most important to them, and make a decision about the center they prefer, they are ready to deal with the process of using the daycare arrangement. Parents seem to be concerned about affectionate, qualified staff, discipline of children, and educational or school readiness (Peters & Sibbison, 1974). They point to personalized care, learning experiences, safety, nutrition, and some participation in the program (Auerbach-Fink, 1977). Preparation for school, both social and cognitive; trained staff; and roles in program governance also have been indicated as important by parents (Roupp et al., 1979), as have the characteristics of staff, the logistics of the arrangement, and the characteristics of the facility and the curriculum (Child Care Information Exchange, 1982). Parents also may have some fears about daycare, such as possible dilution of emotional attachments, retardation of cognitive development, failure to develop self-control, negative effects of peers, and transfers in parenting responsibilities (Kagan et al., 1978).

Other problems or concerns may emerge as the child participates in the care experience. Rutter (1981) has described children's differences in readiness and adjustment to daycare (using considerations of temperament, attachment, age, and birth order), parents' attitudes about their work and work hours, the effect of employment on parenting (time and attention to children), the location of care in relation to the work site, and parents' sharing of household and recreational activities in the family. The USDHHS manual for parents suggests remedies for temporary problems such as children's negative behaviors (clinging, tantrums, wakefulness, thumbsucking, resentment, and so forth) and for differences in expectations and points of view between care providers and parents.

Certainly, the managerial and other personal skills of mothers and fathers can make a significant contribution to the success of the daycare arrangement. For example, parents may be comfortable with daycare if they can monitor it. Auerbach's (1981) book can help parents examine the facility, its emotional and social climates and learning activities, and children's behavior. The USDHHS text and Clarke-Stewart's book (1982) include questions parents should ask regarding the child's needs, staff responsiveness, and the comfort of the setting. Auerbach (1981) also focuses on children fitting into the group and feeling at home, and on expectations and attitudes expressed to parents. Clarke-Stewart (1982) recommends that parents prepare the child with play groups and discussion, provide a gradual entry into the program, monitor the child's experiences and the staff's program, maintain consistency in the child's care, and advocate for daycare resources. She points to the need for a comfortable staff-parent relationship based upon discussion, consideration of feelings, participation, and adherence to commitments such as fees and hours.

The use of relatives for child care arrangements in the child's own home may be a concern of families who select this type of care. According to the U.S. Labor Department figures cited by Clarke-Stewart (1982), some estimated 40 percent of daycare is provided in the child's home by the father or other relative when mothers are working. Twenty percent of these are nonparents such as grandparents, aunts and uncles, older siblings, and so forth. They may have the advantage of the kin relationship to the child, but few are trained in care giving or understand the value of peer playmates and learning activities. They may be inexpensive financially but costly in emotional terms, or they may be unavailable on a consistent basis. Parents who make use of arrangements with relatives may need to select and plan carefully in order to establish expectations and lines of authority regarding activities and behavior so that the child experiences the positives of kin care.

DEVELOPMENTAL PATTERNS, TRANSITIONS, AND PROBLEMS

The child care responsibilities of parents include the guidance of children's growth and development. Good health and adequate physical skills, emotional well-being, successful social relationships, and intellectual/learning competence are all part of the developmental process. Parents' support and assistance, their management of problems, and the family's resources all contribute to the child's acquisition of the abilities and understanding expected in the preschool and primary years. To a significant degree, growth patterns and personality characteristics are predictable and familiar. Variations are typical, however, and are an important feature of development for individual children, for families, and in the context of differing cultural standards. Transitional stages also are expected, where the child and the family make changes and adjustments to fit maturing skills and personality traits. The challenge in supporting the developmental process comes from these two features, the familiar and the different. Somehow, parents and professionals need to monitor development in a way that allows for uniqueness and transitions but also detects and manages problems in children and families.

Parents want and need to know what to expect from children at each age and stage. Descriptions of developmental milestones and characteristics help them to understand and support the child's progress and to note discrepancies from the normal standards. In parent-education programs, these expected sequences are important starting points for discussion. The task of the professional is to emphasize the flexible use of such guidelines so that children are not compared to them in rigid or stereotypic ways. Differences and transitions also need to be described, and often parents themselves can highlight the unexpected characteristics. Problems in development are related in some ways to these differences. Normal boundaries are frequently hard to define because typical differences are present as well. In this section of the chapter, common developmental patterns in physical, personal and intellectual growth will be described. Transitions, adjustments, special situations, and problems also will be discussed.

Developmental Patterns

The period from birth to age eight includes an enormous number of developmental gains. It is a time of both rapid change, particularly in infancy, and more gradual emergence. Physical and intellectual abilities grow rather quickly, although many large marker skills—such as walking, talking, and reading—sometimes appear to develop slowly. Personality is in some ways rather apparent during infancy, but behavioral patterns and general styles of dealing with the needs of self and others take a long time to become established.

The patterns described here are general, with few very specific details. Several texts can be used to supplement this information when needed. Gesell et al. (1974) and Charlesworth (1983) cover the infant through the preschool period, while Bee (1975) and Elkind (1978) include the elementary and adolescent periods as well. Each of these authors describes age-related issues at length, yet they also emphasize that development is a process full of changes and plateaus that do not always reflect the total child. School settings and family relationships are also covered at length.

Assessment scales commonly used at the preschool level include the Denver Developmental Screening Test, the Dial test, the Learning Accomplishment Profile, the Portage Guide, the Preschool Inventory, and the Vulpe Assessment Battery, while the Wechsler and Stanford-Binet scales are typically used at the older ages. Such tests, however, focus primarily on school-related abilities rather than on broader competencies that include social and personal skills.

Birth to One Year: The Young Infant.   The newborn baby experiences
an adjustment period similar in intensity to the one felt by its parents. Once
settled into a feeding, sleeping, bathing, and play schedule, infants begin to
notice the people and events in their environments. A bond of dependency,
care giving and love helps the baby achieve progress in feeding; in longer
periods of wakefulness; and in physical skills such as rolling, grasping, and
sitting. Exploration and inspection of people and objects begin in earnest
once the infant sits, crawls, or otherwise moves about the room. Teething
and weaning may cause periods of distress, and babies may fear strangers
for a time. By the end of the first year, the child is often standing; vocalizing;
engaging in simple, playful games; and in general beginning to become an
active and often amusing young toddler.

One to Two Years: The Toddler.   This period can best be described as
one that is full of activity. The toddler appears to be very busy exploring
new objects and practicing new skills. Walking and manipulating are two
important ones that lead to other adventures in learning and personal
relationships. With people, the toddler is both dependent and resisting,
affectionate and assertive. While quite self-centered, the child nonetheless
enjoys imitating others in gestures and activities. Toilet training and talking
also are beginning, which frequently add to the frustrations and pleasures of
age two. By the end of the first year toddlers are usually showing a very
small amount of self-control, are experiencing longer play times with adults
and peers, and are able to handle very simple tasks requiring thought and
skill.

Two to Three Years: The New Talker.   The second birthday serves in
some ways as a signal of a new era for the toddler. Language development
expands greatly, as do physical skills related to toileting, feeding, and the
use of riding vehicles. This older toddler is still quite limited in attention
span and self-control, but over the year these increase. Adults begin to use
words and reasoning to manage the child, and many simple rules can be
remembered. Self-care becomes important as the youngster tries to model
parents and other children. Coordination for bicycles, wagons, and balls is
adequate for their use, and small-muscle skills mature enough so that
blocks, puzzles, and crayons can be handled. Books and new words are
usually appreciated, and the family can include the new talker in simple
conversations.

Three to Four Years: The Young Child.   When age three is reached,
the toddler can be referred to as a young preschooler. The term conveys the
message that the child has reached the point of possible nursery-school
entrance. Language abilities are well established, even though errors in

pronunciation are common. Physical skills include the ability to dress oneself and care for one's belongings, while social skills with peers and adults are sufficient for dealing with groups of strangers. Intellectually, the young child is demonstrating interests in stories and tasks that require problem solving, reasoning, and other thinking processes for their mastery. While three year olds are still quite immature and sometimes fearful in all of these areas, there is a good deal of success and gain during the year. Vocabulary expands, and pretend or fantasy play is a frequent activity, alone or with others. Independence and self-control are developing well, and the child is beginning to appear as a competent, self-assured individual.

Four to Five Years: The Preschooler. While the previous year functions somewhat as a transitional period, at age four the child is an established preschooler. Independent and self-reliant, the youngster is able to manage eating, toileting, dressing, and bathing fully; knows his or her address; can explore the neighborhood; and can separate easily from the family. Task persistence and memory make some academic learning activities successful and enjoyable. Drawings, paintings, building, and crafts are appreciated, as are dramatic play and fantasy games. Friendships are developing, and the child's self-concept grows in response to these experiences. Sex-role identity is established and even investigated verbally or through exploration. Questions are frequent, and a good deal of knowledge about the world is acquired. Group activities are enjoyed, although self-control of strong emotions is still problematic. Relationships with adults may include affection and discussion as well as challenge when the child's needs are at stake. Reasoning and modeling are usually effective for dealing with behavior, although the removal of privileges also helps to point out right and wrong.

Five to Six Years: The Kindergarten Child. With school entry, children spend a good deal more time outside of the home, with peers and other adults. This is often true even if the child has attended nursery schools or daycare programs. The kindergarten child takes another leap in maturity that is characterized by greater task orientation and more intense peer experiences. Physical skills are well established and find new expression in beginning sports activities. Creative endeavors may include drawing, stories, music, and dance. After-school friendships tend to include long periods of play and visits to other homes. Fads and heroes may capture the child's attention, and television often enhances these interests. Letter and word tasks, counting and adding, science concepts, and exploration of other communities are beginning to challenge the established competence of the preschool period. The child at this age is often outgoing and sociable, pleased with school after an initial adjustment, and able to enjoy outings with parents and friends. Relations with parents may focus on these and on assistance with schoolwork.

Six to Seven Years: The First Grader. The outgoing, active, and task-oriented qualities of the kindergarten child appear to intensify in first grade, but they take on a different tone. This older child may be alternately more assertive and more introspective, more competitive and more sensitive. Social events and relationships are important, and close friendships may emerge from the many previous acquaintances. Academic tasks take on a major focus as reading and mathematics skills are established. Some of these may be confusing and difficult, as families who help with homework are well aware. Language uses do expand, however, and children at this age are capable of extended discussion and processing through the verbal mode. Projects and hands-on activities remain important, however, and these can help the youngster to integrate what is learned in the different subject areas. Humor is important, as is reasoning. The first grader has reached a point where abstract concepts of the world and ideas about self and others can begin to be understood. Moral standards and social expectations become important as well, influencing the parent role toward one of advisement and discussion.

Seven to Eight Years: The Second-Grade Child. As basic educational skills are consolidated and reason is more frequently used, the eight year old begins to look quite grown up. Responsibility for belongings, school assignments, and home chores can be handled. Self-concept and esteem grow in relation to the child's increasing understanding about values and greatly expanded independence. While usually polite and friendly, the youngster also may turn inward and may begin to challenge her parents and teachers. Self-consciousness is apparent in concerns about clothing and personal appearance. The child may develop stronger interests in sports and hobbies, although the frustrations experienced may create problems. Although curious, the child at this age also tends to be self-motivated and directed by individual needs, so achievements may be intermittent. Reading, television, and board games can occupy the child's spare time. Sex-differentiated play begins, often requiring the segregated activities encouraged by the youngsters themselves. Friendships with same-sex children may become long-standing, although popularity begins to be a preoccupation that can lead to some disappointments. Relationships with parents are often centered on school and peer relations, which frequently need explanation and suggestions as forms of parental guidance. When siblings are present, parents also may function as frequent referees in the verbal disagreements and power struggles that punctuate family life. Nevertheless, the child at this age is less dependent upon the family and quite competent in managing his needs.

Summary. The years between birth and age eight include the acquisition of dozens of major milestones in growth and development. Parents' roles and methods change with these maturing skills, but their concern over the adequacy of the child's progress remains throughout. Learning, play, behavior, personality, and social relationships continue to be observed and monitored for needed changes or assistance.

Developmental Transitions

In order to progress from one stage to another, children have to move from a position of comfort and satisfaction to one that is unsettling. Piaget (1970) termed these processes *assimilation* and *accommodation.* In his view children take in information and assimilate it with what they already know. When new experiences are encountered that do not fit what has already been processed, the child struggles to accommodate to it. The adjustments create some instability, but this is necessary and most often temporary. Applied to the developmental process in general, these concepts mean that change is part of learning and maturation and that some upheaval is to be expected. Developmental transitions therefore become almost as significant as the milestones that indicate their achievement.

Transitional phases can probably be detected for every milestone or personal characteristic achieved by children. There are struggles in learning to walk and talk, in putting together a word or joining a game with friends. Progress is a process, a series of efforts and successes followed closely by more challenges. During transitions, children may seem to move backward or regress to an earlier stage, like the grade schooler who reverts to counting fingers when learning to subtract. Or their struggle may create problems for those around them, like the toddler who strives for independence but needs adult supervision. Emotional upheavals may accompany other transitions, especially when children are adjusting to school or a new group of peers. Shifts in interests and skills also produce behavior changes that are transitional but lead to new activities that become a permanent part of the child's repertoire. Some of these require that family members make adjustments in their expectations or their schedules. Outgrowing a nap or taking up a musical instrument are changes that are more enduring. Finally, children may need to respond to differences in the behavior and attitudes of their parents and others in ways that provoke transitions in their growth. A new sibling, a move, or a death in the family require that children adjust and create new personal patterns to fit the changes they experience.

All of these transitions can result in problems for the growing child. Those caring for the youngster have to deal with them in one way or another. Some require attention rather urgently, while others pass by with little intervention. What is important is that distinctions are made between real problems and transitional hurdles of growth that can be accepted and tolerated. Too often transitions are mistakenly seen as danger signs or as obstacles to development. If they are treated as serious problems they may become more difficult to manage. On the other hand, some transitions are not successfully resolved and parents may ignore meaningful signals of trouble. Time is an element that can help to determine what may be happening. The child who persists in grabbing toys beyond the toddler period where language and rules are more limited and into the preschool age has failed to make a transition to more mature and skillful social exchanges. The behavior may be transitional if the youngster is experiencing his or her first group encounters and may be interpreted as an awkward attempt to relate to others. If the youngster does not grow beyond this behavior, however, more strenuous interventions will be required to ensure that the problem does not expand.

Transitions, then, present a mixed view. They are expected as part of the developmental process and as such produce minimal concern. However, problems can be indicated if adjustments fail to be successful during and following these transitional phases.

Developmental Problems

Once parents and professionals have used developmental sequences to scan a particular child's progress, and once transition-related upheavals have been taken into account, the assessment of specific strengths and problems may be required. A wide variety of approaches to testing infants, preschoolers, and primary-school children are taken by different helping professionals. Educators and child care workers tend to focus on general child development, school adjustment, and learning. Physicians and nurses often examine the child's physical health status, self-care abilities, and problems in physical development. Psychologists and social workers may look more closely at behavior, family relationships, and environmental difficulties. All of these areas are important, however, and assessments of possible child development problems should ideally include all the domains.

Some signs of disorders and delays are related to age and intensity; that is, a problem can be labeled as such if a behavior or symptom that might be normal when brief and mild is, in fact, very inappropriate for the child's age or quite extreme in frequency and intensity. Temper tantrums are an example of this. At the toddler stage they are usually normal and not very frequent. If they occur often at this stage or if they continue into the preschool period, the behavior may be evidence of emerging social difficulties that require intervention.

The presence of problems is one method of detection, but it is also important to examine whether or not expected skills and understanding are absent at particular ages. Children who cannot walk or have not started to use words at age two, for example, are at risk even though they may not display overt problems. For these delays in development, many standardized screening instruments such as the Denver test are available.

Other problems may be voiced by parents or care givers only; that is, the child may not seem to demonstrate identifiable delays or disorders, but the adults who care for the youngster may voice complaints or may be unable to manage the youngster's needs and behaviors. In these instances, the child can be expected to have difficulties because the relationship with the adult is not effective or satisfying. For these types of problems, family assessments may be more revealing than those that focus only on the child.

Several authors have identified signs of developmental and personal problems. Crow (1978) has created a profile of 100 signs and symptoms in the areas of physical/organic, emotional, social, environmental, and academic skills, which covers the later early childhood and primary-school years. A preliminary list of 450 items was used with panels of helping professionals and teachers who determined the significance of each symptom. The final list includes problems in schoolwork, learning, coordination, personal habits, peer relations, behavior, health, and parent relationships. Powell's text (1981) on developmental changes and problems deals with the infant-through-preschool period and adopts a family approach to assessing children. The emphasis on updated, more wholistic testing practices, individual differences, long-term observations, and educational intervention makes the materials quite appropriate for a variety of helping professionals. A guide to promoting development is presented that includes motor skills, feeding, sleep, play, language, discipline, toilet training, and dressing. Two texts provide guides to assessing and working with infants and toddlers. Greenspan (1981) describes developmental levels from birth to four years in which the baby's adaptation to its physical and personal environment is the basis for interventions that include social services, family therapy, and infant guidance. Cataldo (1983) provides checklists and suggestions appropriate to group educational programs for infants and toddlers.

A brief list of possible problems is provided in the following age groupings, but the items indicated are very general and designed only to alert the parent and professional to a situation that can be monitored or that requires that a referral be made for more extensive assessment.

Birth to One Year: The Young Infant.   The baby is not thriving and responding to people. Weight and appearance seem poor, and the infant is seldom attentive and alert. Crying is frequent, and sleeping is either very frequent or not occurring in a regular pattern by midyear. The baby seldom plays, vocalizes, reaches, or tries to turn over by midyear. Parents appear overwhelmed or hostile, or may express a great deal of frustration.

One to Two Years: The New Toddler.   The child is not moving about, playing, or understanding words. Sitting and walking are not well established by midyear. The child seldom uses toys or plays games with people. Exploration either occurs rarely or is constant and disruptive. By year's end the child is not uttering words or listening briefly to stories. Parents indicate no control over the child, or they attempt constant restriction. The parents are isolated or overwhelmed to the point of using excessive punishment. Bruises or burns are present beyond those expected from accidents.

Two to Three Years: The Beginning Talker.   The child is not beginning to talk or care for itself. Hearing seems poor, and the child does not indicate needs or desires. Play with people and toys is infrequent or seems very isolated. Little interest in peers is shown, or the child is overly attached to parent. Directions are not followed, and the child is unable to feed itself or attempt dressing. Toilet training is not progressing, nor is language developing. Vocabulary is still poor by the end of the year. The child seems inadequately cared for or is overly neat and fearful of messes. Relationships with parents are strained and seldom enjoyed.

Three to Four Years: The Young Child.   The child is not becoming adept with language and physical skills. There is little or too much fantasy play, and speech is minimal or very unclear. The child is awkward and clumsy. Peer interests are minimal or difficult, including problems with turn taking and cooperation. The child is fearful or tired often and responds poorly to overtures of adults and children. Activity level is overly high, and the child is highly distractible in all situations. Parents are unable to enjoy the child's activities or control behavior to some degree.

Four to Five Years: The Preschooler.   The child continues to avoid tasks and does not complete self-care skills. Toilet training and eating are delayed. Language skills are poor, with little correct labeling or conversation. Rules and directions are ignored, and peer relationships are poor or very limited. Temper tantrums or withdrawal are frequent. Attempts to work with the child are unsuccessful. Parents misperceive the child's characteristics or are unaware of needs. The child may be overly restricted or poorly disciplined. There is no interest in play that is creative or academically oriented.

Five to Six Years: The Kindergarten Child. There is poor adjustment to school, or perceptual problems exist in relation to shapes, letters, and numbers. Vocabulary is limited and speech unclear. The child seldom goes along with activities or else is overly excited by them. Relationships with teachers or parents are overly focused on discipline or learning. Friendships are limited or frustrating. Sibling rivalry may be intense and unmanageable. The child is frequently ill or nervous.

Six to Seven Years: The First Grader. The child is unable to manage learning tasks or behavior, is constantly uncooperative or withdrawn. The child avoids reading and math or makes frequent errors. Self-esteem is low and work habits poor. Limits are frequently tested, or the child is fearful and anxious. Digestive problems are frequent. Memory is poor and disorganized. The child has few friends. Parents are unable to assist in the child's learning or behavior. The child seems physically limited or disordered, including vision, hearing, and motor skills.

Seven to Eight Years: The Second-Grade Child. Work in school is below capacity or stalled, and the child has problems with teachers and children. Nervous habits are common, and the child avoids responsibilities. Listening is poor, and efforts to manage the child seem unsuccessful. Play is limited or fixated. Rules are ignored, and the child seems to be oblivious to others' feelings. Physical problems are frequent. Relations with adults are strained, and parents are frustrated or hostile regarding the child's behavior. The child's concept of self is poor or limited.

Summary. The possible problems described in this section are both general and somewhat extreme. More moderate difficulties and specific problems also are very difficult to manage. These may require individual consultations with professionals and parents having similar experiences. All the problems listed here should serve as warning signs, however, regardless of their perceived significance. It is usually better to overreact than to ignore problems, when children's development is at stake. Advice should be sought from teachers, nurses and physicians, psychologists, social workers, and others who can seek out resources for helping the child and family.

FAMILY CRISES AND UNIQUENESS

Despite the best intentions of parents, crises can erupt in the home that create or magnify developmental problems in children. Many of these are familiar to parents: Illness, death, divorce, stress, substance abuse, and maltreatment all disturb the well-being of family members. Other kinds of challenges to child development take the form of more continuing kinds of difficulty. Uniquenesses in family structure and orientation may create special needs as well as special strengths. Some of these are

Single-parent families	Teenage parents
Blended families	Low-SES parents
Bilingual families	Developmentally delayed parents
Adoptive families	Neglectful families
Handicapped-child families	Abusive parents
Parents of gifted children	Foster families
Dual-career families	Unemployed parents

Special family situations may require sensitive and innovative approaches to providing advice and guidance. In some cases, children's problems may be quite predictable. Poverty often leads to malnutrition, and school tasks are difficult for children whose English is poor. Parents of handicapped children require specialized services, while abusive families need intensive therapy. Teenage parents thrive on supportive group programs, while dual-career families require flexibility in the scheduling of visits and conferences. Children who are adopted may place strains on parents that are similar to those felt by blended families where new sibling relationships create special problems. Parents of gifted children and single-parent families may need assistance in teaching their children at home.

Two kinds of families whose numbers are rapidly increasing and whose needs have received relatively little attention are the single-parent and blended family structures. The single parent, whether he or she has never been married, has lost a spouse through death, or has been divorced and assumes the major responsibility for child care, has a wide range of adjustments to make. The single parent who never married has to begin developing many new parenting skills without the benefit of a partner. Widows or widowers and divorced persons with children must contend with the intense feelings they experience from their loss, while at the same time meeting their responsibilities to their children. The single parent whose spouse has died has problems that are slightly different from those of the divorced parent, who may continue to receive minimal assistance from his or her former spouse. Nevertheless, these two groups do experience many problems which are similar. There are scheduling arrangements to be made in work, family, and personal activities that require skills in managing a heavy load of responsibilities. In some instances, a new job must be found. For the most part, a single mother or father functions as the sole parent who has to develop a wider-than-normal range of child-rearing skills with little relief time for balancing the strain. If there are strong feelings of reduced self-esteem, a loss of social relationships, and little time for personal interests, the role becomes overly heavy, with few satisfactions. Children's needs for care and nurturance are very strong, especially during the adjustment from having two parents to having a single parent. They require demonstrations of love; time with each parent in the case of divorce; and understanding of their feelings of loss, guilt, anxiety, and resentment. Sometimes parents can find support from other family members or from children's programs; these can help to ease the child's distress over a loss, separation, or other form of absence of a mother or father.

In blended families, often resulting from single parents finding new partners, there are other stresses. The stepparent often has fewer strong ties with the child at first, and the relationship may be influenced by previous ones. Children often feel jealous, ambivalent, and overwhelmed by changes in living style. Many issues are hard to resolve in the new family arrange-ment, including sharing affection, accepting discipline, arranging for ex-penses, dealing with conflicts, and getting to know new parents and siblings. Respect for the separated parent is important, and children need to learn how to love, play, and negotiate with all the adults involved.

Resources for working with families in special situations can come from a variety of edited volumes and special texts. Many are available in the reference sections of libraries or at local bookstores. Guidance also may be sought from informed school personnel, social workers, and counselors who specialize in providing assistance to particular families. Parents themselves can be very helpful in identifying their needs and concerns. What is impor-tant is that children be considered in relation to their home situations and that parents' constraints be viewed with understanding.

Family crises present special problems which, while often temporary, are often very disruptive. The loss of a parent creates fears, insecurities, confusion, and serious emotional upheaval in children. Whether the loss involves illness, death, or divorce, the parent's absence is a crisis for the family, whose ability to cope may be seriously challenged. Children can be expected to demonstrate problems with emotions, relationships, learning, development, and physical well-being. The availability of sympathetic adults and friends may alleviate some distress. Where the absent parent is able to maintain contact with the child, the discomfort and fear may be reduced. Anger and resentment are common, nevertheless, and children may need some outlets for these feelings in the form of play, sports, or discussion. Again, many special books and articles are available regarding family loss (Figley & McCubbin, 1983; Gordon & Klass, 1979; Grollman, 1970, 1981; Wallerstein, 1980).

Another kind of family crisis is maltreatment of children, which includes child physical abuse, neglect, and emotional and sexual abuse. These types of abnormal child-rearing behaviors may be complicated by stress, mental illness, developmental delays, alcohol or drug abuse, and a history of abuse during the parent's own childhood years. The maltreated child may be unable or afraid to seek help, and this makes problem management that much more difficult. Family therapy is almost always required, although the reduction of stress through social services is also important. Child therapy should accompany the treatment of parents and should extend beyond simple removal of the child from the home. Support groups of other parents are very valuable in reducing the family's isolation from others and lowering their resistance to change. Social service agencies in local communities are often able to provide resource materials as well as assessment and treatment. A national child-abuse hotline also exists, to help prevent and remediate child maltreatment.

CHILDREN'S RIGHTS

The rights of children have been agreed upon nationally and framed as a U.N. declaration. The following list was widely circulated during the 1979 U.N. International Year of the Child. Family rights to privacy and the freedom to rear children are not challenged by these statements. The list serves as a useful framework for anyone concerned with the care and well-being of children.*

1. The right to affection, love and understanding.
2. The right to adequate nutrition and medical care.
3. The right to free education.
4. The right to full opportunity for play and recreation.
5. The right to a name and nationality.
6. The right to special care, if handicapped.
7. The right to be among the first to receive relief in times of disaster.

*From "Declaration of the Rights of the Child," U.N. Resolution 1386(xiv), adopted by the General Assembly 20 November 1959.

8. The right to be a useful member of society and to develop individual abilities.
9. The right to be brought up in a spirit of peace and universal brotherhood.
10. The right to enjoy these rights, regardless of race, color, sex, religion, national or social origin.

PROGRAM SUGGESTIONS

1. Have parents discuss problems and new trends in today's world that affect child care in terms of providing a safe environment, adequate nutrition, and meaningful learning.
2. Itemize the self-care skills children should acquire by ages two, four, and six years, and explore ways in which these can be taught in homes, schools, and child care centers.
3. Ask parents about their experiences with people who provide supplemental care, such as babysitters, neighbors, relatives, home daycare providers, daycare staff, nursery teachers, coop parents, and recreational center staff. Focus on their feelings about the problems and the benefits of such care, to the child and the family.
4. Analyze the daycare services in your community, including their quality and availability.
5. Have parents think about three children they know well, whose ages range from birth to eight years. Using the list of age-related developmental patterns, expand on the descriptions so that a realistic profile is created for the children.
6. Using index cards, have parents write down three problems they have experienced in their children at particular developmental stages and at transitions between stages. Use the cards to obtain suggestions for managing these problems.
7. Using library resources, examine in greater detail two or three special-situation or crisis families. Make a brief presentation about the strengths and needs of these parents and children and how resources could be provided to them.
8. Describe how the ten U.N. rights of the child relate to the home and to the daily care of children. How could these rights be strengthened or made more meaningful?

7

Children's Play

Play is a major childhood occupation. It is usually pleasurable and often serves a learning function. It may be solitary or sociable, free flowing or organized. Because it occurs so frequently and is so engaging, play assumes a significant role in child development. The nature and value of play has been explored by many psychologists and educators, yet definitions of play and concerns about its use continue to be debated among parents and professionals. In this chapter, play is viewed as a necessary avenue for child growth. Types of play, adult roles, and play materials will be discussed along with some issues and definitions.

THE NATURE OF PLAY

One of the many difficulties in defining play is that purposeful, tasklike forms of play and those that appear to be pleasurable or entertaining are considered to be dichotomous and separate processes. Can a child who is having fun experimenting also be engaged in meaningful learning? Do robust or imaginative play activities serve any useful pruposes? If a child elects to take on a difficult problem with toy materials, is she still playing? Are snuggling and talking experiences considered to be forms of play? The answer is yes to all these questions, because such activities contain playful elements that dominate the situation; however, play can be described more specifically.

Broadly defined, play is seen by most authorities to be enjoyable or satisfying and different from required, directed, or less pleasant activities. The "fun" element of play has been emphasized by Chance (1979), and it appears as though children themselves use this criterion to discriminate work and play (King, 1983). Play also involves some free choice and some release from structure and purpose as these are imposed by real-world people and situations. Chance (1979) describes the "nonliteral" or "end-in-itself" character of play; Apple (1979) focuses on the nondirected, noncompulsory, and somewhat unscheduled qualities of play; and Fowler (1980) emphasizes the free-flowing, informal aspects of free play in which there is a disregard for purpose and reality. These qualities do co-exist with others, however, in which mental activity, socialization processes, and developmental progress are emphasized. Caplan and Caplan (1976) describe the historical role of play from Pestolozzi to Bettleheim, and include many other pioneers in play. Although play is seen as voluntary, containing freedom of action, it is also a dynamic learning medium. It is a source of socialization and innovation (Sutton-Smith & Sutton-Smith, 1974); it is a challenge (Chance, 1979) involving mental activity and creative, symbolic, purposeful tasks (Fowler, 1980); it is influenced by factors in the personal and physical environment (Sponseller, 1982) and is necessary to mental health (Axline, 1978). Most of these authorities value play for its contribution to the child's learning and physical and personal development and see it as a process that includes acquiring knowledge, exploring strategies of problem solving, and testing skills. In Fowler's (1980) analysis, play is exploratory, instrumental, constructive, symbolic, and linguistic in focus.

The role of the adult in children's play seems to be supported by early childhood practitioners. In the earliest years, adult-child play is encouraged in model programs and parent-oriented curricula (Cataldo, 1983). During the school years, however, adults tend to overorganize and routinize play by using it as an extension of work or sanctioning only play that occurs during recreational periods (Apple, 1979). Thus the nature of play and the role of adults may change over time.

On the basis of these views, play can be defined in three ways, all of which reflect its value for children's growth and well-being. First, play is a pleasurable or satisfying pastime which the child selects or joins. It serves as a stabilizer, cathartic, and energy modulator. The positive affect associated with either robust fun or quiet enjoyment, for example, provides an alternative experience for the child who also encounters activities involving difficult emotions. Pleasure and satisfaction balance stress and unhappiness so that children are not overwhelmed by negative emotions that tend to wear down their confidence and competence. This stabilizing effect of play is important to mental health, especially since the child typically seeks it out or voluntarily joins in. As a cathartic, the pleasurable and fanciful, unstructured play often allows for a variety of personal expressions. In the rather safe context of play, where adults and order may be absent, children can release ideas and feelings in verbal, physical, and fantasy modes. They can play out fears, disarming their power to cause distress, or vent frustrations by demonstrating some mastery over playmates and toys. They can dramatize almost any situation that excites or concerns them and obtain some sense of emotional release, in part because such play, like dreams, is free of many constraints. As an energy modulator, the pleasurable nature of play serves as a time in which physical and mental resources can be renewed. It is a rest period or a change of pace from other forms of play or necessary activities that tax children's energies of one type or another. Robust play, for example, may renew children's interest in cognitive tasks; quiet, solitary play can serve as an energy modulator for social interactions that require attention to others.

Play is also a learning and developmental medium for children. This second aspect of its definition must be interpreted very broadly in order to include a variety of defined or open-ended, concrete or imaginative, incidental or child-oriented learning episodes either occurring naturally during play or planned as game activities or structured as tasks using play modes. The physical learning that occurs during play, from infancy to adulthood, is often acknowledged. Babies playfully grasp and shake rattles or laughingly struggle to crawl and walk. Toddlers happily climb sofas or stairs and learn to undo whatever enclosures parents devise to contain them. Preschoolers become adept with blocks, balls, and bicycles, all of which involve complex motor skills acquired in playful situations. In terms of intellectual learning, play experiences that often appear exploratory, repetitive, engrossing, and even frustrating to children also tend to include cognitive activity. Such play involves mental perceptions of the sensory qualities of objects and toys and the effects of manipulations upon them, the intellectual classification of materials into categories, the thought-producing resolutions of problems encountered in obtaining and using play materials, and the verbal labels and expressions associated with imaginative play and toy–person interactions that are processed and remembered intellectually. Most activities in homes and children's centers that are referred to as play also consist of cognitive stimulation in varying degrees. The learning function of play can be influenced by the materials available, by children's own tendencies to explore toys and create playful tasks, and by the adults' interest and skill in supporting and mediating such play in a way that adds information, ideas, vocabulary, and other contributions to development that are intellectual in nature. It can be said that the learning content of play can often be increased without losing most playful features of the activity. This is especially true in the earliest years; however, adults may need special skills in combining learning and play, as children focus on academic learning (see Chapter 10).

The third basic feature of play is its value as a socializing medium. The personalities of young children are newly emerging in the early years, and this includes the growth of independence and of unique styles of interacting with others. Social learning is more often a part of play than is generally realized. Toddlers who play apart from each other may be seen to observe and duplicate each other's activities. Preschoolers who appear to be oblivious to their friends' stories or behaviors in a corner of the nursery school may repeat their phrases and acts later at home. Pretend play and games in kindergarten provide social models to peers who watch or participate. Although some play is solitary, it may involve the rehearsal of socially oriented activities. Even when no social elements are present, the child's personal involvement and satisfaction when playing alone may have later implications for relationships to others. During the many naturally occurring play episodes in homes, neighborhoods, and child care centers, there are social exchanges of ideas and behaviors that teach children about the peer culture into which they will grow. Adults may not be aware of these useful peer interactions and social learnings unless problems arise. But even in situations of conflict, children are learning how to deal with others' behaviors and feelings as they also learn to manage their own needs. They are constantly provided with models they can study, duplicate, or reject, with play partners who generate ideas or follow along with their own suggestions, and with friends whose growth and play interests parallel theirs over a period of time (see Chapter 3). Their interactions with adults contribute to socialization in similar ways. While peer interactions reflect the society's characteristics, in the case of adult-child interactions society's expectations and norms are transmitted more formally. Parents demonstrate constructive modes of play, interjecting judgments about the appropriateness of the youngster's expressions or behaviors. Their supervision or involvement generally assures that the play activity is a positive one for all participants. In this way, standards of social exchange are demonstrated and rewarded. Children learn concepts of fairness, cooperation, and respect for others when parents and teachers model and discuss these during play.

What, then, is play? A young child engaged in play is demonstrating enjoyment or satisfaction, is learning, and is developing personal and social skills. It is likely that the activity is self-chosen or at least agreed to, and that it does not include routine care or a nonplay focus. It is participatory, and the child is not completely directed by an adult. It may be experimental or task-oriented, fanciful or serious, social or solitary in format. Play makes children feel good, and it helps them learn. It serves a role in their personal and social growth because it enables them to understand themselves and deal with others. Play values can be enhanced through supportive adults, materials, and settings.

TYPES OF PLAY

Definitions of types of play have emphasized their social, educational, and functional aspects. Chance (1979) includes physical, manipulative, symbolic, and game modes of play. Fowler (1980) focuses on the developmental contributions of play as exploratory, instrumental, constructive, and symbolic functions. Sponseller's (1982) reivew of play identifies symbolic, linguistic, motor, and social types. Shapiro (1981) includes experimentation, skill testing, role rehearsal, constructing-inventing, and information gathering. Taken together, these descriptions provide a background for pinpointing types of play likely to occur in homes and children's centers and for discussing parents' and teachers' roles in relation to play. The various types, summarized in Table 7 and discussed in detail here, are not mutually exclusive; they may occur simultaneously in a given play situation.

Table 7
The Value of Types of Play

Types of Play	Characteristics and Value
Exploratory	Provides new experiences and varied approaches to objects and people. Reflects curiosity and requires some freedom.
Skill	Builds new skills and rehearses existing ones, especially physical and intellectual. Reflects persistence and requires energy and patience.
Affectionate	Is an expressive pleasure that is positive and reinforces good feelings. Reflects love and acceptance and requires flexibility.
Imaginative-Constructive	Provides creative and representational expression. Reflects thinking and uniqueness and requires fluid materials.
Social-Pretend	Contributes to personality and self-awareness, and provides role rehearsal. Reflects concepts and requires imagination.
Social-Interaction	Develops behavioral models for language and interpersonal skills. Reflects personality and requires peers.
Communicative	Enhances language development and use. Reflects verbal and personal skills and requires involvement with others.
Organized Games	Encourages social exchange and develops intellectual or physical skills. Reflects alertness and requires reason and memory.
Media	Has the potential for enrichment, information, and socialization. Reflects personal interests and requires supervision.

Exploratory Play

Infants and young children often become involved in detailed explorations of themselves and other people, of toys and objects serving as playthings, and of their surroundings. Think about children using sand, water, blocks, or a musical instrument. Their activity engages the senses and explores the capacities of the material. It may comprise a new adventure or reflect a continuous series of investigations using the same materials. There may be trial-and-error experiences or more organized modes of play. The child directs the activity, however, according to his curiosity and varies it in a rather spontaneous fashion. Exploration of this type is often sensorimotor in nature because young children use physical manipulation in studying people and objects. They handle them in a variety of experimental ways, gathering information through the senses, especially touch, hearing, and sight, and processing it in their minds. Their exploration may be motivated by curiosity or a need to be actively involved in their surroundings. Intellectual or linguistic concepts also can be explored, using learning games, words and songs, and more abstract toy materials such as counting cubes, picture books, and even microcomputers. Exploratory play is particularly valuable for children because it helps them gain new experiences. It is also important to encourage and protect this type of play, regardless of the confusion or disorganization that may occur when youngsters probe new limits and materials.

Skill Play

Repeated practice with intellectually oriented and physical playthings is common in preschool children. This activity often resembles concentrated study, with occasional variations or progressive changes shown by the children as their skills mature. Its repetitive nature appears to provide a sense of satisfaction in those abilities mastered, mixed with interest in achieving at a higher level or in new areas of activity. The toddler who struggles several hours a week to make a new tricycle function smoothly or the preschooler who takes apart and completes the same puzzle over a period of days are both engaging in skill play, as is the first grader who is heard singing the same song over and over again. Some exploratory play may be involved initially, but the child's attention seems to focus quickly on building up a particular physical or intellectual skill through constant, playful rehearsal. Often there is a spontaneous shift to another similar ability using the same or a related plaything. It is important to encourage and monitor this skill play. The child's excitement may take her beyond an acceptable or safe limit, or it may lead to frustration and rejection if expectations exceed capacities.

Affectionate Play

The delight and satisfaction experienced by adults and children of all ages is apparent to anyone who witnesses affectionate play. Its strong positive flavor is one of its values. Affection provides tension release and relaxation, along with a successful and reinforcing interaction with another person. Social and emotional development is enhanced with this type of play, especially if it is moderately robust and satisfying. Overly strenuous physical affection or very challenging verbal exchanges that become upsetting should be avoided, however. Touching and hugging and funny words and expressions add additional spice and laughter. Because youngsters are often unable to recognize their frustration or saturation, adults need to monitor affectionate play and provide distraction when the child is fatigued. This type of play alters less over time than does exploratory and skill play, which accommodate to higher ability levels. Tickle, chase, and funny sounds and faces all tend to look the same from infancy through grade school, and their appeal seems to remain strong even in adults, who also benefit from affectionate play with children and loved ones.

Imaginative-Constructive Play

The creative expressions of preschool children take the form of constructions that are more or less realistic in form. Simple block configurations, made-up songs, scribbles with crayon and paint, and clay or sand arrangements and designs are all instances of imaginative-constructive play. The child as creator directs the process of making some form or shape that is unique and may even express a concrete idea. As toddlers, these valued processes may produce little that is recognized by adults, and that is expected. As the child's skills and interests mature, the creative process may begin to reflect some elements of the adult world, but most concepts and configurations tend to remain childlike and original. The developmental process influences the designs seen in the earliest years, with children progressing from very primitive to more sophisticated figures and settings in their productions. Uniqueness abounds and often reveals a child's experiences and concerns. To emphasize the imaginative-constructive play process, adults should most likely allow children to express themselves freely, with little direction or modeling. When specific products are the focus, such as in crafts and special projects, children's constructive play may be limited in imaginative elements and similarly limited in play value. Materials using a variety of textures and many media, such as water, paint, chalk, soap, and so forth, can be provided, even in the toddler years. Adults should accept the child's expressions as special, regardless of form. Clean-up habits and restricted areas for use of these materials also should be encouraged.

Social-Pretend Play

In using their imaginations, children also are exercising representational skills, releasing tensions, rehearsing behavioral roles, and developing personality. Social-pretend play is constructive and reconstructive in nature. Children create and participate in situations that are very fanciful and not always reflective of the real world. Sometimes people and events are rather completely made up; on other occasions children may pretend to be someone whose words and activities are familiar and easily recognized by others. Youngsters engaged in this "play acting" or drama may be employing a wide variety of intellectual, social, and physical skills. Their play may be rich in vocabulary and problem solving, or it may be highly creative and inventive, full of new ideas and unique people. Because pretend play is not usually controlled by adults, children tend to exercise a good deal of conceptual and behavioral freedom. They can be queens, kings, firefighters, storekeepers, doctors, car drivers, spouses, parents and siblings, all within the same play episode if they desire. Choices and roles tend to be open, regardless of age, experience, and, hopefully, the gender of participants. Adults can encourage this play best by exposing children to many places and events outside the home and center and by providing opportunities and some props, such as discarded "dress-up" clothing and implements used by community helpers such as mail carriers, plumbers, or cooks. Adults can point children in the direction of social play through their approval of pretend activities, but they should probably remain apart from the children and their peers once play is established. Supervision to help resolve problems in turn taking, sharing, and equality of roles may be needed. Stereotypes may be common; adults can observe these and encourage alternatives through books, discussion, and visits where children can see many different people employed in familiar roles.

Social-Interaction Play

Although similar to pretending, children engaged in social-interaction play are focused upon another child's specific actions. There is a good deal of observation and duplication of the behaviors of a peer. The youngster is copying a model demonstrated by another. In toddlers this copy-cat activity is very obvious: Dad's sweeping and Mom's cooking are repeated rather accurately with toys or real implements. At the nursery school, preschoolers attempt the same style of climbing, block building, drawing, or other activity seen in peers. During the early elementary years children learn a great many peer games, verbal expressions, and general interaction styles from others. The value of this play is the learning of a behavioral model, or an assortment of them, from which a child selects behaviors of her own. An actual interaction may not occur between actor and observer, but the activity may be absorbed and reproduced later. When there is an interaction, the children may alternate copying one another. Modeling also occurs between adults and children, and this includes a great many play-oriented learning activities such as reading a book, trying a science experiment, or using a new board game. Appropriate behavior is also modeled, such as table manners or the proper way to hold a pet. Unfortunately, behaviors also are modeled that may be disruptive, damaging, or hurtful. Often these can be used as learning experiences by adults, who can explain how the behavior needs to be changed. After experimenting with the many acts they witness in play, children typically come to prefer those that are approved and useful.

Communicative Play

Sounds, gestures, words, songs, and phrases tend to be included in both solitary and social play among young children. Babies and grade schoolers may talk to themselves in either situation. When a playmate is available, verbal communication often accompanies the children's activities. Such exchanges have the potential to contribute a great deal to the development of vocabulary and concepts and the use of language as a tool for expression and for resolving conflicts that arise. Through accumulated experiences of this type, children gain some understanding of the effectiveness of language and of its richness in social exchange. When activities continue to be described verbally, children's interest and ability with written words may help them to become more successful in the acquisition of reading skills and the enjoyment of books and stories. Communicative play at the earliest ages is expressed as informal parent-infant games, where babies coo and gurgle with particular delight in response to mothers' and fathers' utterances. Toddlers duplicate many words, later creating phrases that are quite effective in communicating their needs and reactions. Preschoolers and first-graders use language in a great deal of their peer play as a way to direct activities, express ideas, or manage rules they have established. Such conversation often reveals children's interests, concerns, and even their developmental-social skills. Structured language activities such as stories, nursery rhymes, songs, and drama are also valuable activities. Adults can encourage communicative play in much the same way as they do other types, with special attention to providing new vocabulary and experiences and to avoiding intrusiveness when adult supervision is not necessary.

Organized Games

Formal games begin in toddlerhood but cannot be handled well by most children until the age of five or six. Simple turn-taking and matching games may be tolerated by three year olds, such as ball rolling and shape matches. Four year olds appreciate circle games of brief duration if they are not overly competitive, such as "Ring around the roses" or "I spy." Physical games or sports may be played if they are modified to be simple and relatively easy to succeed at. Board games also can be used, such as picture lotto match-ups, counting and color-selection games, alphabet guessing, and so forth. By grade school, children are familiar with many sport and adult-oriented games involving skill and strategy. Games of this nature may be played into adulthood. They provide a formal, fun-oriented mode of interpersonal exchange and personal skill testing. The rules involved in structured games provide both intellectual and physical challenges to players. In addition, social and personal characteristics are developed such as fairness, patience, tolerance, and self-acceptance. Adults and older peers may fulfill a significant role in learning to manage and enjoy organized games. For young children, the process should be gradual and tied to child and family interests, with a generous measure of reinforcement through success and praise.

Media Play

Radio, television, phonographs and tape recorders, theater, movies, personal microcomputers, and home video and other electronic games are included in this type of play. In many instances, the child's role in media play is that of a relatively passive observer, even though there may be a good deal of mental and physical activity. Where children are able to execute some control over a media program, the toy quality improves greatly. Children also may create or use pretend models of these items in their play, such as children's toy TV's, wind-up radios, movies, and phonographs, and in these instances their play may resemble the imaginative type. Electronic toys may duplicate some board games, but these often are used as solitary activities requiring skill in eye-hand coordination and memory. Media play is as traditional as radio and as newly challenging as microcomputer software. Benefits and risks to children have been associated with these activities as well, with debates among teachers and parents as to how such play should be monitored. Television has engendered the greatest amount of controversy, in part because of its availability in most homes and many children's centers. Moody (1980) has compiled research findings on the effects of television. In some instances there are learning and enrichment, socialization, and educational impacts on children. Programs such as "Sesame Street"; "Mister Rogers' Neighborhood"; "Captain Kangaroo"; science, art, and nature specials; and children's cable stations can be quite useful when mediated by adults and viewed in moderation. But TV also is seen as contributing to aggression, stereotyping, limited communication, and inappropriate learning patterns. Singer, Singer, and Zuckerman (1981) have described how television can be used as a constructive teaching tool. They also argue for adult monitoring to reduce negative effects from frequent family use of TV and too much emphasis on media as significant to family life. Frequent discussion and criticism of television characters and events may be very helpful at the preschool and elementary level. Special educational programs can be encouraged in moderate amounts.

Movies and theater can be viewed as somewhat less influential to the young child because relatively few are exposed to any but special children's programs. In homes where cable television brings adult-oriented movies to the young child, parents must find an effective system for monitoring their viewing and explaining any exposure that is confusing or frightening. Even G-rated films (for all audiences) may contain episodes that young children find upsetting. Parents and teachers may need to inform one another about these movies prior to children's viewing.

Video games, electronic toys, and microcomputers offer a special challenge during the early years. The capacity for child control and mastery makes these materials very appealing as play and learning aids. Where strategy, imagination, skill rehearsal, and information are involved, this form of media play can be quite useful. Toddlers are capable of using electronic toys and software that produces a response for any key that is depressed or that permits a simple method of drawing. Preschoolers can rehearse beginning skills in problem solving, reading, and mathematics, while school-age youngsters can expand their use to good programing, creative simulation, or logic-oriented games. Conflict-oriented programs, such as attack-and-destroy games, should probably be avoided because of their emphasis on negative socialization. The length of time children spend using these materials may need to be monitored in order to avoid eye strain, emotional stress, and preoccupation with these sedentary activities. Sharing should be encouraged; indeed, most young children seem to prefer an adult or peer playmate in their media play.

ADULT ROLES IN PLAY

Some adults enjoy playing with infants and young children; others may encourage or merely tolerate their play. The roles assumed by adults in relation to children's play appear to influence both the immediate activities of children and any developmental implications that follow from the quality of play experienced during these years. Even if reluctant to get involved with children, adults can and should make an effort to ensure that play occurs and is improved with needed materials and supervision. At the very least, it can be argued that children's play keeps them busy, allowing adults to spend their time attending to necessary routines. The developmental value of play, however, in physical, intellectual, and personal-social terms, should not be underestimated by adults. Everyone benefits when youngsters extend their play competence to success in school. This helps adults as well as children to feel good. Expectations for adults in playing with children are not overly demanding of their time and attention, and good play can enrich everyone's life, at home or school. The following six general descriptions reflect parent and teacher behaviors that are not difficult to acquire or maintain. Special attention may be needed, however, for parents of high-risk or handicapped children, because of unique problems experienced by these families in managing children's play.

Play Atmosphere

Adults can influence the emotional-social atmosphere in which children's play occurs. Their support and encouragement, for example, will make a child feel relaxed and cheerful enough to want to play and to respond to playful overtures made by others. A negative attitude with many restrictions and punitive responses to play is very likely to result in minimal activity or in very passive, less valuable forms of play. An appropriate atmosphere is facilitative, but it is not completely free of rules and corrections. Children need to understand the limits of their playfulness. They should be firmly discouraged from play that is damaging, dangerous, or hurtful. Within a few clearly defined boundaries, however, an adult's obvious enjoyment and interest in play activities encourage youngsters to play well. Supervision can be moderate and timed to coincide with children's own transitions from one activity to the next. Parents can visually check up on the youngsters without interrupting them and can remain within hearing range in the event of conflicts, which can be handled calmly with the goal of resuming the activity. Support for play can be expressed by helping children create a comfortable setting in the home or center; by obtaining materials, toys, and props; and by praising youngsters for play that appears constructive, imaginative, cooperative, and moderate in degree of excitement. Refreshments can be supplied, along with discussion about what is happening. Smiles, hugs, and compliments express approval. Parents and teachers can review the children's experiences later in the day, reminding them of the pleasure they had and the learning they acquired.

Play Organization

Since adults are responsible for daily arrangements of time and space in the lives of young children, they fulfill an important role in the organization of play. A safe and comfortable setting is needed, a place where children can spread out their toys and make some noise. Some youngsters are fortunate enough to have a playroom, finished basement, family room, large bedroom, backyard, or nearby playground where they can engage in robust or quiet play. Even in more restricted settings, children can be allowed a corner of a kitchen, bedroom, or living room where play can occur without too much disruption. In nursery schools and daycare centers, a great deal of attention is devoted to the settings where children's activities are continuous and valued. It is also important to parents and professionals that clean-up responsibilities are included when play is finished, especially where settings are used for more than one purpose.

In addition to physical space, play opportunities also tend to be organized by adults. This includes time each day, at several intervals during the day, for play. Since infants and young children also spend time on feeding, dressing, and grooming routines, play periods may consist of many brief ones interspersed with care giving, household chores, and errands. Of course, play can be a part of these activities, and effective adults tend to use play in just this way. Nevertheless, time and opportunity for the child's own self-directed play are needed and can easily be organized to coincide with adult activity. In early morning, before or following lunch, and mid and late afternoon there are often one-hour blocks where children can play while adults are busy or relaxed enough to join them. Early evening is frequently a family playtime where a working parent and otherwise active siblings can play with a young child.

Play Materials and Playmates

Preschoolers spend a great deal of their time with playthings or people. Play materials include not only toys (see next section), but play objects and natural substances. Safe household containers, utensils, and furniture often stimulate exploratory, skill, and imaginative play. Water, playdough, sand, wood, leaves, pebbles, and so forth provide a good deal of play opportunity when simple containers, shovels, vehicles, and figures are added. Infants enjoy play using rattles, soft objects, and the many available action-oriented "busy box" toys; older babies like to investigate stacking, open-shut, and container-type toys in addition to balls, mirrors, and soft blocks and creatures. Toddlers expand their activities to include walking-riding toys, simple puzzles, books, vehicles, dolls, records, and telephones. Preschool children enjoy all construction toys and art materials. They like games of many kinds, pretend and board types, as well as "play sets" that provide miniature settings and people figures reflecting adult roles. Science, reading, mathematics, and craft-oriented materials become favorites toward the grade-school years, as do musical instruments and sports-related equipment.

What these playthings provide are outlets for expressing skills and understanding and sources for new concepts and exploration. They are the concrete units upon which children build fantasies, practice skills, and gather information. They are also a meeting ground, an activity center that attracts other children and adults, inviting them to join the play situation. Playmates may be peers, siblings, or adults. In many ways, another person is like a toy, serving as a stimulus and a vehicle for play. The personal characteristics of people during such activities provide additional challenges and delights. There may be conflict or confusion when two individuals play together, but there are also the dynamic elements of words and actions that contribute in exciting and unpredictable ways to the situation.

Playful adults are particularly important during infancy, when the child's limited abilities create a dependence upon someone else's interest in engaging them. Parents and care givers have to make overtures and sustain them with the very young. They remain involved in games and sports at older ages when children need direction and mediation in their play. Peers are excellent playmates because they reflect similar interests and abilities not usually present with adults. Siblings also may function as playmates, although there is a tendency for patterns of dominance and submission to arise and overshadow the activities. Nevertheless, other children are invaluable playmates, and parents may need to make arrangements for friends, relatives, and neighbors to play with the youngster. Indeed, some families enroll children in play groups simply for the playmates they contain, and staff members in these situations are prepared to help children play well with others.

Play Modeling and Teaching

Sometimes play has to be taught or demonstrated. Adults tend to assume this role when children have difficulty with a toy or need encouragement in trying a new activity. Parents and teachers can use children's ability to copy or imitate to this end. They show the youngster, by example, how to make a toy work, or they complete a game while the youngster observes. This form of modeling and teaching is quite effective in the context of play, and children can learn a great deal from the demonstrations. Two risks are involved; that adults will reduce the child's explorations with play materials by predisposing them to the one use they model, or the child will lack the ability to use a toy in the manner shown by an adult attempting to teach the

child. These limit children's play or lead to frustration, neither of which represents good modeling. Adults should probably demonstrate what seems appropriate at the child's level, and they can praise additional uses of toys that children themselves discover. This type of adult role is important, however, because it can lead to enrichment and learning in play, advancing the youngster's developmental level by providing increasingly more mature and competent play.

Play Involvement

To join a child's play and participate at his level can be extremely satisfying to adults and children. Real involvement in play may not completely resemble the actions of peers in the same situation, but there is a sense of sharing and mutuality between adult and child. Within reason, the adult can color, build block structures, move about miniature cars and figures, and otherwise conform to the expectations of the activity. Such participation will not compromise the adult's status as supervisor and authority figure as long as the play situation is relatively neutral or equivalent in tone. If a youngster wants to control or direct others fully, then dolls or action figures should be substituted, with adults expressing their preference for play where everyone is active and contributing.

In more formal games, it is likely that adults will be helping children learn rules and also providing some source of competition. From observations of this situation, it seems that adults have to avoid the two extremes of indulgence and outright competitiveness. Because there is already an unequal power distribution between children and their older playmates, and because the adult is also functioning as teacher, the challenge to the youngster should remain at or slightly above his or her level of ability. The exception is for games involving chance elements where winning can be experienced in turn by all participants. With moderation of the adult's superior skills and enthusiasm for joining children's play, these experiences will often be appreciated and remembered as special times. Such sharing brings adult and child into a neutral zone of interaction, a play situation that has mostly positive elements and builds a bond of affection from participating together in a pleasurable experience.

Monitoring

Finally, adults also fulfill the role of supervisor and mediator of children's play. Young children lack the ability to understand fully the consequences of many of the things they do. Adults teach a great deal when they monitor play by helping children to notice others' feelings, to wait for a turn, to use self-control when frustrated, to invite others to join in, to simplify activities for increased cooperation, to express themselves verbally rather than physically, to set up a new activity, and so forth.

For safety, parents and teachers need to keep a constant check on the children's surroundings as well as on their activities. Damage or injury can occur rather quickly, even when precautions have been taken, simply because young children in small groups can become excited, distracted, or emotionally upset, with accompanying behavioral ramifications. Adults need to find ways of avoiding conflicts before they occur and must remain nearby to help children to resolve them successfully. For infants and most toddlers, parents and teachers should be particularly vigilant; pushing, grabbing, throwing, hitting, and biting are characteristic of some and attempted a few times by most. Preschoolers can play somewhat further from constant adult supervision, but problems can still be expected rather frequently. In the kindergarten and first-grade years, play can be quite independent, with adults offering more distal mediation and suggestions.

TOYS AND PLAY

What is a good toy? The definition tends to vary with developmental stages, teachers' and parents' goals, and the child's own special interests. Everyone has their own qualifications, including availability and price of the item. The criteria for toys to be included here reflect a concern for good play (satisfying and beneficial) and for toys that represent the most types of play. Skill practice, imaginative and social forms of play, games, and some exploratory activities involve toys. Affectionate play; activities with artistic, electronic, or musical media; and a good deal of exploratory play do not require toys as such, even though materials or equipment may be needed. Toys, then, can be distinguished from playthings, which are broader in purpose and available in different forms. Toys are objects specifically designed for play. They may serve as learning aids, but the play or game element must be primary. They may engage children's interests and abilities in any or several areas of development, such as the physical or imaginative, and they may be commercially produced or created by parents, teachers, or children themselves. To extend this overall definition of toys several criteria for good toys will be discussed.

Elements of Quality

There are at least ten characteristics of toys that indicate high quality or value in children's play and in the degree to which they earn adult support, including acquisition and involvement.

1. *Good toys are safe and durable.* They are able to withstand use by children of corresponding age, even if abused or experimented upon by older playmates. Safety elements include unbreakable materials, rounded edges, nontoxic substances, appropriately sized pieces, securely attached units, and safe moving parts. Sturdiness should be judged by use over time and in varied circumstances. In addition, toys should be checked for ways in which they might trap or damage a child's body parts. This would include examining the spaces between crib rungs and the ends of implements likely to be poked near eyes, placed near head and ears, tested with fingers, or used by feet. Take-apart and small-sized toys should be given only to older children if the components are capable of being ingested. Heavy toys should be used only with supervision, to avoid accidents by dropping or swinging. Electrical toys are usually inappropriate for young children. Firing toys and spring-activated ones likely to be used near the face should not be allowed. Brochures regarding updated safety criteria are available from many health and consumer agencies concerned with toy safety.

2. *Good toys are intrinsically delightful and satisfying.* Some are appealing immediately, while others take longer to establish themselves as valued playthings. Brightly colored dolls, balls, and trucks please children spontaneously; blocks, musical toys, and board games may take longer to satisfy but may be extended in pleasurable use beyond immediate interest.

3. *Good toys can be used in a variety of ways.* Children can try several alternative uses for them beyond the purpose that seems to be primary. Construction toys allow a great deal of choice, as do materials for physical and creative activities. Other exploratory toys can be designed for many uses; for example, dolls and vehicles with movable parts and props can stimulate much more action than those without such extras. Toys containing assorted pieces or textures help children make more observations and discoveries and try out more play ideas.

4. *Good toys can be used across several ages and stages.* This is true of many creative, imaginative, and open-ended construction toys, board games, and sports equipment. Children can use play clocks, puppets, game props, audiovisuals, alphabet-number toys, science toys, and so forth, for several years. Playthings for infants and toddlers have less value over time,

but good ones are used quite heavily during these years of rapid change in ability. For these littlest children, more complex sorting toys, picture books, and simple vehicles are good throughout the preschool stage. Some wind-up toys are used and saved over years because of their delightful animation and special charm.

5. *Good toys successfully involve the child.* These require sensory, motor, and thought responses. The young child's concrete actions or manipulations are observable signs of success. Such toys may be limited in the range of response, such as a hammer bench with no nuts and bolts, but the child gains a sense of mastery in producing a concrete result. This involvement and response can be seen in peek-a-boo toys, magnetic drawing boxes, action boards, and similar toys that invite active manipulation and success.

6. *Good toys are informative or provoke curiosity.* They stimulate intellectual and verbal exploration. They may contain simple problem-solving or strategy challenges, or they may encourage verbalization that leads to improved information. Matching picture cards and dominoes for example, are capable of expanding ideas while the youngster engages in play. Layered toys and those with interesting decorations also stimulate curiosity and add concepts.

7. *Good toys fulfill the promises made by their creators and producers.* They are honest toys that children can use appropriately. Those that appear wonderful to adults may be flawed in design for children in whose hands they fail to function. Sometimes adults need to examine toys closely prior to their purchase, or watch closely and return toys that frustrate children. Age-stage designations should be accurate and instructions clearly described.

8. *Good toys may be used by both boys and girls, without stigma.* Their packaging and advertising promote nonsexist play. Figures included in construction toys and cars are female as well as male, and those packaged with playhouse materials include males as well as females. Reading and math-oriented games should be appealing to both sexes, and storybooks, puzzles, and other picture toys should depict females and males in varied occupations.

9. *Good toys are nonviolent in form and play use.* On occasion, children misuse toys, making neutral materials serve aggressive ends. But weapons and destructive implements are not likely to be used well in children's play. Toys that are exciting but promote positive actions can easily meet the same needs for assertion and strength. Rescue figures and vehicles often satisfy children, who can rehearse positive rather than negative leadership yet engage in heroic gestures or find gadgetry stimulating and novel.

10. *Good toys are beneficial to children in some way.* They add to the quality of their present experiences and should appear to contribute to future competence. They are worth their expense in time and money because

they generate pleasure, stimulate progress, or contribute to the quality of life at home or school.

Other Issues about Toys

Some judgments about toy value have to be made in perspective. The following are a few issues concerning toys, presented in bipolar terms, that will help adults to think more clearly about them.

1. *Is the toy homemade or produced for purchase?* Many exciting and educational playthings are made by skillful parents or teachers. These include rocking horses, climbers, ABC games, texture books, and so forth. These are valuable additions to play, provided they are safe and useful.

2. *Is the toy convergent or divergent?* Both are needed. The open-ended toy has no fixed solution but allows children to experiment and still succeed (blocks, paints), and the self-correcting toy can be used in predetermined ways, such as rattles, puzzles, and crafts.

3. *Is the toy for solitary or social use?* Each has its advantage. Construction toys, climbers, playdough, and many games are designed for use by children and their friends. Small vehicles, puzzles, and sorting toys tend to be used by children alone.

4. *Is the toy designed for skill practice or imaginative use?* On the one hand, children need a great deal of experience developing their perceptual-motor skills, and adults like toys that teach. But children also benefit from engaging in fantasy and role-rehearsal play, which help them to grow in understanding the world in which they live.

5. *Is the toy complex or simple?* Rattles are quite limited in scope; play figures produce varied activities involving people and animals. Both fulfill a role in helping children to be active players at different developmental stages, even though more complex toys can be used to a greater degree.

6. *Is the toy realistic or abstract?* Some adults and children prefer toys that are quite detailed or that duplicate real objects as much as possible. Others believe that realistic features limit the child's imaginative use of a toy. Trucks are a good example; some are plain wood and fixed, while others contain precise details and moving parts. It is not clear which type are used best in children's play, but families may prefer both.

7. *Is the toy traditional or innovative?* Some playthings are classic toys, such as balls, dolls, wind-ups, boats, cars, and blocks. Others are quite new in concept, such as a child's magic show, space creatures, rockets, electronic toys, and computer games. Each can contribute to play, and each is probably excellent for the toy collector.

In summary, it is important that parents maintain a reasoned perspective on toys. They are valuable additions to play, but they need not be expensive and complicated. Children can create many delightful and useful play situations, and parents who encourage play can use their own ideas in designing playthings. If toy choices were reduced to a bare minimum, children could still thrive using balls, blocks, cars, dolls, and crayons, provided that adults helped them to think imaginatively. Toy fads are exciting, but they need not cause concern among parents when a toy cannot be acquired. Holidays and birthdays can be made special in a variety of ways, the most traditional of which is time together using the simple amusements of outings, conversation, and affection among family members.

PROGRAM SUGGESTIONS

1. Discuss the three basic features of play, and compare these for children and adults. How are they similar and different?
2. Using Table 7, construct a list of important toys for each type of play. Compare the final list with the materials found in an early-childhood program or in individual homes.
3. Debate the pros and cons of encouraging exploratory and pretend play, especially the controversies about messing up, sex roles, and any problems in using fantasy.
4. What can go wrong with children's playful uses of media? Ask parents to identify the dangers and how they have attempted to prevent or minimize them.
5. Talk about adults' roles in children's play, and find out which are preferred by particular mothers and fathers.
6. Present suggestions on how adults can use toys to teach children a variety of skills and concepts.
7. Examine the list of ten elements of toy quality, then use these to evaluate toys that parents identify as favorites of children and adults.
8. Create a worksheet containing bipolar descriptions of the seven toy issues in the text. Have parents place checkmarks along these dimensions for the toys used by their children, in order to find out what characteristics apply most often to the toys.

8

Children's Behavior at Home and School

The behavior of children is a primary concern of adults. Behavior carries meaning and reflects the child's affective and developmental status. Behavior also impinges upon others—it requires a response from them and influences their behavior in turn. Discipline and child management are focused on behavior, and many efforts of adults to understand children, to guide and teach them, center on their physical acts and emotional reactions. Behavior is the pivotal issue in situations involving conflict, distress, communication, moral development, and learning.

Behavior is not easily separated from any other aspect of the child, especially personality. One signals something that is happening in the other. However, the early childhood years are an emergent, formative period during which children experiment with a variety of behavioral concepts and models. So much is being acquired in the formation of rules and patterns that it is difficult to make interpretations about the links between behavior and other personal states. Young children are not yet fully socialized and are strongly influenced by what is happening in their environments. Much of their activity results in new learning, which contributes to their eventual skill in managing feelings, needs, and behavior. For these reasons, some of the concepts and issues related to children's behavior are examined in this chapter apart from other aspects of personality. As a distinctly important component of child rearing and parent education, behavior also is discussed elsewhere in this book, in sections on rearing models, parenting skills, peer relationships, feelings, and education. In the sections of this chapter, behavior is viewed in terms of its meanings and management, with special attention to issues around discipline for teaching as well as for behavioral stabilization.

THE MEANING OF BEHAVIOR

Infants and young children communicate primarily through their behavior. They interact with others using body and vocal displays and employ actions in situations of conflict or stress. Their activities are used as indicators of developmental growth and environmental influences upon children. These meanings of behavior are important to parents and teachers who work with children. Because the young are dependent upon the perceptions of adults yet relatively unskilled in communicating their needs, interests, and conceptualizations, behavior serves as a regularly occurring vehicle for understanding messages, social skills, personal needs, and development.

Communication

The behavior of infants and young children provides an essential communication link between the child's needs, feelings, and interests and the adults' awareness of these. Such messages to parents might reveal a baby's pleasure or pain, a preschooler's frustration, or a school-age child's pride in learning a new skill. Facial expressions and body movements are particularly important in infancy; it is by such means that otherwise helpless babies can communicate. Wiggles and smiles, quiet staring, clenched fists, and rigid bodies serve as signals for necessary adult responses. Crying and cooing might accompany these nonverbal behaviors. At the preschool level the child is more adept with words, but physical gestures still tend to capture much about their affective and cognitive state. Laughter and hugs, avoidance and rejection, throwing and hitting, involvement and persistence—these are all behavioral cues, data about children's well-being, needs, and interests. At the primary-school level, the pleasure, disappointment, or frustration of children in regard to their work and their social relationships is still quite gestural, while at later ages verbal communication assumes a more primary role in revealing children's concerns. Behavior is still foremost to teachers and parents, who tend to view it as an initial indicator of learning and social difficulties, especially where children's acts are disruptive to others or harmful to self.

The communicative functions of behavior have been emphasized by early childhood educators since the child-study programs of the 1930s. Cohen and Stern's (1978) current and earlier editions have served as a classic guide for teachers in understanding individual children through the use of observation and recording in varied situations. Almy and Genishi (1979) also discuss the uses of child study for behavioral evidence of adjustment, learning, language growth, and social relationships. The relatively open and enriched environment of the early childhood program provides many opportunities for observing and analyzing children's learning and behavioral characteristics and needs.

Clinical psychologists who work with children also have come to rely upon behavioral indicators of the child's degree of healthy functioning.

Beller's (1962) classic text in this field emphasized a range of behaviors, from normal to abnormal, in interpersonal and program-related categories: general appearance, activities, emotions, and responses to routines; reactions to teachers and children and to toy and learning materials; evidence of thinking and fantasy; and impressions of unique character traits. These behavioral categories were used to establish strengths, disturbances, program objectives, and recommendations for individual children under observation.

Other, newer child development journals focus on the behavior and mental health of children from birth to three. In general, such indicators include babies' failures to grow, adjust, play, and interact and parents' reports of extremes in child activity, temperament, and their own attitudes about babies' needs and their ability to cope with parenting.

Researchers in child development have completed studies of early behavior in relation to parents and peers. Examples of these include studies of infant sociability, emotion, relationship to the parent, play with toys, interactions with other children, and responses to environments. Each investigator typically uses a coding system for recording a variety of behaviors, then analyzes any patterns that are revealed.

The messages obtained through the observation and study of young children's behavior thus communicate important information about the child's general personal and program-related needs and interests and provide implications to parents and care givers about what might be required to enhance the child's personal and learning environment.

Social Skills

Children's behavior also has meaning in the area of social relationships. Experiences with other children, responses to parents and teachers, and interactions in varying social settings all reveal the child's developing socioemotional skills and difficulties. The emergence of these unique personal styles is part of healthy growth. It can be seen in the many tasks of childhood or the challenges accompanying maturation that require children to master new skills to match their experiences.

Documentation of the sequences of maturing social behaviors, characteristics, and skills, from infancy to middle childhood, has provided some guidelines for those who work with children. The Gesell Institute's (Gesell et al., 1974) standards and descriptions of age-related marker behaviors have anchored the observations of decades of early-childhood educators and parents. Based on studies of large numbers of normally developing children, their averaged age-stage characteristics inform parents and others of what to expect as the child grows and changes. The profiles can be misleading, however, in cases where children develop in uneven spurts. For example, children may acquire physical skills early and accompanying language abilities later. Pronounced temperamental differences and subtle handicapping or environmental conditions also can create uneven patterns that do not coincide with the behavioral norms. For the most part, however, these socially oriented descriptions are useful in understanding children at each stage. Gesell et al. (1974) describe changes in behavior, individual differences, relationships, intelligence, tensions, fears, school, the media, and eating and sleeping behavior. General behavioral descriptions also are provided by Elkind (1978) and many other parent and teacher materials. These focus on children's characteristic interests, social relationships, and abilities to negotiate in the home and school setting. They give an almost affectionate narrative of infants and young people at various stages of their lives, without specifying precise criteria for examining the child's status.

At the youngest ages, Willis and Riccuiti (1975) have developed infant and toddler behavior scales with descriptions in many categories concerned with people, temperament, and daily activities. Children are scored according to their resemblance to these. Parent-child relations, especially in the years before preschool, are considered to be the important precursors to social growth, and measures of these can be helpful in identifying potential and actual problems (Bromwich, 1981; Giffin, 1981). Included are some educational or clinical treatments, as well as follow-up assessments of the effectiveness of them. The focus in these descriptions of parent-child behavior is often upon their reciprocal social interactions, including affection and developmental assistance, that create a satisfying relationship in support of children's growth and well-being.

At the preschool level, social skill measures have emphasized the child's status in school adjustment; acceptance by other children; ability to manage self-care and behavior independently; and some attitudes relating to self-concept, sex roles, and confidence (Goodwin & Driscoll, 1980). Social maturity is an aspect of growth in this area, but it is not as behaviorally oriented as are peer play and adult-child relationships. Recent developmental checklists tend to include sections on some of these social skills. White and Watts (1973) have established that certain observable social behaviors are linked to general competence and intelligence. Children who are developing well are described as able to get the attention of adults and use them for help, express positive and negative feelings, lead and work with peers, compete and demonstrate pride, and role-play adult activities. Thus, children's social behaviors have meaning in several areas of growth. Ratings, observations, interviews, and reports about self and others provide information and guidance to teachers and parents about these important behaviors.

Distress and Conflict

One of the most important groups of behaviors to deal with in young children are those related to opposition, distress, and conflict with others. These highly negative behaviors are very disturbing to parents, teachers, and daycare providers because they tend to produce strong negative emotions in other children and to disrupt the social and learning environment. They require immediate attention and are usually difficult to manage in ways that satisfy everyone concerned. They also may contribute to reduced self-confidence in parents and burnout in professionals. Taxing as they may be, however, conflict behaviors in the young have a purpose. They fulfill a role in development because children are confronted with social problems they must attempt to resolve. A disagreement, frustration, or overwhelming feeling of distress has to be expressed and handled. Adults and peers respond as well, and the child has to learn to use his personal resources in dealing with the problem situation.

Conflict is to be expected in adult-child relationships, peer play, and sibling interactions. It is considered normal most of the time in these circumstances. With playmates, such conflicts represent a cycle of mistakes and learning, of moving out and withdrawing, of testing boundaries, and of developing protective and sometimes aggressive strategies for defending one's own interests. Observations of these reveal the behavioral options the child has adopted or failed to develop. A particular child's temperament and activity level and the dynamics of the specific pairs or groups of children also play a role in how each individual reacts. A child who grabs a toy or hits a playmate may generate a stare, cry, or physical exchange from the recipient. The initiator may learn from the conflict and make adjustments, or the pattern may become habitual.

With different personal and environmental characteristics, it is difficult indeed to determine the behavioral meanings of conflict. Nevertheless, children can be expected gradually to acquire skills in minimizing conflict and finding behaviors that are acceptable for peer-group interactions. The preschooler, for example, becomes less physical in obtaining a toy, electing instead to ask for it, wait, or find a temporary substitute. Verbal exchanges become alternatives to hitting, even though they may express similarly negative feelings. The modeling, limit setting, explaining, and praising that parents and teachers find effective for most conflicts eventually modify children's behaviors and enable them to engage in more productive play. The degree to which an individual child is able to manage a peer situation provides behavioral evidence of that child's social learning and personal state of mind. It may reflect individual differences and the amount of acquired learning in playmate exchanges.

Distress and conflict between individual children and their parents also vary in meaning. During infancy, where a baby's needs for food or comfort conflict with mother's and father's needs for rest and relief, the adults are called upon to shape behavior and teach alternatives to children. By the end of the first year, most toddlers have learned a little about parents' limits of patience endurance. They can play with a toy while food is being prepared or go to the other parent when one parent ignores a tearful demand. Learning to balance emotional needs among family members is a difficult process, however, and behaviors alter over time. For some parent-child pairs problems may become serious enough to contribute to child abuse, neglect, emotional and social stress, or the failure of children to develop self-control and a normal regard for others. In other families parents and children may have a comfortable relationship that supports an affectionate, sociable nature in the child. Some parents share activities with children, and their common interests ease conflicts in other areas; other mothers and fathers become particularly skillful in dealing gently, humorously, and firmly with conflicts. The behaviors expressed by children to their parents are often intense and frequently difficult to manage. For many families, however, behavioral conflicts rise and fall in frequency and duration across all the child-rearing years, with some crisis points. Eventually an established pattern between child and parent for achieving understanding and for coping is created and maintained, and the behavioral evidence of this can be noted.

Sibling rivalry is an additional source of behavioral conflict in many homes. Brothers and sisters can be expected to compete for parents' attention, test behavioral strategies, react to each other's personalities, and have difficulty coping with outright conflicts in a variety of daily events that affect them. Even when parents make the effort to prepare children for new siblings, to give each child a percentage of their time, to balance each person's needs, sibling conflict is a fact of family life. Verbal behavior, physical gestures, and other kinds of actions that express or provoke conflict may occur often. Many authorities have discussed the benefits and disadvantages of these conflicts (Leichter, 1975; Sutton-Smith & Rosenberg, 1970) and related them to birth order, sex, achievement, and personality within the family. Some of the systems for managing children's behaviors with parents may be effective with brother-sister interactions. The meanings of such behaviors are complex but often useful for parents and teachers in understanding and working with children. A preschooler, for example, may become upset by a new baby at home yet learn to be nurturant and verbal in helping to care for the child. A school-age youngster may develop physical and intellectual skills more rapidly than others by virtue of the repeated teachings of an older sibling. Such trade-offs may be quite meaningful, enabling brothers and sisters to develop skills and characteristics not learned elsewhere.

Behavior and Development

Children's behavior is used to determine their developmental and social status. For teachers, this tends to be one of the most important functions of behavior. Measures of ability and growth such as the Bayley, Denver, and Stanford-Binet scales, the many published checklists, all depend upon behavioral responses to the test items. Whether verbal or physical behavior is used, assumptions are made about the children's achieved understanding and skills, based upon what the examiner sees and hears from the children. Behavior is thus a yardstick by which their status is assessed. It is used as evidence for the acquisition or the failure to acquire the expected skills and understanding of each age.

In the preschool classroom, and to a certain extent in children's homes, it is relatively easy to obtain information about developmental status. Children's behavior with toys and equipment, with tasks, and in relation to others reveals many of their strengths and needs. Their successes with fitted shapes and containers, their use of language with books, their negotiation of a playground climber, their use of board games, their understanding of simple addition, and their attempts to read words all can provide evidence of growth in successive stages. Likewise, children's failures to play creatively, to persist in a task, or to remember simple concepts are indications of some difficulties. Eventually such behaviors are formally linked to age-related norms so that a more precise profile of developmental status is established.

The specifics of these sequences of growth will be discussed in Chapter 10. It is important to mention in this section on behavior that children may demonstrate very inconsistent actions and reactions as they progress in development. The transitions between stages and children's approaches to the achievement of major milestones may be accompanied by much upheaval and confused behavior. Successes that are evident on one day may vanish the next, replaced by activities far below the child's capacity. Sometimes emotional outbursts are part of the struggle to learn something new. Occasionally children withdraw socially when they are attempting to figure out how to succeed at a new task. Children's gains in understanding their behavior in relation to others and coming to terms with their personal qualities and limitations also may be accompanied by very troublesome behavior alternating with more positive activities. Signs and symptoms may vary greatly at home and in school. All of these transitions related to developmental progress tend to be viewed as more or less serious, depending on the child's previous history and the adults' experience. Some take the position that such "hurdles" are normal and require a basically optimistic perspective. Others believe that even minor developmental problems require attention and adjustment. Developmental behaviors nevertheless have meaning for parents and teachers, both in academic and behavioral terms.

Behavior and Circumstance

One final aspect of the meanings of behavior consists of the circumstances in which behavior occurs. People, settings, materials, and events influence the actions of infants and young children. When early childhood professionals develop their curriculum and classroom design, some of their primary concerns are the physical arrangements of space, the type and level of materials, and the way in which adults use the environment with children. It is clear to them that babies and preschoolers are affected by what they experience around them. Their behavior is shaped and observed by the context in which they interact.

Poorly arranged classrooms tend to contribute to behavioral difficulties and sometimes to learning problems. Inappropriate materials, too little or too much structure, inadequate or poorly trained staff, lack of privacy, conflicting traffic patterns and activity areas all may result in frustration, distraction, boredom, stress, and a variety of behavioral patterns associated with them. Well-designed classrooms and properly trained staff, on the other hand, may result in a smoother series of activities and fewer behavior problems. In daycare programs, group size, staff training, and other physical features of the environment have been associated with children's behavior and progress (Belsky & Steinberg, 1978; Roupp, Travers, Glantz, & Coelen, 1979).

In children's homes there are similar relationships between physical and emotional aspects of the environment, in terms of behavior and competence during the infancy and preschool years. Parents who make arrangements for children to be actively involved in learning and play and who encourage independence may have fewer instances of conflict and social difficulties. At older ages when children require a great many outside activities and relationships, they also may be influenced by people and events. Neighborhoods vary in facilities and opportunities for constructive play with peers. Children who have few agemates may be unable to find sufficient outside interests, turning instead to passive amusements such as television or more disruptive, attention-getting acts. Crises such as family stress, substance abuse, divorce, poverty, or death may occur at times in children's lives when they cannot cope successfully. Their behavior may subsequently reveal the impact of these experiences.

Thus, each child's individual circumstances during the early years will influence her behavior differently. This context in which development, learning, and social growth occur may be supportive or negative, temporary or permanent. In understanding behavior and its meaning, parents and teachers need to consider in which direction the child's life context of people, environments, and events is guiding her behavior.

THE PURPOSES OF DISCIPLINE

In the early childhood years, discipline has more to do with teaching and guidance than with punishment. It is also more related to socialization and understanding than it is to behavior management as such. Yet the word "discipline" has carried connotations of harshness and inflexibility, just as the term "management" has been associated with unsympathetic techniques of behavior modification and control. It is difficult, indeed, to find an appropriate term for the limit-setting and teaching functions of loving and flexible adults in dealing with the emerging behaviors and needs of infants and preschoolers.

It is just as difficult to define the word *discipline*. Discipline is purposeful. It is not simply a punishment for wrongdoing or a way of making children behave in the way that adults insist is correct. It is focused on the child's social and cultural adaptation to society. Broadly defined it is an important process whereby children learn approved ways of dealing with feelings, of interacting with others, and of gaining internal, self-directed standards of right and wrong. Even though children are frustrated by corrections, they also are able to observe models of response to negative emotions and view the consequences of their behavior. Prosocial behavior is developed by using reasoned discipline that points out alternatives and builds self-control. Thus, the educational goals of discipline are considered to be as important as the goal of dealing with behavior.

Issues Related to Children and Adults

Several issues are involved in early childhood discipline. Because of the vulnerability and the limitations in understanding, communicative abilities, and physical capacities of very young children, many familiar discipline techniques are ineffective and even harmful. Reasoning cannot be used with an infant whose needs are urgent. Toddlers are not physically capable of waiting for attention or of expressing themselves verbally. Preschoolers do not, as yet, understand abstract notions of right and wrong. Some school-age children are unable to manage their responsibilities or cope with peer pressure. The developmental limits of young children have to be taken into account when discipline is forthcoming. Adults who fail to consider these are likely to have unrealistic expectations about whether children can respond to what is being asked of them. Both parties may feel frustrated and disappointed needlessly. Understanding such limitations may result in fewer incidences of ineffective discipline.

The social-emotional needs of infants and children are related to discipline because failure to fulfill such urgent requirements can create additional disciplinary situations. A tired or hungry baby is soothed with rest and food. An active toddler who is taken for a walk is less likely to bother her parents. A bored preschooler may be handled best by providing an old magazine and scissors, while a first-grader who is upset by his friends may need a friendly hug. There may be a variety of methods for meeting these kinds of needs, some of which are special to the particular adult and child. Certainly, parents and teachers should not always be at the child's disposal or feel that they are responsible for immediately attending to every perceived need. But to bypass or ignore some powerful, pressing requirements creates a cycle of additional behavioral problems. Often the first step in discipline for the very young is to determine the need and reason behind the behavior. Solutions that satisfy both adult and child may modify the behavior of each without the use of discipline as such.

There are often many different reasons for a given adult act of discipline. These purposes will be discussed in more detail later in this section. However, the overall goal in managing the behavior of the very young can be described as educational. Because children are just beginning their socialization, just becoming involved in conflict, and making their first mistakes, their discipline has to inform, guide, or teach them. As yet, their histories are brief and their understanding limited. They gradually have to build self-control and the ability to respond to adult demands. Adults teach by modeling, limit setting, explaining, and even punishing children with their disapproval. It is a lengthy, time-consuming, and complex process. There are few shortcuts in effective and enduring discipline. The teaching process in relation to behavior is taxing but often rewarding, especially in the early years, where such an educational foundation can benefit not only the child and adult but ultimately a society that depends upon adherence to democratic rule systems.

By far one of the most effective teaching methods that an adult can use with young children is praise. Physical affection, positive facial expressions, and verbal praise serve as rewards in the teaching process. Behavior can be shaped by praising children when they attempt and partially achieve understanding and acceptable behavior. Teachers of young children know how well complimentary remarks work in getting cooperation. A child who is

praised for putting one block away tends to help in putting them all away, while praise for taking turns typically results in more of this behavior. This positive approach to discipline as teaching is an important concept for young children and will be mentioned often.

Every child, parent, and teacher is different, in personal history, feelings, and the ways in which each deals with people and events. This makes it extremely difficult to know how someone will act or react. Often people do not even know their own feelings and tendencies until they see themselves behaving in a particular way. Infants and children, parents and teachers are all unique individuals whose very differences from one another influence how they will discipline and how they will respond to discipline. Teachers have always found that each group of children they encounter can be expected to react differently to them. Parents often struggle or rejoice in finding that their second child shows a different set of behaviors when a particular discipline strategy is used. Those who work in the child welfare field sometimes find a difficult relationship reflects a mismatch of temperament in a given child-parent dyad. The issue of individual differences in adults and children complicates any form of discipline, creating unpredictable patterns of successes and failures in handling behavior. It is important to keep this in mind when recommendations are made about discipline.

Another aspect of the individuality of adults and children is the perspective from which each person views a given action or set of behaviors. The attitudes and beliefs of a particular parent or teacher influence their judgments in situations. Research has demonstrated that such mindsets serve as perceptual screens from which adults operate. McGillicuddy-DeLisi and Sigel (1983) have used videotaped behavioral interactions between parents and children to determine what belief systems are influencing adults' judgments of and responses to the child. Others (Porter, 1980; Rosenthal & Jacobsen, 1970) have established that teachers' behaviors are strongly related to their attitudes about what children should do and are capable of doing. If these mental screens determine the disciplinary and teaching activities of the adults who work with children, it may be necessary to examine them in the context of developing effective discipline. An awareness of such beliefs, attitudes, and perceptions could help to resolve some issues concerning individual actions and reactions, some whys and wherefores of discipline.

Some Dilemmas in Discipline

Offering Consistency and Flexibility. One of the many reasons why discipline is a difficult topic to discuss is that there are several contradictory adult behaviors associated with managing children. One is the consistency-flexibility dilemma. On the one hand, the need for consistent rules and adult responses to children's behavior is clear. To obtain the same disapproval for wrongdoing, the same praise for evidence of self-control, the same messages from most adults about right and wrong creates a pattern that helps children to learn. There is little doubt that behaviors to which everyone reacts the same, negatively or positively, are better understood. If the child is capable and interested in bringing behavior in line with standards expressed this consistently, the educational goal of discipline is more easily achieved. On the other hand, rigidly applied rules and disapproval can create an opposite effect. Children sometimes need adults to be flexible, to bend and give in, when there are extenuating circumstances or when rules become unreasonable or overwhelming. When the toddler is too engrossed in play to come when called, the preschooler forgets to hang up her sweater, or the first grader refuses to wear a hat he dislikes, the adult may need to be flexible. The willingness and ability to suspend a rule temporarily, to provide a reminder instead of a punishing consequence, or to ignore a challenge is sometimes more important than consistency. Other issues such as children's limits, needs, and individuality may take precedence. The dilemma occurs when adults have to decide between consistency and flexibility. Judgments have to be made based upon the specifics of the situation and the adult's own priorities and perceptions about the child. Sometimes the confusion is resolved well; other times difficulties may persist.

Expressing Positive and Negative Feelings.   Another dilemma that makes decision making difficult is that of being loving, affectionate, accepting, and supportive of the child, yet sometimes withdrawing positive regard and firmly correcting, expressing negative emotions, and making the youngster aware that feelings of love can be replaced by firmness and disapproval. Adults are usually aware of the value of unconditional regard for the child. Love leads to trust and the desire for approval. A strong positive relationship is very much a part of managing children's behavior, partly because of its power to maintain motivation for acting appropriately. Yet parents and teachers sometimes have to put aside the affection that ties them to children, in order to discipline them. The concern, disappointment, sadness, or even anger of the child in response is not easy to deal with. Especially in the very young, tears, refusals, and seeking out others for comfort create feelings of doubt and distress in adults as well. But firmness is necessary to successful discipline, and the rejection of inappropriate, hurtful, and dangerous behavior helps point out to children that the feelings and rules of others around them are important. To resolve this dilemma is difficult indeed, and adults often have to "feel their way" through a given situation. Signals from the children may help to guide them; so also will discussion with other teachers and parents caught in very similar dilemmas.

Distinguishing Feelings from Behavior.   A different set of problems is related to the inner versus outer child, or the feeling versus behavior issue. In early childhood education, teachers often attempt to teach children that there is a distinction between feelings and behavior. Both are aspects of personality, but one's inner feelings and thoughts are not subject to disciplinary actions, while behaviors are. One's behavior has an impact on others. If it is hurtful, damaging, rejecting, or otherwise outside boundaries people establish, then others can respond and most likely will. Private feelings and thoughts are not open to discipline when they remain private. As children begin to understand this, it is likely that they will learn to manage some of the behavior associated with a feeling and the words tied to a thought. As they become comfortable with this distinction they are better able to express themselves to others without being disciplined. They can continue to entertain personal feelings and to respond inwardly, but they must modify those outer behavioral displays that are not acceptable.

Of course, the notion of this difference between feelings and behavior is not an easy one to grasp, and others tend to define us in terms of our actions rather than our feelings. Indeed, even with such awareness, the control of behavior is part of a long social and personal process. Many adults remain unable to acknowledge and control their own behavior. It also is unhealthy to separate these aspects of self so much that emotions are hidden and suppressed. The dilemma for adults rests in moving between these extremes and finding a comfortable, healthy way of conveying these notions to children.

Accepting Uneven Results. One final difficulty in using discipline is that even when a particular strategy appears to be effective and educational the "sometimes it works, sometimes it doesn't" syndrome may appear. Experienced preschool teachers are very well aware of the potential for this to occur, even when using their best techniques. Parents have doubtless had the same experience with their favorite methods of disciplining children. It may be the case that this inconsistency simply comes with the territory, that inherent in the successes and challenges of dealing with the young there are complications that cannot be seen ahead of time. Sometimes the very familiarity of an adult's methods eventually produces a lack of response. On occasion, there are problems the child brings to the situation that newly complicate it. Although discouraging, parents and teachers may need to repeat what they do until success is achieved. Or, they may need to substitute an alternative. Uneven results are part of what makes discipline such an emotion-laden subject, requiring the determination to seek solutions continually as children and adults grow and change.

Reasons for Discipline

Discipline is part of rearing and educating children. Every adult who works with the young becomes involved in activities called discipline, behavior management, socialization, and so forth. Whatever term is used, the major concern is to handle behavior effectively, in an educational, beneficial, and enduring way. The specific purpose of a given act of discipline may be one or more of the eight reasons described in this section. An examination of these goals is helpful because discipline plays an important role in children's development and because adults may provide more effective discipline if the reasons behind their actions are clear.

Primary Goals. Three primary goals of discipline that lay the foundation for later action are (1) the development of a loving, trusting relationship; (2) the building of self-esteem; and (3) the modeling of understanding and respect for others. These goals are important because they form the secure base upon which children can perceive the feelings of others. A loved, confident child whose parents and teachers demonstrate regard and respect for others is more likely to understand why behavior that is hurtful or offensive to others has to be stopped. Such a child can relate to the feelings of others because she has experienced the distress and ultimately the guilt that accompanies wrongdoing and the consequent interruption of such a loving relationship.

During the infant years, for example, parents respond rather quickly and lovingly to their babies, holding them when they cry, providing the breast or bottle when they seem hungry, and helping them sit and play with simple toys. Good feelings grow. On occasion, continuous cries and demands for attention are deliberately ignored, at least for a small period of time. A mother or father is too busy or too tired to respond. What the child begins to learn is that, even though adults are loving and can be trusted, they have their own needs and priorities and they can get impatient and saturated. Very slowly the child is required to wait a little for the bottle or play alone briefly, and the loving relationship continues.

The obvious demonstrations of love and the occasional withdrawal of approval for a period of time are an early form of discipline. As the child grows and adults maintain a primarily positive relationship, gains in esteem and self-confidence continue to build understanding and respect for others. The child's strong positive feelings also generalize to others. The loving, respectful behavior modeled by parents is imitated. The loved, respected child loves and respects others. The toddler copies a parent's hug, a preschooler offers to help in the same manner as he observes the teacher, and the first grader confidently explains an accidental shove because she intended no harm. The goals of love and respect are thus very basic to discipline throughout the early years.

Setting Limits.   Another immediate and long-term purpose of discipline is to set limits, or boundaries, for children's behavior. It may very well be the case that the learning of limits established in the very early years provides a healthy explanation of discipline. Limits begin to become very important during the toddler years, when new physical, cognitive, and intellectual skills enable the child to try new behaviors. As these experiments occur, adults begin to establish limits and boundaries. Certain activities are not allowed; the toddler cannot touch certain valuables, run into the street, or have only cookies for dinner. Such external limits have to be taught by the adult and remembered by the child. Gradually the baby understands that some behavior has to be brought under voluntary control. The "no-no's" are distinguished from other activities. By the preschool years these are becoming internalized or governed within by the child's conscience. The rules that are accepted are made a part of the child's personal-social style. During the grade-school years, most youngsters are very clear about the boundaries under which they must operate, even if they disagree with them. They have become rather automatic, and self-control in regard to limits is fairly well established. It is important to remember, however, that children's developmental capabilities influence the growth of self-control. The role of adults is to make limits clear, simple, and possible; to be fairly consistent in enforcing them; and to use praise to reward children's attempts to keep their behavior within such boundaries.

Developing Social Skills.   Discipline is part of building children's social skills. Socialization is the process by which young people become aware of and accept the values and expectations of their families, schools, and culture. It is important to the smooth functioning of the home and classroom, where others need to learn and interact without an undue amount of conflict in attitude and behavior from inadequately socialized children. Standards regarding these expectations are expressed to young children by the adults around them, many times in terms of right and wrong. This emphasis builds the child's sense of morality, an abstract notion brought down to the youngster's level through disapproval, correction, guilt, punishing consequences, and verbal explanations. Other values are expressed as behavioral rules forbidding particular activities, especially in relation to specific times and places. Manners are both positive and negative rules, in that they provide standards of what to do and what not to do.

Social rule systems come from parents, teachers, and neighborhoods, although conflicts may occur among these people or between groups of adults and other persons representing society in the media. In socializing children, teaching them values, and developing a moral conscience, there are many inconsistencies that can be experienced. One set of adults, for example, may approve of physical aggression or object to messy self-feeding, while others encourage verbal resolution of conflict and early independence. The teaching of values may require some skill in decision making, as well, so that children learn to distinguish among the expectations and decide which ones best fit the standards most important to them.

Finally, the authority and power relationships that children grow to understand will play a role in their socialization. Some adults insist on a very high degree of conformity to their standards, and the child's obedience is expected in every relevant situation. Sometimes the child's individuality and ability to make decisions is lost in the face of absolute standards. Fortunately, this is rare and children are reasonably well socialized during the early years.

Encouraging Problem Solving and Conflict Resolution. Discipline also is intended to guide children into solving problems and using reason to resolve conflict. Positive discipline is characterized by explanation and direction and by thoughtful planning and the rational conduct of acts of discipline. It is a valuable goal because it directs children into appropriate behavior and helps them find solutions for problems that arise. Early-childhood teachers are trained to provide a great deal of guidance to children throughout the preschool day, using a "let's figure this out" orientation. The child's needs are sorted out, and the teacher suggests an alternative behavior that is more acceptable. The child who wants another's toys learns how to ask for it or where to find a similar one. Parents often provide guidance similarly. A child upset from school is asked to explain what happened on the way home and is given suggestions for avoiding a similar incident the next day. When parents and teachers remove an unruly child, interrupt a dispute in a game, and praise a child who exercises restraint, they typically explain in some detail the issues around their discipline. All of these activities aim to build children's problem-solving and reasoning skills so that discipline is less frequently needed because the youngsters are able to resolve a matter independently.

Teaching the Consequences of Behavior. Sometimes an adult who needs to discipline a child provides or arranges a negative, punishing consequence. Logical results of inappropriate behavior, such as the withdrawal of a privilege in which a misbehavior occurs, are usually effective in demonstrating disapproval, producing discomfort, and ultimately changing behavior. If there is a logical relationship between the child's behavior and its consequence, the punishing aspect of the consequence may be masked. The child sees it as naturally occurring rather than under adult influence. The tie to the behavior in question is, to the child, very straightforward and often rather unemotional. This keeps attention focused on altering the behavior that is at fault.

Other kinds of consequences are, to the child, less logical. Emotional and physical consequences tend to create very distressing situations. The angry or disappointed adult response is a consequence in and of itself. The child feels the force of such reactions and may produce either an immediate change in behavior and a recognition of wrongdoing or else a change and an accompanying resentment or failure to understand what has happened. The strong emotions involved may teach or they may block the ability to learn. Physical consequences also may produce varied results. In the earliest years, before the child understands explanations, adults tend to use distraction, physical restraint, removal, and spanking as punishing consequences for unacceptable behavior. The child's reaction to mild physical actions from adults may result in hesitation and change in similar circumstances. This is especially true for concrete misbehaviors such as fingering electric outlets, climbing on high furniture, or biting a playmate. Frequent or extreme physical consequences or those used in connection with expectations children cannot manage tend to produce little change at great expense to a positive parent-child relationship and sometimes to children's health.

Encouraging Responsibility and Fairness.   Finally, the goals of discipline include the prevention of aggression and irresponsibility and the development of children's sociability and sense of fairness. To function as a social being requires an interactive style that helps individuals get along with and enjoy one another. Babies who gurgle, coo, and smile at one another; toddlers who can play near their peers; preschoolers who create intricate games of pretend together; and first graders who are eager to join one another in a project are all examples of sociability. Such comfortable relationships, with minimal aggression and a sense of responsibility for one another, are an ideal of many homes, schools, and societies. Discipline that tends to encourage children in this direction provides valuable supports for harmonious group living. Even when assertion is necessary to a child's growth and well-being or when self-interest is important for achievement, an attitude that expresses a basic pleasure in interacting with others and treating one another fairly and equally is helpful in society.

Certainly, such feelings can be encouraged in group care programs, where children's playmates and teachers may serve as extended family members. Sociability is important to any elementary school, where the ups and downs of daily living require some stabilizing harmony. Discipline that does not create resentment or denial of wrongdoing also may promote sociability. The child who gives up feeling frustrated and angry following correction by an adult is more likely to behave with fairness to others. Youngsters who can admit being wrong and accept responsibility will be better able to rejoin their friends in a positive and sociable frame of mind. Discipline that supports these attitudes may lead to a better social life for everyone.

SYSTEMS FOR MANAGING BEHAVIOR

Most published materials dealing with the management of children's behavior use a format of structure, suggestions, and explanations organized in a particular point of view. In general, the authors describe a system for interacting with children that is expected to produce improved parent-child relationships and acceptable behavior. Some systems have to be rehearsed, preferably under the guidance of a trained group leader, while others provide parents with a text that enables them to develop such skills on their own. Most are oriented toward older children and have to be adapted for youngsters at preschool age.

The systems that will be described in this section can be useful when examined for their relevance to the early childhood years. An analysis of these systems may be very helpful in understanding varied points of view about children and the ways in which adults manage them. Basic differences center on four aspects of behavior: (1) concepts of what controls behavior, (2) uses of reason and power, (3) the role of children's interests and environments, and (4) views of motivation to behave in particular ways. Each system looks somewhat differently at behavior along these lines, but, despite such diversity in orientation, several similarities exist across them. All the techniques for managing children's behavior assume that parenting skills can be improved and family relations can become more harmonious. Establishing two-way communication and understanding is encouraged by most. Some are more open to the values and goals of a particular family and tend to allow for a degree of personalization of the program to a set of parents and children. Effective implementation of adults' standards and interactions with youngsters requires consistency.

There are four categories into which behavior-management programs will be placed in this section. The first is predominantly concerned with the social skills of children over the long term. Communications programs, values clarification, decision making, conflict resolution, and problem-solving systems all attempt to build children's understanding and abilities in dealing with adults and peers. A second type of approach is oriented toward the immediate control of behavior and the uses of authority. Applied behavior analysis, logical consequences, and assertiveness training focus on ways to influence actions and reactions toward self and others. More than any of the others, these are management systems for shaping adult-child behavior. A third type of program deals with the emotional aspects of behavior, using positive regard and self-esteem to create relationships in which behavior is monitored by feelings. Methods encouraging self-esteem and growth of self, including transactional analysis and Ginott's (1968) use of praise and limits, all focus on building self-awareness and esteem. The fourth kind of approach is oriented toward children's growth and activities, comprised of resources that encourage adults to focus on their activities with and provisions for children. Some offer curriculum or scripts for gaining skills, while others provide advice relating to diet, play, learning, and social relationships. These tend to be early childhood materials in which the behavior of infants and preschoolers is examined primarily as it reflects developmental progress and the activities of adults.

We turn now to a discussion of each of these four categories of behavior-management approaches.

Social Skills and Behavior

The specific programs that can be placed into this category have an orientation that makes them distinct from others. Several are formal, packaged programs used in schools and agencies with groups of parents. Parent Effectiveness Training (Gordon, 1970) and Systematic Training for Effective Parenting (STEP) (Dinkmeyer & McKay, 1976) both rely heavily on improving communications between parents and children, using structured programs gaining information and improving understanding and skills. Each has a parent handbook and separate materials for group leaders. Parents are encouraged to attend to the meanings of behavior, provide attention to children's needs, and see behavior as a method by which children communicate and express themselves.

The STEP program uses a system of encouragement and logical consequences as an esteem-building alternative to punishment in developing children's sense of responsibility for their behavior. Parents are problem solvers and decision makers whose authority is democratic. They are expected to be understanding, responsible, and supportive with children. The STEP study groups cover material in nine sessions with other parents, using a handbook, posters and charts, taped cassettes, and activity assignments. Illustrated problem situations are examined in order to practice the approach. For parents of young children, the STEP program may be very useful in helping them focus on understanding children, developing their esteem and social skills, and using supportive discipline. It also may build a sense of family unity and mutual respect from the early years throughout childhood. Such attitudes and valuing of children may produce long-term benefits in their behavior and social relationships.

Parent Effectiveness Training (PET) relies heavily on the use of interpersonal communication in resolving problems that occur between parents and children. Active listening to messages that pinpoint feelings is the primary route to resolving conflicts between the needs of parents and children. Solutions are explored and evaluated for their success. A distinction is made between real communication and other messages intended to win a disagreement or to manipulate the listener. For young children, parents are helped to tune in to behaviors that express their needs and are advised to provide supports that enable children to deal with some needs without their help. The use of power in relation to children is considered limited in effectiveness because it does not teach appropriate behavior. Solutions to conflicts are considered acceptable when they satisfy adults and children. PET is relevant to the early childhood years in several ways. It can help parents to reveal and to attend to children's needs, to focus on a positive relationship, to build children's independence, and to teach children social skills they can use with others.

Conflict resolution and problem solving are approaches to dealing with behavior where the focus is on the successful determination of basic whys and hows in social interactions. A child's problem behavior is seen to have a consistent context and some solutions. This approach is an integral part of several other systems for managing parent-child behavior; however, its behavior-relevant theme has been described in relation to group discussion, classroom management, and systems theory (Rutherford & Edgar, 1979). Problem solving and conflict resolution are processes by which parents can both improve their responses to children's behavior and model an interactional style their youngsters can use with others. Problem-solving methods are used for finding the problem and arriving at a solution that resolves conflicting feelings and behaviors. The people and settings are seen as part of the situation. Adults diagnose or identify the behavior that is problematic, the context in which it occurs, and what changes are needed. A solution is developed in which adults and children plan how and when to respond and which behaviors to accept, reject, or modify. The child participates in creating alternatives. Problem solving and conflict resolution thus are terms used for several processes, including the organized observation of children and the change-oriented handling of their behavior. One of its best uses may be the conscious definition and neutral discussion of behaviors that create difficulties among family members.

Values-clarification and decision-making approaches to children's attitudes and activities (Simon et al., 1972) are also processes that make people more conscious of their feelings and actions. Behavior is seen as either consistent or in conflict with people's beliefs or values. The decisions that are made in selecting actions and reactions also may be unrelated to values and be problematic because of this. The process of acknowledging values, selecting behaviors, and acting in ways that reflect values requires several steps. The value has to be stated, then discussed, defended, and redefined. Alternative behaviors are considered, and those most consistent with the value are selected. The decisions are many, and, once made, the final chosen behavior is expected to be used consistently. In cases where adults' and children's values conflict, problem-solving and other strategies might be used to determine where differences exist and how to find solutions that respect values. Parents of young children are often beginning to acknowledge their values and child-rearing philosophies. Their awareness might be very useful in making decisions about handling the behaviors of their toddlers which they feel are unacceptable. Parents and teachers can use this system in communicating with one another. Explanations of values and conscious decisions about behavior also could prepare children for later social experiences with peers, when their rejection of wrongdoing can be based on expressed values.

All of these approaches or systems can provide concepts and procedures both for dealing with children's behavior and teaching some enduring social skills for use with adults and playmates. Because they all require some communicative and reasoning skills, however, their appropriateness for young children must be qualified. The modeling of clear values that are reflected in behavior and the verbalization of beliefs can be understood gradually by young children.

Behavior Control and Uses of Authority

Control and authority are major issues for parents and teachers in dealing with children's behavior. More than the growth of social skills, the focus in these systems is upon bringing behavior into line with standards set by self and others. The use of others' authority as a weight or force behind self-control and self-defense is a major element. Motivation, communication, ability, and feelings are considered, but only as modifiers, not targets, of the methods. Rewarding and punishing acts and consequences are seen as part of the conscious manipulation of behavior and the protection of territory.

Behavior modification or applied behavior analysis is a carefully administered system for managing the behavior of individual children (Becker, 1971; Patterson & Gullion, 1969). The antecedents of a problem behavior are systematically recorded to provide baseline data by which to judge a change. Organization and reinforcement are then used to produce a predetermined change. Adults structure the environment so that the child receives cues, guidelines, and rules for determining which behaviors produce what consequences. The consequences are given to children by adults immediately after the corresponding behavior is demonstrated. Positive reinforcements include praise and concrete rewards (tokens, treats) for approved behavior, and punishment includes disapproval, restriction, or withdrawal of a treat, for problem behaviors. Punishment is used because of its assumed suppressive effect on unwanted behavior. However, verbal statements, loss of privileges, and time-outs are used in preference to physical punishment. Positive reinforcement also is considered to be more effective generally and less limiting than punishment because it avoids consequences such as children's withdrawal and emotional outbursts and the modeling of aggression.

In the early childhood years, applied behavior analysis may be useful for persistent destructive behaviors. Characteristic elements such as brief negative verbal statements and time-outs also can be helpful as nonjudgmental, clear consequences for children who often become involved in negative situations they appear unable to handle. The high level of control and use of authority in this system, however, is not always appropriate for either adults or children. It also requires a great deal of close monitoring, which some adults are unable to provide.

A behavior management system that is more oriented toward using reason and fostering independence in children is that of logical consequences (Dinkmeyer & McKay, 1976; Dreikurs & Grey, 1970). Adults maintain their authority, but situational factors play a greater role in the control of behavior. The "natural" results of misbehavior are used as punishing consequences, even when these are engineered by adults. Most such consequences would occur if parents did not interfere, since often the behavior violation itself brings a penalty. Parents can use these as consequences if they remain as neutral advisors and fail to provide remedies. They also can set up a situation in which children are required to fulfill a commitment prior to being granted a privilege. If the child does not meet the goal, the privilege is automatically withdrawn as a logical consequence. It is different from punishment per se because it is firmly tied to behavior and has a shaping effect on it. Yet it serves as the price a child pays for a mistake, and in this way it is a punishing consequence.

For young children, this system can be a useful contribution to many behaviors affecting others. It is not geared solely to repeated problems but can help children to understand how their behavior is tied to their activities and to its impact upon others. It contributes to parents' authority in that they must be firm and specific when children are confronted with a consequence of their behavior. Provided the young are not dealing with emotions and situations beyond their ability to handle, these techniques may help to develop responsibility and self-control.

Assertiveness training and protective parenting represent other types of behavior control systems, but they are basically a protective technique for adults in dealing with the behavior of other adults and children (Bakker & Bakker-Rabdau, 1973; Kiley, 1978). Behavior is described in terms of actions and reactions to the territories belonging to people, such as their personalities, possessions, rights, and other domains that are private, psychological, and behavioral (action or competence territory). Skills associated with protecting these aspects of one's self are managerial, defensive, bargaining, and acquiring new areas of growth. In dealing with other adults and with children, a parent or teacher analyzes incidences of invasion, recognizes behavioral weapons, and then expresses clearly his or her desires and bargains for what is required. Such assertiveness has been viewed as an aspect of self-knowledge and actualization in which positive change improves behavior, feelings, and social status. For young children, such a process of awareness and self-esteem in parents can lead to a greater understanding of other people's needs, abilities, and goals. In terms of discipline, parents can advocate for their own needs wherever children's behavior impinges upon them. Of course, the young do require a great deal of latitude, and families often place the needs of younger members first. Within this framework, however, mothers and fathers can recognize some manipulations in children and help them account for this in others.

Emotions and Behavior

The management of children's behavior is seen by some authorities as very much tied to the affective relationship between parent and child. In their view, love, acceptance, and the growth of self-awareness and self-esteem create a social environment in which children begin to understand feelings and actions. Within this atmosphere, discipline is expected to serve as a positive shaper of behavior that encourages children to be respectful and considerate of one another while developing their own personal interests and abilities.

One approach that is based on feelings, personality, and behavior has been described by Ginott (1968) and presented in other forms by Brooks (1981) and Faber and Mazlish (1975). Parents function as sympathetic advisors who teach children to communicate their feelings, who establish and enforce limits of acceptable behavior that account for children's needs, who use praise and feedback in monitoring behavior, and who demonstrate methods for positive expression of emotions. Feelings are separated from behavior in that children's personal emotions are accepted but behavior that falls within established approved, unacceptable, or questionable zones is open to parental action. Negative emotions are acknowledged as natural, and their display is permissible within limits. Children are viewed as competent, valued persons whose place in the family is important. Choices are encouraged, as is the sharing of feelings with one another. For young children, this affective monitoring approach may help to create the loving and accepting home environment needed to nurture their growing skills. Socialization also is accented by the manner in which feelings and behavior are related to one another. The child's freedom-within-limits may be particularly appropriate for ensuring mental health and encouraging children to develop personal and social competence.

Transactional analysis is an interpersonal therapeutic program that has been adapted for parents and children (Babcock & Keepers, 1976; Harris, 1969). The roles of mothers and fathers include managing daily activities such as caring for children and monitoring their growth and behavior. It also includes the provision of "strokes" by which positive feelings are expressed to others. Strokes can be whatever makes the child feel good, from physical affection to verbal praise and requested privileges. Parents also are expected to deliver strokes to themselves and each other. The methods presented in Babcock and Keepers (1976) specifically describe the characteristics and parenting tasks of the infant, toddler, and preschool stages. Strokes are unconditional for babies, whose indulgence is important, yet parents are advised to take good care of their own requirements and gradually permit the child to develop an independent ability to self-stroke. Toddlers, who require a great deal of exploration, who are often ambivalent and highly active, are able to respond to parents' conditional strokes gradually and gain positive feelings for themselves.

Parents who provide a safe environment and opportunities for activity will enhance the child's growth at the same time that they conserve their time and energy. At the preschool age, children separate more from their families, encounter more challenging physical tasks, are required to deal with strong feelings, and understand thought processes. They also are exposed to life scripts of parents and society that attempt to program them into particular molds. They need to learn they are okay and acceptable according to their own values. Parents' ego states also influence their behavior, as they may act and react as a child or a parent, sometimes reversing the roles and creating mixed messages that interfere with effective parenting. Awareness of one's state of mind and the appropriate use of strokes in relation to behavior help to create parenting satisfaction and effectiveness that nurture children's skills, independence, and positive feelings.

The value of direct attention to self-esteem as a means for helping children become successful people is described by Briggs (1970). There are several themes in this approach toward managing children. One is that a climate of love, respect, and empathy provides the basis for self-esteem. Another is that high esteem has a positive influence upon behavior. Third, the development of self, in terms of intelligence, creativity, and social relationships, is viewed as assured through children's self-respect and regard. Some of this self-esteem approach is a reflection of the self-actualization theories of Rogers (1970) and Maslow (1971). Social competence through mental health is encouraged. Constructive discipline is seen as democratic, empathic, and oriented toward seeking solutions to problems. Strong feelings, both negative and positive, are discussed. Parents are advised to examine their own self-images, especially their defenses against weaknesses. Negative feelings such as anger and jealousy are seen as reactions that can be prevented by greater awareness of their causes. Children's misbehavior is viewed as a consequence of a negative self-concept or a reaction to adults' emotional states. Gains in intellectual and physical skills as well as improved self-esteem provide avenues for developing competence and happiness.

For young children whose personalities are in formative stages and whose growing abilities are sources of admiration from adults, the use of self-esteem in relation to behavior seems quite appropriate. Parents' awareness of the constructive role of self-esteem might be very valuable in creating strategies that nurture this feeling in children. Good self-concepts might result in reduced incidences of behaviors that require discipline and might help to resolve conflicts more effectively when they do occur.

Behavior and Children's Play Activities

A fourth type of behavior management system is one in which attention is focused primarily upon the play and social activities of young children. Play, exploration, adult-child games, experiences with other children, toy use, and so forth are described for each age group. Parents are expected to arrange for and enhance these activities. Behavior management is related to these activities, but the emphasis is upon directing the child and adult into useful, learning-oriented or creative exchanges. Discipline is not a primary factor because the children are engaged in activities. When problematic incidents do occur, they are usually discussed as a facet of social growth and healthy trends toward discipline.

There is a great deal of advice material available for parents of young children, primarily in the form of books. (See other chapters for more details on these.) There seem to be four types: step-by-step descriptions of development with complementary suggestions for toys, games, and parent-child activity; encyclopedias of information and activities; pediatric and developmental reference books that include a range of subjects related to basic care and nurturance; and topical, question-answer resources that cover a variety of issues in some detail, including behavior, development, and activities.

An illustration of one of the most often used types of materials is step-by-step scripts for parents of infants and preschoolers, such as those of Caplan and Caplan (1976), Karnes (1979), Sparling and Lewis (1979), Watrin and Furfey (1978), and White (1975). Each provides the parent or care giver with comprehensive descriptions of development throughout the first three to five years of life. The child's particular age-stage is easily located, and normative descriptions of activity, behavior, and skill achievement in physical, language, and intellectual areas are provided. Parents are expected to use the information to identify games, toys, outings, special experiences, and so forth, which are designed to enhance growth and stabilize behavior. They are encouraged to follow the suggested curriculum activities as a script at each step in the child's growth. In effect, parents learn to teach, using the material as a guide; and they learn to understand behavioral evidence of the child's progress in development. The approach is useful as a means for reducing negative behaviors associated with child boredom and lack of adequate learning challenges.

Table 8
A Guide to Discipline for Teaching and Managing

Elements	Techniques
PROBLEM PREVENTION (through care and attention)	Provide affection, understanding, attention, rest Build self-esteem, security, independence Reduce frustration, interruption, hazards Arrange play time and space, privacy Avoid competition, aggression Supervise and monitor peer relationships, sitters
LIMIT SETTING (using boundaries and reinforcements)	Establish clear, simplified limits and don'ts Use praise, rewards, successes, humor Build expectations, standards, do's Remain firm, clam, fair Accept some mistakes, confusion, adjustments Use reminders, repeats, media, books, discussion
PROBLEM SOLVING (for needs and solutions)	Identify needs, feelings, causes Locate alternatives, new choices Understand fears, confusion, frustration Provide cues, help, support Listen to points of view, body gestures Insist on resolution, compromise
MANAGING BEHAVIOR (in conflicts and problems)	Restrain, distract, discourage, prevent Direct to substitutes, alternatives, choices Demonstrate disapproval, unacceptability Ignore negative behavior when is attention getting Give comfort, time-outs, privacy Maintain patience, order, reason
TEACHING (for values and socialization)	Model cooperation, coping, sharing, compromise Explain reasons, rules, others' views Teach responsibility, rights, democratic authority Label feelings, needs, limitations, abilities Highlight consequences, cautions, problems Deal with societal standards, expectations

Summary

The many complex ideas and issues presented in this section are compiled in a simplified form in Table 8 by grouping key words and phrases into five operational categories of discipline. It is hoped that this table will serve as a guide in sorting through the abundance of theory and advice regarding the disciplining of children.

It is important to point out that the behavior of children can be managed in ways other than through the use of direct control or power assertion. Parents and teachers can learn several different tactics that can be varied for the particular behavior and circumstance. While social skills and play activities serve as a foundation, problem solving and firm control can be used when children's behavior is difficult and when consequences are needed to substantiate moral teachings. Parents should try to understand all of these issues in order to develop a child-rearing style that is effective as well as comfortable and humanistic.

PROGRAM SUGGESTIONS

1. Ask parents to observe a group of young children playing together, focusing primarily on nonverbal interactions among them. Ask parents to identify the children's communicative and social skills, their needs, and their developmental status.
2. Arrange for a teacher or guidance counselor skilled in testing children to demonstrate the use of nonverbal tests and how testers use behaviors in this situation to help them identify problems.
3. Discuss and create a list of disciplinary dos and don'ts for each of the dilemmas included in the text.
4. Using suggestions of both parents and teachers, develop a chart of reasons for discipline that are relevant at each developmental age or stage, from birth to age eight.
5. Locate four parents or teachers who have taken courses in or attempted to use behavior management systems. Ask what they have learned and how their families were affected.

6. Using Table 8, discuss the techniques that parents and teachers are likely to find the most effective.
7. Obtain additional information and materials for behavior systems that are social-emotional and for those emphasizing control. Arrange for parents to compare the philosophies and methods of these.
8. Discuss the role of society in helping parents to teach moral and social behaviors to children. Where do the behavioral expectations come from, and how can families select those they feel are significant?

9

Feelings and Personality

Children's feelings are immediate and overpowering to them, affecting their behavior and shaping their growing personalities. Emotions are more or less a part of every child's activity and interaction, and they reveal patterns in the children that soon become recognized as characteristic. Adults contribute to this process through their responses to affective needs, temperamental trends, emotional displays, social styles, and other signs of feeling in children. In each family and school the children's mental health and personal-social style may be viewed differently, some accenting self-esteem or creative expression, others emphasizing independence or cooperative play with peers. Regardless of the variety of points of view, most adults are quite concerned with children's feelings and personality growth, wanting to ensure their mental health and harmonious relationships with others in the present and over the long term.

The reason for creating a separate chapter that examines the affective realm is to allow for some depth in our exploration of child rearing and schooling as they relate to the world of children's feelings and personality. Like the chapter on behavior, the intention here is not to imply these are distinct parts of the child. In fact, behavior and feeling mirror one another in much of the child's activity. But mental health and the child's individuality as a thinking, feeling person are vital to discuss in relation to parent education and good home-school relationships. Sections of this chapter will deal with children's needs for emotional security, their personality development, personal differences, and the expression of feelings.

CHILDREN'S EMOTIONAL WELL-BEING

Children need to feel loved. Their very growth and development depend upon their emotional security. Parents' expressions of love toward infants through cuddling, feeding, and soothing; their tolerance and respect for toddlers; their support of and assistance to preschoolers; and their understanding of and interest in their first and second graders all show evidence of love. Dependable and nurturing adults contribute to children's security and self-esteem, building their confidence and ability to interact successfully with others. Love and regard protect the child's mental health and nurture the growth of personal and social skills.

Showing Love

Most parents, care givers, and teachers feel a strong sense of love and attachment toward the young children they care for regularly; indeed, it is something they may seldom think about. Still, taking love for granted could create confusion for children if adults felt it yet failed to show it. Infants and preschoolers have to experience visible signs of love in order to know it is there. Often the value of demonstrating love and regard has not been emphasized to parents and teachers. It may seem to them a trivial matter, even though they may provide comfort and praise when their children appear to need these. Adults also may believe that demonstrations of love toward children produce spoiling or self-indulgent attitudes, that coddled children will be unable to cope with the difficult times in their lives. For them, loving expressions may be more subdued and less spontaneous, tied to specific praiseworthy acts of children or similar evidence of earned affection. Other parents and teachers may be accustomed to showing love only when children appear to require it. Hugs, verbal encouragement, special privileges, and so forth may be provided only in relation to youngsters' communication of need and desire. Some adults, however, are so accepting and adoring of children that loving expressions accompany their first interactions with them and continue as part of their child-rearing style. Regardless of particular family or school attitudes concerning the emotional security of the young, it can be said that love may be expressed in a variety of ways, under many different circumstances, as long as the message to the child is clear—that he or she is valued and cherished.

To ensure the child's emotional security, love can be associated with physical care and emotional nurturance; that is, parents and teachers can convey many positive feelings toward children throughout the course of a typical day. During the infant years, parents may stare at, stroke, kiss, smile, and sing to their children during feeding, diapering, playing, and putting them to sleep. Their acceptance of needs, delight in the baby's special qualities, and willingness to spend a pleasant time together represent love. At toddler stages, parents and teachers often are challenged by the child's interests in exploring, in trying new activities, and in resisting some limits. Yet they also can be proud of new accomplishments, entertained by many independent personal traits, and enamored of the toddler's unqualified affection for them. Parental love is more complicated at this age, mixed with some disapproval and apprehension, but adults can still provide physical affection, praise, attention to needs, involvement in play, and respect for the child's growing uniquenesses. At preschool and middle childhood, parents' verbal expressions of love can be added to physical gestures, and genuine play and recreation together may coincide with their attention and indulgence of special interests. Even in difficult situations, in exchanges that are negative or upsetting, even in periods when parents themselves are struggling to cope with their own emotional states, a few moments of affection, a word of regard, or a brief mention of love can help to create an atmosphere of security and respect. Even in the busiest or most unhappy of times, most adults can spare this time to establish and maintain the feeling of love that is so basic to the health of young children.

Attachment and Security

Definitions of love need to include children's relationships to adults. Between children and their parents, the bonds of love have a kind of developmental history. Attachment and emotional security, the products of love, grow over time. They are tied to the daily behavior and feelings between babies and parents. Some authorities feel that strong emotional bonds are created as soon as mothers and fathers look at and hold their newborn infants. For many, the days and weeks following birth tend to be periods of excitement and exhaustion, but gradually parents and babies come to know each others' looks, smells, touches, and sounds. They show responses to small signs and signals that create an intimacy and deep feelings that form a strong tie. This attachment or bonding process serves some essential purposes. Some authorities on early development feel that this relationship of love is necessary to the child's development; without it, the youngster will not thrive. Each writer in this field has a particular point of view, most of which are too complicated to be presented here in detail. (Some other developmental texts that have extensive discussions of attachment theory are Arnstein, 1975; Bee, 1975; Bower, 1977; Rutter, 1981; and Willemsen, 1979).

Attachments of many types are noted. The ways in which attachments are formed can be described in an overview of several theories that, taken together, contribute to a whole, rounded picture of love. One such view is that attachment results from daily, routine care giving to babies by parents. Their satisfaction of children's needs creates a mutual dependence that ties them together. Another view is that physical warmth and touching contribute to the growth of love, perhaps more than meeting babies' needs for care and food. In many cultures, the child is held by an adult for a major portion of the day. The promptness and consistency of parents' responses to the infant's cries and their support for the toddler's growing independence and abilities are seen by some as the source of trust and self-confidence. This type of relationship between parent and child expresses love and furthers growth.

Attachment also is related to communication. Infants and parents learn to "read" each other's signals, creating a responsive pattern of interaction. Adults attend to facial expressions and bodily gestures, while babies learn to feel, hear, and see a familiar caregiver; this results in communication and love. Related to this is the view that reciprocal responding between parent and child contributes to attachment. As each attends to the other, they take turns reacting to whatever behavior or signal is expressed. Much of this occurs during play and care-giving routines.

Sociability is another factor in establishing attachment relationships. Outgoing, attentive, entertaining adults may capture the child's interest, making their relationship a strong, positive one. Play with children may fulfill a role as well. Fathers, mothers, and care givers who engage the child in simple games or gentle roughhousing tend to form a satisfying bond with them. Likewise, regard and approval of the child are thought to create self-esteem and affectionate, democratic relationships within the family. Finally, although parents are the beneficiaries of the most primary loving bonds, others can share the child's affections. Multiple attachments with several adults may be established when children have experiences with care givers, teachers, and extended family members.

Following this early period of life when relationships of attachment and love are formed, children continue to develop such bonds with adults and peers outside of the home. In child care settings, a familiar and consistent adult who is trained to understand early emotional patterns assumes an important role. The care giver helps children adjust to and enjoy the program, establishing a relationship with them that is essential to their acceptance of a new and sometimes frightening environment. The attachment provides some assurance of personalized care that nurtures individual characteristics and meets a variety of needs. The care giver's feelings also are involved, since the relationship must be valuable to both adult and child. Most staff members in centers and daycare homes do, indeed, develop just such a loving bond that sustains them both.

In early childhood centers and elementary schools, teachers of young children fulfill a nurturing, parenting role as well as an educational one. Relatively strong affective relationships are established and maintained partly because of the children's need for individual attention. This balances demands made upon them to function as group members and to complete a wide range of curriculum tasks. Gradually, as the children are able to care for themselves, relationships with teachers become less dependent and emotional. Children look to themselves and their peers when they require comforting or recognition. The teacher serves as a more neutral consultant and resource on academic matters, or a friend in particular situations that may arise. Obvious attachments with adults decline as peer relationships assume greater significance, with the result that love is expressed in different forms.

Self-Esteem and Security

While it is difficult to measure the level of positive self-regard, self-concept, or self-esteem in young children, it is possible to indicate the value of these feelings. Certainly children who feel good about themselves also feel relatively secure and confident. Temporary discouragements and occasional problems encountered by confident children are less difficult for them to handle. It can be expected that the adult's enhancement of self-esteem will contribute to the child's emotional security.

A number of meaningful dimensions of self-esteem can be identified that are open to the influence of parents and teachers.

Self-Concept.   The first dimension is self-concept, or the child's definition of self. Favorite activities; special interests; and the child's physical features, family, and home all are aspects of the child's self-knowledge. Adults need to help children to gain this kind of information.

Pride.   The child's feelings of being acceptable, okay, and a person who is valued contribute to a sense of pride in one's self and one's accomplishments and activities. Parents and teachers help to build feelings of pride by praising children and highlighting special things about them.

Emotions and Moods.   The child's awareness of and ability to identify and label a particular feeling or a set of emotions is important. Play experiences that dramatize feelings, their beginning and ending, and their normal part in growing up can help children to recognize that they are very much like others.

Needs and Self-Control.   Related to emotions themselves are two other aspects of esteem—expressions of need and self-control. Language, facial and nonverbal gestures serve to communicate needs that others help to fulfill. Adults later require children to verbalize what they want as an important part of their socialization. It contributes to their competence and confidence in interpersonal relationships. Self-control in children enables them to manage their feelings, thereby minimizing frustration and improving self-esteem. The youngster who elects to use socially acceptable means for expressing feelings or needs has acquired a good deal of skill in self-management. Adults can help through reasoning, modeling, and supporting efforts at self-control.

Friendships.   Friendships and other peer exchanges contribute to self-esteem when children behave in a constructive and prosocial manner with others. Their cooperation, sharing, turn taking, and ability to resolve conflicts are part of a continuous learning process. Positive, enjoyable interactions with others promote feelings of worth.

Independence.   Autonomy in mastering tasks similarly builds good feelings. Success in caring for oneself, in selecting and completing an activity, and in helping others to accomplish goals leads to self-confidence. The child who feels competent is able to approach new challenges and derive satisfaction from what has been mastered. These are rewarding and very appropriate routes toward self-esteem that teachers and parents can foster.

Discipline.   Adults assume a central position in the relationship between discipline and feelings of worth. Some methods of handling unacceptable behavior can be effective in teaching and controlling behavior yet also support self-esteem. Clear and manageable class (and home) rules, options for handling conflict, respect for feelings and dilemmas, and so forth help children to avoid difficulties and to accept consequences gracefully when discipline is necessary.

Acceptance.   Adult acceptance and generally affectionate attitudes toward children are related to this. Children can be expected to gain esteem when they regularly interact with an adult who expresses positive feelings toward them, who shares experiences and appears as a real person, and who attends to each individual each day.

Family.   Neighborhood and cultural ties also play a role in generating respect and regard. The child as family member can be emphasized in order to demonstrate the importance of home, family, and neighborhood. Pride and recognition of the child's parents and siblings and of the surroundings of the child's life are important to the young and are convenient sources of discussion, home-school exchanges, and curriculum activities.

Ethnic Background.   A final dimension of self-esteem is the youngster's ethnic background. Information about special activities, clothing, food, celebrations, and so forth provide respect for cultural values and strengths. For many children such obvious demonstrations of respect engender self-esteem.

CHILDREN'S PERSONALITY DEVELOPMENT

From infancy to the middle childhood years the child's unique personal-social style emerges and solidifies. Characteristic behaviors and patterns of interaction with others become associated with each schoolchild. Personality resembles a mosaic developed from hereditary and environmental features, chance events, planned activities, and individual differences. It parallels predictable maturational sequences but does not always reflect them. Children are born with biological patterns, inherited characteristics, and varying dispositions and temperaments. Their parents and homes provide restrictions and opportunities. Outside the family, they are exposed to people and events who also impact upon their abilities and personal styles. No one knows how it is that personality is actually shaped by all these factors, although some theories and studies have provided useful information regarding some influences. This section of the chapter contains a brief overview of theories of personality formation and social growth in the first years of life and the preschool period through middle childhood. The focus is on understanding parent, teacher, and care-giver roles in supporting this development.

Formal views of the origins and formation of personality contain rather complex descriptions of contributing elements and processes, used primarily for the study and treatment of children and adults. For this text, an overview of some of these features of socioemotional growth may lead to greater understanding of the child's changing needs and characteristics. Some issues regarding personality may sound familiar. Theorists have discussed the roles of heredity, social contexts, purpose and motivation, physiology, unconscious influences, learning, patterns of interaction, morality, cognition, temperament, early versus later influences, language, behavior, peers, and education. Varying theories address different issues, and those wishing to understand the young child may want to explore more deeply those concepts that are meaningful to them. For the advanced reader or those interested in greater detail, more comprehensive discussion can be found in Hall and Lindzey's (1985) classic text and in similar personality and child psychology books (Baldwin, 1967; Bee, 1975; Lamberth, Rappaport & Rappaport, 1982).

In every theory about how people feel and interact, the roles of several basic elements are usually analyzed. The physical characteristics of humans, the social environment in which they grow, the realization of their inner abilities, and the maturation and continuous development of their understanding and skills have all been part of one or the other theory. They also have served to distinguish among them; that is, groups of theorists have focused their attention generally on one of these elements as a primary determinant or characteristic of personality.

Physiological, Learning, Dynamic, Trait and Person-Centered Factors

In the view of some authorities children's development is influenced a good deal by physiological characteristics and innate abilities. Some of these gradually mature over time, while others emerge in predictable stages that are evident in every human. Growth proceeds somewhat on its own, taking some shape from learning experiences and patterns of social exchange with others, but primarily progressing without constant nurturance or motivation from parents and others. Personality is the reflection of a structure of stages, traits, and a learning history. The person is the product of these combined factors.

Morphology and Physiology. William Sheldon's (1940) theory emphasizes the influence of structural characteristics on human feeling and behavior. Constitutional factors are present in the child at birth. The morphology and physiology of the body, in particular, are rather fixed and less open to change than attitudes, habits, and other modifiable features. A frail, linear physique, or an athletic body, or a plump type are each thought to determine personality or temperament. Thus, traits such as sociability, self-indulgence and affection, assertiveness and energetic behavior, restraint, and resistance are a function of body type. Degrees of varying physical attributes in a particular person contribute different measurable aspects to that personality (Sheldon and Stevens, 1942). Environmental and interpersonal relationships may compound these physical limitations and strengths so that the child's feelings and relationships become unique to her. Children who have such strong physiologies may require that parents and teachers take into consideration not only the influence of their bodies but also other characteristics and needs possibly overshadowed by obvious constitutional factors.

Reinforcement Theory. Reinforcement theory is used in several approaches to personality that view it as an organized system of learned feelings and relationships and behaviors. Names such as Pavlov, Watson, Thorndike, Hull, Spence, Dollard and Miller, Wolpe, Eysenck, Bandura, and Skinner have been associated with these theories. Behavior, including the interpersonal area, is thought to be a function of laws and conditions that are experienced and shape and control the child's development. Positive and negative reinforcements tied to stimuli and events help them to be acquired. Conditioning principles are used in understanding the growth of children's intelligence, physical and language skills, and interpersonal relations. The child also learns habits and information from the ways in which basic and secondary drives are reduced. Cues provide directions for the child's actions and reactions, and adults use them to manipulate learning events. As the child grows, a hierarchy of responses to patterns of stimuli is constructed that serves as a repertoire of possible behavior. In acquiring these learned patterns, adults play a significant role in guiding and directing the children through their administration of reinforcements, by organizing experiences and modeling particular behaviors. Whatever produces a positive reward or punishment, even in a complex series of activities, has the potential to contribute to personality.

Trait-Factor Theory. Another form of personality theory where organized sets of information or characteristics are believed to be the source of socioemotional growth and behavior is called trait-factor theory. Rather than the learned stimulus-response units of reinforcement theory, trait-factor theory employs descriptions of general and specific traits that make up a personality. Cattell, Thurstone, Eysenck, and Guilford are names prominently associated with this view. Rating scales and questionnaires are employed in determining ability and temperament factors that appear to characterize a person. These are part of a lattice of traits that, when analyzed, are expected to define and predict an individual's feelings and behavior. Family members play a role in the development of these factors, as do situational events and the ways in which people gratify children's interests and motives. Some neurotic-versus-normal and extraversion-versus-introversion factors are thought to be significant dimensions of personality. Creativity and intellectual competence are examined as factors composed of personal and ability traits organized along several dimensions. Guilford (1967) has created a three-dimensional model that describes the structure of the intellect. In this model, mental abilities are classified as operations, contents, and products. Across these three dimensions he generates a total of 120 specific traits. Parents and teachers assume an important role at the level of each trait and can attempt to develop characteristics that will result in a desired pattern of personality traits.

Psychoanalytic Theory. Not as well organized and physiological as those approaches already described, psychoanalytic theory considers personality as the result of innate instincts tied to biological characteristics which evolve in a predictable and cumulative manner. Freud's classical theories are familiar to most parents and teachers in one form or another. The assumption of the unconscious origin of personality, the id, and its companions the realistic ego and the value-laden superego is the cornerstone of psychoanalytic theory. As the child grows, he or she becomes, with parental influence, increasingly capable of controlling instincts and drives toward pleasure and self-satisfaction and handling interpersonal behavior. Identification with loved others, particularly of the same sex, helps to develop some personality features. Defense mechanisms such as repression and projection, and emotional outlets such as dreams and expressive activities, enable the individual to examine and handle strong feelings and play a role in the socialization process. In the early childhood years, children progress through oral, anal, and phallic stages where love objects, especially the mother, satisfy some needs and deny others, thereby influencing feelings and behavior. Little boys and girls have differing experiences (oedipal complex and penis envy) that affect their ultimate socioemotional development and attitudes toward love.

Other theorists who later based their work in psychoanalysis included Erikson and Jung. Their views of stages of growth and personal histories as part of a person's constitution place their viewpoints within this group of personality theorists. However, their extra-self and socially oriented analyses of feelings and behavior also place them within the social, environmental and developmental group to be discussed in the next section.

Person-Centered Theory.   A theory that is both innate and social is the person-centered approach of Carl Rogers. His view of personality formation includes a heavy emphasis on the characteristics and abilities with which a child is born. Within each person there are all the essentials for becoming an emotionally healthy and socially successful individual. As the child grows, this inner being encounters experiences and parental teaching that come into her phenomenological field. To actualize or become the self that is within requires unconditional positive regard and valuing from others and the desire to relate and communicate. Self-knowledge and acceptance between child and adult lead to the emergence of the child's actual self. A healthy child experiences congruence between inner and outer feelings and behavior. Thus, the role of the adult is to move the child toward her own fulfillment, toward progressive behaviors that are in tune with the youngster's innate self and help to nurture its emergence.

Social, Environmental, and Developmental Factors

Even though many social and developmental personality theorists describe biological contributors to an individual's socioemotional characteristics and style, they primarily emphasize the ways in which children and adults develop from their interpersonal and environmental experiences. Creative and unique aspects of the self, humanistic and positive influences, the nature of striving, and the control of one's personality are all discussed in varying ways.

Neo-Freudian Theory.   Social psychological theorists such as Adler, Fromm, Horney, and Sullivan discuss the interplay of a range of interpersonal processes and individual characteristics. For Adler (1931) people are composed of unique patterns of goals, needs, and strivings that make them distinctive. They consciously make the effort to achieve particular goals and are capable of planning and guiding themselves. Superiority feelings, inferiority and compensation, basic interests in interpersonal relationships, individual styles, and the creative self all play a role in determining one's personality. Birth order and early childhood memories are seen as significant factors as well.

Fromm (1955) discusses how people are lonely and need to relate to others, establish roots, and create a personal frame of reference. They have a sense of identity and endeavor to transcend their early drives with loving and satisfying social experiences. His ideas along these lines also include the ways in which a person is part of a society, adopting a style that fits the needs of this broader social context.

Horney (1945) describes social strategies children develop for dealing with "basic anxiety" as reflected in feelings of isolation or helplessness in relation to adults. Needs for approval, partnership, restrictive borders, power, exploitation, prestige, admiration, achievement, independence, and perfection are sources of inner conflict that can create healthy or neurotic personalities. The child may move toward, away, or against people in attempts to achieve an idealized self-image. Parents who provide security, love, and respect can contribute to healthy growth.

Sullivan (1953) views personality as the dynamic center for processes that are part of a person's interpersonal field. The self-system develops in relation to the behavior of others and the need to guard one's own feelings and image. Personifications that characterize others are created by the thinking child, whose anxiety and tension motivate mental and physical activity. The stages of infancy and early childhood witness the emergence of dynamisms that characterize abilities and transitions. Some of these are feelings of apathy or attachment, cognitive skills in understanding relationships and language, views of others as good or bad, growth of learning and self-awareness, independent need satisfactions, and coordinated physical skills. The child's play activities in dramatizing others and in using language to understand others better are considered important to healthy growth in these areas.

Psychosocial Stage Theory.   Erikson (1950) is a psychosocial stage theorist who describes the stages and changes in children's development as related to interpersonal experiences and some maturation of abilities through the early years. His focus is on the child's growth as expressed in feeling states that need to be more positive than negative. The proper ratio of opposite qualities or behavioral concepts, however, is thought to result in the growth of hope, will, purpose, competence, and self-awareness. During infancy the child develops feelings balanced between trust and mistrust as a consequence of parental management of needs. In toddlers, the muscular-anal stage, a middle road between autonomy and shame/doubt contributes in healthy ways to self-will, self-control, and understanding of right and wrong. At the preschool age, the locomotor-genital stage, a sense of con-structive purpose grows through adult responses engendering more initia-tive than guilt. Toward early middle childhood, competence can be the result of feelings of industry as an alternative to inferiority, so that the child is prepared for work in home- and school-related tasks. Erikson's stage de-scriptions take the individual into adulthood, where the healthy ego is creative, strong, and aware of itself. In late adulthood, the final stage of life, the healthy person demonstrates an integration of the ego which results in wisdom.

Field-Environmental Theory. Environmental theorists include a vari-ety of individuals who have emphasized the importance of the context, surroundings, or experiential field in which a particular person functions. This environment contains demands, forces, historical precedents, and be-havioral expectations that influence the immediate activity and the develop-ing personality. Some names associated with such a view are Jung, Lewin, Barker, and Boss. Gestalt psychology, phenomenology, and existentialism are also terms that reflect this orientation toward the whole arena in which person and environment interact.

Jung's (1968) analytic theory, while stressing some of Freud's instinc-tual themes, also highlights the collective history of humankind which is expressed in the collective unconscious in the form of predispositions to personal behavior. These predispositions of people influence their destiny in that some human characteristics are seen as archetypes and images that are applied to the child's present experiences. Thus, it is the interplay of genetic history as potential and the present situation that determines behavior. Thinking, feeling, sensing, and intuiting are other processes that influence the personality. Additionally, psychic energy leads the child forward toward progress and self-realization.

In Lewin's (1951) field theory, the person operates within a life space containing events, people, and forces that influence feeling and activity. It is a dynamic space with increasingly complex elements and tensions. Through processes of differentiation and integration the child is able to recognize and organize these elements and influence the boundaries and conditions that are encountered. Barker (1968) has used this work to describe the ecology or context ("behavior settings") in which people behave, including parental and peer expectations, uses of resources, and other conditions that help or hinder the child's developing abilities and personality.

Existential theorists such as Boss (1963) also discuss the space in which people operate. From the point of view of the child, existence is a state of immediate experience, of phenomena that are being sensed. The child's feelings and behavior are tied to the space, time, bodily senses, persons, and moods that impinge upon him or her. Choices can be made about which phenomena to accept and respond to, so that the child is responsible for determining what they will be and do. To live authentically, adults can help the child to be open to experiences and possibilities within whatever given conditions are present.

Ideographic Theory. Another group of theorists could be said to emphasize the unique person, the self that functions autonomously, demonstrates needs and motives, and grows in a wholistic way toward health and competence. Murray, Maslow, and Allport are names associated with various approaches to the person as an interesting and analyzable unit.

Motivations are the central theme of Murray's (1951) work. People are, in his view, striving, seeking, and directed. Their needs serve as organizers of their awareness and motivation. Primary and secondary, overt and covert, focal and diffuse needs are related to one's attention, emotion, and behavior. Some examples of needs are achievement, affiliation, autonomy, deference, nurturance, play, order, aggression, and understanding. People and environments press upon the person and influence the manner in which needs are expressed. Some examples of these forces are family discord, discipline, illness, danger, loss, and nurturance.

Maslow (1970) also discusses needs and tasks that affect people, in particular occasional peak experiences that have significant influences upon children and adults. To grow up well means individuals self-actualize or distinguish themselves. Some elements in this process are self-acceptance, spontaneity, realism, problem-centeredness, autonomy, appreciation, humanism, intimate relationships, democratic values, humor, creativity, and individuality.

Allport's (1937, 1966) focus is upon aspects of selfhood that are associated with autonomy and consistent behavior. Motives, traits, and dispositions are seen as highly varied, growing out of a complex of systems in people. In the first three years of life, the child develops a sense of bodily self, a beginning self-identity and pride or esteem. In early childhood, the self-image and self that extend to others are developing; in middle childhood, self-awareness in relation to reason and thought becomes prominent. These are part of the consistency in a personality and are reflected in attitudes, intentions, and evaluations. The child grows toward self-sustaining, independent behavior, goals and purposes, and a unified personality. Parents and others facilitate development of the individual from a biological creature to a mature and organized personality who can extend herself, relate warmly, and be realistic and self-accepting. Much of this growth is seen as self-fulfilling or moving toward the positive, rather independently of specific adult intervention.

Person-Environment Interaction. Piaget is the last theorist to be discussed in this section. Most of his work focused upon the cognitive area of development, but the emphasis on person and environment is important to personality theory (Piaget & Inhelder, 1969). The child's growth is viewed as gradual and tied to both maturational and environmental events. What the child experiences during the early stages helps to shape his understanding of relationships in space and time. As the child adapts to new sensory impressions by way of physical and mental manipulations, more complex operations and thoughts become possible later. Maturing abilities are enhanced by these encounters with objects and people. The youngster progresses through predictable stages, taking in impressions and forming ideas (assimilation), then changing these as new experiences require (accommodation). Frequent interactions are important, and adults can assist children by providing these.

During the earliest sensorimotor stage, infants are very busy explorers and actors, interested in investigation and imitation and rather attached to other persons. In the preoperational or preschool period, the child has a greater awareness of the separate self and attempts to make judgments about what is experienced. It is an age of establishing some intuitions about how things work, of an egocentric view of self, of some mastery, and of beginning moral development. In the school-aged period of concrete operations the child has gained systems of concepts or frameworks for understanding events and relationships. It is a more integrated stage marked by reason and logical thought. In terms of personality, the child is oriented toward rules, others, and the use of reason only when past age seven.

Parents and teachers may be able to work more effectively with children if these gradual changes in ability are understood. Indeed, Piaget's theory emphasizes that children think differently from adults, that they may be unable to comprehend some rules, moral ideas, and feelings of others until they have progressed beyond the preschool period. The child's need to be actively involved in his own learning, to experience firsthand the qualities of objects and their workings are also important keys for adults in understanding children.

Personal Differences

In addition to theories about personality, it is also important to consider some developmental issues that relate to children's emotions and to their social interactions during early childhood. Experimental studies, case histories, and observational research have pointed to several influences upon how the child's personality develops. Many of these are factors beyond the direct or even indirect control of parents, teachers or other caregivers. Yet, their effects may be detected in the characteristics demonstrated by the growing child whose uniqueness is shaped by them.

Each child's personality is different from that of his or her relatives and age-mates. Parents and teachers have long recognized the challenges and pleasures of such uniquenesses. On the one hand, individual differences require that each child be understood on his or her own terms. It means that personality growth, behavior, educational needs, and so forth, will be different from one child to the next. Of course, youngsters also make differing demands and provide a variety of satisfactions to parents and teachers. Every developmental stage may present adults with a profile of needs and strengths that is different for each child. These can be magnified or reduced in relation to special family and school factors. The end result of these processes and relationships is a unique personality, tentative and changing in the earliest years, but firmer and more obvious by the end of the preschool period.

As we conclude our discussion of specific theorists' views of children's personality development, we turn to an examination of several other special factors that must be taken into account regardless of theoretical approach. There are external and internal factors, that is, those existing outside or within the child, that have been accepted as providing a significant influence upon children's overall development and success in schooling.

Socioeconomic Status (SES).   One factor is socioeconomic status, although it is made up of several others. Parental education and income determine to a large extent the family's social-class membership. Ethnicity may be included in this, especially if systematic discrimination from other groups is seen as a major social and economic influence. Personal growth and social relationships can be affected by social status because it determines some of the family's experiences (neighborhood, diet, resources, friendships, schooling) and thereby the child's. Studies of the effects of SES have been conducted by a great many scientists, and SES is viewed as a predictor of intelligence, achievement, culture, lifestyle, and some attitudes and behavior patterns. In terms of an individual child, however, there may be parental and personal characteristics, family history, and other factors that counteract SES. A high-SES family, for example, may produce a poorly adjusted, inadequately achieving child while a low-SES youngster may grow up to be a successful professional, partly because his family was able to capitalize on any available resources or had a family history that generated dignity and competence. (See Singer & Singer, 1969, for a discussion on social class and development.)

Sexual Status.   Being male or female also is considered to be a major influence upon the child's development and personality. Even though it is difficult to separate those effects of sex that are hereditary from those that result from the way parents and others treat girls and boys, there are nonetheless observable differences. Although they are disputed, many authorities consider that differences in skills, preferred activities, and styles of interacting with others are due to the inborn predispositions of boys and girls. Others argue that individual children in specific families with particular physical and intellectual abilities will escape traditional perceptions and roles associated with membership in one sex or the other. The biological differences between girls and boys do, nonetheless, present children and adults with corresponding developmental challenges. As youngsters become aware of their differing physical characteristics they can be expected to adopt many behaviors associated with others of the same sex. Being a boy or a girl becomes part of one's identity in early childhood. In an environment relatively free of stereotypes and/or prejudices in relation to sex, children may grow to feel proud of themselves and be free to develop their interests and abilities regardless of their biological sex. (See Heatherington & Parke, 1975, and Nash, 1970, for further discussion on sex and development.)

Birth Order.   Another major influence on personality consists of the child's birth order in the family. Research and personality theory have emphasized that first-, second-, and third-born children have quite different child-rearing experiences that are related to their position among their siblings. Even though parents may strive to treat each child with equal amounts of regard, privileges, responsibilities, and so forth, their children can be expected to have emotions and interpersonal exchanges influenced by the sequence in which they are born into the family. First-born children tend to be the highest achievers in the family. In terms of personality, oldest children may tend to be more assertive, have greater self-esteem, and be more competent in language skills. Perhaps the first-born's early, undivided attention from parents helps to create a more dominant personal style.

Later-born children, of course, have both the advantage of a frontrunner sibling and the frequent disadvantage of a negative appraisal from the older child who serves as idol, teacher, and privileged critic. Nevertheless, in any specific case, the middle or third-born child may strive and succeed in moving beyond any possible handicaps by virtue of birth order. (See Adler's theory in Hall & Lindzey, 1985, and discussions in Leichter, 1975, and Sutton-Smith & Rosenberg, 1970.)

Temperament and Intelligence. Two factors thought to contribute some innate features to the child's development and socioemotional growth are temperament and intelligence. Certainly IQ has been viewed, particularly by middle-class people, as an inherited trait, where children are born with intellectual advantages and limits that at least partly determine their ultimate achievement and status. The extremes of giftedness and retardation seem particularly to be inherited. The middle ranges of intelligence, however, may be influenced by the richness or deprivation of children's experiences as these are managed by parents, care givers, and teachers. The debate between the roles of heredity and environment continues, with many parents and educators having the most to say about the possibilities of improving children's status. Of course, intelligence is important as a personality issue because it is thought, not proven, to be related to happiness and success in life. Some authorities have pointed out that overall competence, which includes social skills in concert with intellectual-cognitive ones, is a more appropriate description of ability that allows the child's particular experiential history to fulfill a role in its development and maintenance. (See Bee, 1975, Heatherington & Parke, 1975, McClinton & Meier, 1978, and Nash, 1970, for discussions about the development and measurement of IQ.)

Temperament has been discussed as both an inborn trait and a long-term characteristic developed during the earliest years of life (Thomas, Chess, & Birch, 1968). It is an important personality dimension that helps to characterize the very young child's general mood and style. Temperament includes activity level, rhythmicity of daily cycles, distractibility, openness or withdrawal to approaches, adaptability, attention and persistence, intensity of feelings and reactions, degree of response, and quality of mood. Constellations of these descriptors have been used to explain various types, such as the easy, the slow-to-warm-up, and the difficult child. Indeed, many of the phrases included in temperament analysis have been used in clinical descriptions of young children as well. It is fascinating, indeed, to find that these are enduring traits. Parents, care givers, and teachers may be much better able to understand personalities of children with an understanding of the contribution of temperament factors.

Culture.   Certainly one of the most obvious and sometimes problematic influences upon the young child's emotions and social exchanges is her family, specifically, their culture and lifestyle. (See Heatherington & Parke, 1975, Singer & Singer, 1969, and Stevens & Mathews, 1978, for a discussion regarding families.) The attitudes, knowledge, behaviors, and cultural membership of the family may very well play an essential role in creating individual differences that finely tune the child's personality. Certainly the cultural-ethnic orientation of the family may be expressed by even the young child as preferences in food, friends, recreation, and so forth. Children may take up whatever values are presented in relation to culture, from the use of manners to sex-role characteristics to attitudes toward teachers and schools. Many generalizations about particular cultures can be prejudicial, however; and such characterizing of all members of a group as possessing particular values may confuse rather than aid understanding.

Related to culture and ethnicity are the general affective mood and style of a family. Some mothers may be sociable; others may be altruistic. Some parents are more active; others show a restrained and very calm exterior. Some fathers participate in direct child care and play; others seldom do. Different relationships and patterns are experienced by children, who, particularly in early childhood, are likely to develop the responses, expectations, and limitations of their parents and other models such as care givers and teachers. Individual behaviors and attitudes follow from many of these family traits.

Parenting Style.   Another family variable is parenting style, and it can be viewed as a behavioral pattern, a set of beliefs that influence the handling of events, or a byproduct of knowledge and understanding (see Chapter 2). Parents who are authoritarian or democratic, who are interested and involved or hostile and indifferent, who actively teach or discourage children's learning can be expected to provide differing child-rearing environments. Children who are abused, for example, duplicate this pattern themselves, while nurturant, indulgent parenting may result from child confidence and self-esteem. The beliefs that parents hold about children's development and behavior—how best to enhance, control, and teach them—determine much of their parenting style, according to McGillicuddy-DeLisi & Sigel (1983). Educational and social supports also are thought to contribute to parents' understanding and nurturance of personality and development (Cataldo, 1980; Cochran & Brassard, 1979). Although the connections between parenting style and children's socioemotional growth and health are not clear, it seems appropriate to include them when developmental issues are involved.

Schooling and Exposure to Media.   Additional factors that may affect personality are children's daycare and schooling experiences and their exposure to media in the form of television, books, and movies. The activities and people that young children encounter in educational settings present to them a wide range of feelings and behaviors that are both similar to and different from those found within the family and neighborhood. For most youngsters, this environment is stimulating and satisfying, helping them to develop new skills in managing feelings and dealing with others. On occasion, a child who is overwhelmed or insecure may be unable to grow interpersonally outside the home. Schools do make many useful contributions to personality, however, particularly when teachers place a premium on supporting individual children and gently guiding them into successful social interactions.

Television, books, and movies have been known to delight and inform, frighten and frustrate young children. Certainly in the area of violence and sex roles, the media have been criticized for failing to hold up acceptable images and standards for the young. Others believe they have the potential for contributing to and assisting socialization and education when properly monitored (see Chapter 7).

FEELINGS: THEIR EXPRESSION AND MANAGEMENT

For parents, care givers, and teachers the importance of children's feelings is apparent. They are part of every period of time spent with a child. Varied in urgency and manner of expression, young children's feelings nevertheless dominate most of their interpersonal exchanges and much of their ongoing activity. Emotional expressions do not always require adult help; indeed, children may benefit from some degree of affective space in which they can feel, act, observe consequences, and make adjustments independently in relation to emotions. The contented gurgles of babies briefly alone in their cribs, the footstomping retreat of a disciplined toddler, the elated laughter of a preschooler watching a clown, or the quiet tears of an embarrassed first grader are all healthy emotional displays that belong to the children. But an understanding of the range and power of feelings, the role of language and communication, and the emotions of adults as these influence the personal-social growth of young people is important for those who interact daily with them. The effective management of emotions may contribute to the child's mental health and constructive relationships with others. In addition, adults can be helped to balance their responses to many emotional signals within a family or classroom and between an adult and child. Priority given to self-expression and esteem also can be tempered with understanding and respect for others. A good starting point is a discussion of children's feelings.

Feelings in the young are relatively apparent in their behavior, even given some individual differences in children's tendencies to emote openly. Since behavior as an expression of affect is discussed in Chapter 8, here the feelings themselves will be given attention, even though it is not always possible to determine the nature of children's feelings or to uncover the causes or circumstances that led to their expression. Sometimes the puzzle is quite complicated because each personality and set of social relationships is unique. In general, however, a number of difficult and satisfying feelings may be recognized and managed with a degree of success.

Difficult Emotions

Distress.   Perhaps the most disturbing "negative" feeling for adults to face is that of children's obvious distress. Crying upsets almost anyone. Even two year olds react with sympathy to the tears of children and adults. Yet infants, toddlers, and some preschoolers cry several times a day. The source of distress might be hunger, fear, pain, tiredness, hurt, frustration, or disapproval. Holding, talking, and concrete "gifts" such as a bandaid, toy, or other distraction may reduce and sometimes eliminate distress. On other occasions the adult may be able to resolve a dilemma or help to alleviate an upsetting situation. Sometimes distress is responded to promptly by adults; other times a decision is made not to show a reaction. If the soothing and problem solving of others are not effective, then the child may be encouraged to call upon her own resources to reduce distress; she may fall asleep, find an alternative activity, or permit another person to provide comfort. Generally, the younger the child, the more adults are needed to manage distress directly. By the primary-grade years, children are often able to satisfy themselves or accept verbal suggestions for dealing with situations before distress becomes unmanageable. Parents and teachers, however, do need to continue to be available to help children with this feeling.

Fear.   Another powerful and overwhelming negative feeling that usually requires adults for its resolution is fear. Both the child with an immediate fright and the one with a generalized anxiety in particular circumstances need parents and others to soothe, explain, and be available to them. Fears about loud sounds, strangers, animals, the dark, new friends, failures, loss of loved ones, and so forth, are commonplace in the early years. For the most part, it takes time and repeated support from others for children to overcome fears. Discipline and ridicule may produce emotional conflict and added fears. Physical affection, verbal reassurance, modeling of other responses such as curiosity and acceptance, and a gradual adjustment to whatever caused the fear are all useful strategies. Of course, some fears are useful. Adults want children to avoid dangerous situations, and moderate amounts of fear help them to do this. As children grow, many fears can and should be discussed openly so that feelings are aired and youngsters can observe how other people have managed this emotion.

Dependency.   Dependency can be described as a negative feeling in one respect, but it is basically a normal part of everyone's personality. Children are, in fact, dependent; nevertheless, the feeling of helplessness and need for others can be strong and somewhat uncomfortable in the early years. Clinging, shyness, remaining near a parent, resisting independent playtimes, and similar dependent behaviors all occur from time to time. Adults need to provide reassurance that they will be available or that others will care for the child if needed. Parents who are insecure themselves may unwittingly transmit this feeling to the child by failing to express confidence that their needs will be met. Occasionally, the adult may respond so inconsistently to feelings and interests that mistrust develops and the child becomes anxious and overly dependent. Whatever the cause, the normal balance between feelings of dependency and security can be expected to tilt somewhat to one side or another during the early years. As long as the child feels reasonably secure, fewer feelings of helplessness and need can be expected. Adults can encourage this by noting and praising signs of independence, by exposing children to others who are self-sufficient, by helping children to learn to take care of themselves, and by teaching them gradually to accept more responsibility for their own activities.

Anger and Aggression.   For those who are on the receiving end of these feelings, anger and aggression are difficult emotions. Since frustration is an inescapable part of growing up, anger can be expected to occur. It may, however, be expressed in ways that are more or less acceptable to others. Children may learn to use anger to their advantage, or they may develop an understanding about differences in the forms that anger takes. Rules at home and in school are generally very clear about prohibitions on hitting, pushing, throwing, biting, or grabbing. Anger in the form of tears, shouts, walking away, or refusals to participate are usually permitted. This helps the child express feelings too powerful to keep inside yet maintains rules for group living. Anger that is associated with conflicts or aggression between children requires a series of tactics to prevent, comfort, redirect, and model appropriate behaviors. Over a period of time children learn to use a variety of other modes of dealing with their own angry feelings and those of others. Materials for self-expression, such as art, music, pretend play, and construction toys help to release and channel angry feelings. Verbal models used by adults to redirect anger and aggression calmly also teach appropriate alternatives to children.

Rejection and Hurt. Two feelings that preschoolers begin to encounter at home and at school when either adults or children refuse their social overtures are rejection and hurt. Busy parents and teachers may ask the child to make do without them, or playmates may deny them entry to a game. If these events occur often or if the child's self-esteem is not yet adequate, then feelings of rejection, of not being liked, may establish themselves. Certainly, rejection occurs for everyone at one time or another, and children cannot be shielded from this experience. If the dose is not overwhelming, occasional rejection can help children to cope with others, to find alternative activities and relationships, and to begin to understand their own personal characteristics as others react to them. Within an overall accepting and loving atmosphere, feelings of rejection and hurt can be handled rather matter-of-factly with discussion, suggestion, and occasional intervention by adults. In situations that are overly negative, parents and teachers may need to observe what is happening, provide some monitoring that can break the cycle of rejection, or prevent the situation from recurring.

Self-Doubt. Feelings of doubt, confusion, and lack of confidence are also difficult emotions for children, even though they are not always easily observed. Those who feel that they are incompetent, who doubt their own abilities and values, or who are confused about expectations or standards are likely to demonstrate their feelings by avoiding others, behaving very inconsistently, or displaying attitudes that are rather difficult to handle. The child may be tense or overwhelmed, lonely or withdrawn, overly compliant or sometimes aggressive and demanding. Parents and teachers may be able to help with a consistent, affectionate, and long-term program of encouragement, praise, explanation, and demonstration. The extra time spent on these feelings may result in changing a negative cycle into a positive series of affirmative experiences. Even the youngster whose temperament appears to lean toward the reserved or less easily adapted may benefit from this kind of adult assistance.

Jealousy. Jealousy is a feeling that occurs not only in relation to a new brother or sister; children may envy a friend's toys, a parent's affection for someone else, or any other situation in which others seem more privileged. It can be eased with understanding and sympathy, but jealousy is likely to be a part of the child's many emotional experiences. It is not resolved by providing whatever the child covets, because this creates a pattern of demands that can seldom be met. Firm but affectionate responses may allow the feeling to be aired, whether or not the child's jealousy subsides. Parents and teachers usually find it helpful to provide role-play or pretend props for the youngster to use in acting out these situations. In the case of siblings and jealousy between playmates, the child who receives a reasonable share of attention and regard will usually bring these feelings under some control. Rivalry may nonetheless continue into later years, and some bickering can be expected to remain as part of social relations.

Tension. One last difficult emotion that requires attention from adults is that of tension, the feelings of nervousness, anxiety, insecurity, or stress that lead to a state of suspense and unhappiness, making it hard for the child to play, interact, or feel happy. Tension can lead to passivity or aggression, but it is usually accompanied by behaviors such as jumpiness and distractibility, teeth grinding, thumbsucking, tics or other nervous habits, and difficulties in relationships with adults and children. Tension can come from many sources, including emotional problems and stress at home or school and anxieties about war, disaster, divorce, and death, which have become commonplace in recent years. Some highly active children appear to be tense in many situations and need some calm activities, fewer distractions, and gentle handling to help them through the day. Children under stress, who, for example, are experiencing a crisis at home, are overwhelmed by school demands, or unable to handle peer pressure, may need a great deal of affection, assurance, and personal attention from adults in a comfortable, relaxed environment for at least a portion of every day. It is hoped that the youngster will begin to develop the ability to cope with stressors so that the tension-producing situations may become resolved, keeping feeling levels reduced and within the normal limits that children can manage. Certainly, the complexity of daily life for many children today makes it important for adults to examine additional ways of reducing stress at home and school.

Satisfying Emotions

Love. Those who spend time with young children are likely to notice one very endearing and satisfying emotion that is demonstrated with a good deal of regularity. At this age, children feel a great deal of love. Their attachments, bonds, and similar positive ties to others are established and expressed openly. Physical affection, including touching, cuddling, wrestling, tickling, kissing, and verbal statements of feeling are enjoyed by those who interact with young children. For some, love is expressed very early in the relationship and in more obvious ways than for others. This may reflect both the child's temperament and a family style. In the case of infants and toddlers, loving expressions are part of daily, routine care giving and play. For preschoolers and early-primary children, love may be demonstrated with verbal as well as physical gestures. Later, the meanings of love become clearer, so that children begin to adjust their feelings and become more indirect and restrained. The spontaneous love that parents and teachers receive nevertheless makes such relationships rewarding and enjoyable. Its childlike, appropriate demonstration can be returned in kind and cherished for its genuineness.

Comfort and Well-Being.   Infants and young children need many positive feelings to carry them through the ups and downs of developing new skills and understanding, of interacting with adults and children. Two such important feelings are comfort and well-being. The nurturance and responsiveness of devoted parents, care givers, and teachers engenders these feelings that, in turn, make it possible for the young to grow well. Feelings of comfort and well-being, of trust and security are produced in an environment where children are valued and cared for with consistency and affection. Adults often obtain pleasure in creating such an atmosphere, in providing the means whereby an infant is comfortable and a preschooler secure, in acknowledging that they are needed in order for children to feel this way. Such positive feelings are general and pervasive but not always permanent. Despite the actions of parents and teachers, children have temporary discomforts and feelings of doubt about the dependability of adults. In general, though, the positive side of these emotions is well within the experience of many children and the goal of most adults.

Happiness and Joy.   Happiness and joy are satisfying to see in anyone, but particularly in children. From the first full smiles of the three month old to the deeper joys of the happy second grader, one of the best experiences for parents and teachers to have is to fulfill a role in producing such feelings. Many children exhibit a generally sunny disposition, a pleasant temperament that is nurtured and enjoyed by adults. Others may need a great deal of deliberate and conscious effort in demonstrating happiness. Often children go through stages where good feelings are apt to alternate with distress: Teething, schedule changes, new care givers, illness, and family crises typically bring sadness, negative moods, and generally trying times for both adults and children. At other periods in development there is likely to be a sense of fun and enjoyment in play and social relationships. Adults who work with the young know that they can expect happiness in waves and that some activities are likely to produce more of it. Joyful experiences are planned by teachers and sometimes by parents. A favorite

food, a new toy, a robust game, an entertaining event, and other standbys such as peek-a-boo, ice cream, or a trip to the zoo can be expected to result in good cheer. Such happy events satisfy everyone's need for these refreshing feelings. Certainly, happiness can and should be part of every child's day and every adult's.

Self-Confidence and Mastery.   Other important, positive emotions for children to have about themselves are self-confidence and a sense of mastery. At the preschool and early-primary levels, such feelings play a major role in assuring that children persist in developing skills and understanding when they are confronted with difficult material and confusing behavioral options. In the case of young children whose control of their lives is highly limited, feelings of "I can do it" are needed in order to overcome the many obstacles that present themselves at home and school. Self-confidence is behind the child's persistence when dealing with complex learning tasks such as reading, writing, and mathematical operations. It is also vital when new friendships are being formed or when children work with a new teacher. Adults can aid children by providing activities that can be mastered with modest degrees of effort, by focusing on successes more than failures, and by allowing children to have some choice in what they are required to accomplish so that their own interests and levels of ability can be included. Parents and teachers also need to avoid confusion and unrealistic demands, hurtful criticism, and negative attitudes, all of which can operate to shake children's confidence.

Pride and Self-Esteem. Everyone needs to have feelings of pride and self-esteem. Regular doses of praise, expressed regard for the child, respect for products and efforts, and the modeling of self-pride all contribute to these valuable emotions. Children who express pride in their accomplishments and who feel good about themselves tend to grow up mentally healthy and socially skilled. Even when mistakes are made, errors are acknowledged, and personal struggles are obvious, the pride demonstrated by adults for the special qualities in each child leads to acceptance and a sense of being a valued, contributing person. Certainly it can be said that every child has something to be proud of, something that parents and teachers can point to with satisfaction. Children do offer a great deal to adults, helping them to expand their skills, develop new attitudes, see themselves differently, embrace their own strengths and needs, and so forth. Children's progress is a source of satisfaction to most people. Pride and self-esteem, then, can be a mutual emotion for adults and their young, serving to make each admire and cherish the other.

Developing Language

The development of children's ability to communicate with gestures and vocal expressions begins, to a certain extent, with the first cry. Over the days and months that follow, babies and their parents learn to understand each other's needs, feelings, and behaviors. By the time a toddler utters his first words, there has been a gradual but extensive development of the ability to communicate and an accumulation of understanding about concepts, purposes, and rules for using language and deriving meaning. Language describes feelings, contributes to personality, and is a signal of intellectual growth; therefore, this area of children's development is one of the most integrated with other strands. It is tied to social relationships with parents and others, to personality as a communication of ideas and feelings, to intellectual growth as indicated by concepts and logical thought, and sometimes to physical development, as when language is used to motivate and praise children's efforts. Because of its significance in all these ways, a discussion of language and communication could be placed in sections under parents' educational roles, their management of behavior, or child care and play. Here, the subject seems quite appropriate to socioemotional development and, more specifically, to the communication of feelings.

Early signs of language such as crying, cooing, and babbling most frequently occur in relation to feelings. Babies use their bodies, including their vocal cords, to make their needs known. Parents respond with food or cuddling that is frequently accompanied by soothing sounds, nonsense words, or actual conversation directed at babies. Voices, sounds, and touch begin to become familiar signals of satisfaction to the child, and parents, in turn, become more adept at hearing different gurgles and cries that indicate distinct needs. The communication system thus developed is very useful in keeping baby and parent in tune with one another. It also serves as a precursor to the "real" language of words, phrases, and sentences.

By the end of the second year of life toddlers are generally quite able to understand many words, simple phrases, and even sentences parents and care givers use while caring for and playing with their children. The child's actual use of words may vary greatly; some youngsters join conversations, point out interesting things around them, describe their play activities, and ask for things they want quite clearly. Others may understand much of the verbal world around them, but displays of these skills come much later. By age four, most preschoolers speak rather clearly and use language in a wide variety of ways, even though they continue to make errors in their pronunciation and sentences. Verbal expressions are ongoing in their play and learning and in social exchanges with parents, teachers, and friends. Books, songs, and other language activities also build up their understanding of the reading process so that, by kindergarten age, spoken words can be deciphered from written ones. As reading skills are practiced, additional vocabulary growth occurs and the use of language in thinking, in teaching, and in figuring out problems becomes primary. By second grade, children are generally required to use language in all of their school subjects, and it is the established mode of teaching throughout later schooling.

The relationship between language and thought has been studied extensively, and theories about this aspect of growth are debated by those in the field. For some, language is viewed as a series of learned associations between words and the objects, events, and people they represent. Children imitate their parents and others, then practice words and phrases they hear. Adults teach and provide an array of these learning opportunities on a daily basis, and children gain in understanding and the ability to use language by repeated practice and refinement, with parental encouragement and praise for their efforts. In this view, speech is acquired through a process of learning, which involves stimulation, reinforcement, and practice (Skinner, 1957).

Another view of language development holds that the process is more complex and creative, more dependent upon the active participation of the child. Children learn the rules and structures of their language from exposure to other speakers. The child is seen as having a predisposition for language that, with maturation and environmental stimulation, allows her to understand the principles of language and meaning and then relate (transform) these into the words and sentences they have heard. The child depends less on imitation and repetition and more on discoveries and modified verbal expressions that reflect what the child understands about language. Youngsters' perceptual and intellectual abilities in concert with parents' casual verbal expressions provide the basic ingredients for this development. The child's skills develop somewhat apart from direct adult involvement, yet adults' support and stimulation may play a role in the child's motivation and use of language models (Chomsky, 1965).

These theories about how language develops may influence adults only minimally. Probably most parents and teachers use both learning principles in teaching specific words and psycholinguistic encouragement in allowing the child to experiment with whatever verbal expressions arise from their own maturing abilities. The emphasis upon language, however, may be very strong, partly because some adults recognize its relationship to so many aspects of growth, especially cognitive development. In programs for the very young, teachers often make conscious efforts to encourage vocal utterances; to teach words for things children experience; to extend and expand verbal expression; to play with language in song and rhyme; to build vocabulary, phrasing, and sentences with conversation and stories; and to use language for expressing feelings and thoughts (Cazden, 1977; Dale, 1972; McClinton & Meier, 1978; and Tough, 1976).

In addition to theories about how young children acquire language, it is also important to examine how words and meanings can be used by children. Along with valuable intellectual meanings, the social and emotional expressions conveyed through language help children to understand and deal with themselves and others.

The labeling of feelings is part of the interactional strategy of those concerned with self-esteem and nondirective assistance for children (see earlier sections of this chapter). By asking children about their emotions they may gradually be able to understand the causes and management of feelings. When conflict occurs with other children and adults, an awareness of emotions and the use of verbal modes in resolving them or finding alternatives is generally effective, even with the young child. Words can serve as substitutes for actions, or at least as a first line of defense. In child care centers and schools, this function of language is quite important if children are to negotiate successfully for themselves. Yet the conscious, verbal exploration of feeling with children is not easy for many adults. Props such as puppets, stories with animals, role play, and so on help a great deal in openly talking about strong feelings. Play therapy and games involving identifying and neutralizing emotions have been used with young, troubled children. Language in these situations, both verbal and gestural, serves as a way of grasping and examining feelings. Sometimes this simple exposure eases the pressure of an emotion; in other situations even casual discussions of feeling may help to create a healthy, verbal approach to handling one's emotions.

Language uses have been studied by Tough (1976) and Cazden (1977) in an effort to appraise and enhance the quality and complexity of children's language. Several functions described by Tough (1976) include: first, language that is self-maintaining, enabling the child to care for himself in relation to others; second, language that directs or monitors actions in which the child is engaged; and third, language that reports or mirrors ongoing experiences. Fourth, at higher intellectual and linguistic levels, language is used to analyze and reason, to help children figure out what they encounter. Fifth, projecting and predicting involve the use of language for thinking beyond immediate or personal experience, such as forecasting an event or predicting consequences and related possibilities. Finally, language may be imaginative and empathic, where the child renames materials, creates an imaginary set of circumstances, or expresses concern for another person's feelings.

Parents and teachers may consciously or inadvertently assist children in using language in such complex ways. During play activities, stories, or actual discussions, preschoolers can talk about themselves and their friends in a way that includes many of these functions. Adults who use inquiry in relation to a picture or event may be particularly successful in helping children to understand feelings and behavior. Such language uses build personal, social, and intellectual skills in ways that can be exceptionally satisfying and informative to adults.

SUMMARY

To summarize this chapter on feelings and personality, it can be said that there are numerous theoretical orientations attempting to explain the composition and structure of personality. Further, there are many determinants that appear to be instrumental in shaping a child's feelings and characteristics. These forces that operate on the child are summarized in Table 9.

Table 9
Overview of the Child's Growing Personality

EMOTIONAL WELL-BEING

The child requires demonstrations of love and regard.

The child needs to feel attached, secure, and accepted.

The child's mental health is aided by feeling valued, esteemed, and appreciated as an individual.

THE ORGANIZATION OF THE PERSON

The child's body type is related to personal traits and temperamental characteristics.

The child's development is shaped by acquired learnings and response patterns that are reinforced.

The child's personality is made up of ability and temperamental factors and intellectual traits.

The child's instincts become controlled and organized through social processes and emotional stages.

The child's inner being emerges through positive relationships with others.

THE SOCIAL DEVELOPMENT OF THE PERSON

The child's personality is composed of goals, needs, strivings, and an identity that adopts a style or self-system for dealing with others.

The child matures in stages of experience and ability in the direction of competence and purpose.

The child's space or environment of expectations, forces, and historical precedence guides thought processes and psychic energy towards self-realization and authentic living.

The child's autonomous self is directed by needs and motives and through social pressures to distinguish or actualize itself.

The child's development is gradual and tied to experiences that promote adaptation and progress from egocentrism to reasoned thought and moral behavior.

PERSONAL DIFFERENCES

The child's personality is influenced by social status, sex, birth order, temperament, intelligence, culture, parenting style, schooling, and media experiences.

FEELING STATES

The child has experiences with difficult emotions such as distress, fear, dependency, anger, rejection, doubt, jealousy, and tension, all of which contribute to personal skills.

The child has experiences with satisfying emotions such as love, comfort, well-being, happiness, self-confidence, and pride, which support personal development.

COMMUNICATION

The child's communicative and language experiences help to form and express personal concerns and a social style.

PROGRAM SUGGESTIONS

1. Have parents talk to a preschool and a primary-school child about the different needs for emotional security described in the text. Ask the children when they feel good or bad and how they and their parents respond.
2. Examine in more detail the personality theories of two different theorists. Use the information to make recommendations to adults guiding young children.
3. Arrange for parents to do a case study of a child, using Table 9 to identify outstanding personality characteristics and explain their value.
4. Examine the qualities described in the Personal Differences section of this chapter. Ask parents to analyze how they were affected by one of these and how they might have been different emotionally and socially in other circumstances.
5. Request that parents talk to their own mothers and fathers about how they were as children, compared to the personalities they now demonstrate. Arrange for a round-robin series of reports about what changed or remained stable, including photographs from the early childhood years.
6. With parents' suggestions create a list of techniques for relieving each of the difficult emotions in their children.
7. Ask parents to remember three of their own past experiences with the satisfying emotions described in the text.
8. Develop a list of labels of feelings and find their dictionary definitions. Have parents use these to describe a strong feeling they experienced recently in relation to their children.

10

Families
and the Child's
Education

The child's education begins at home. Early learning and social skills develop within the intimacy of the family. Parental nurturance from infancy through the preschool years includes a wide variety of activities that are educational in the broadest sense. Daily experiences with objects and events, personal relationships, and the home environment itself all function as instructional methods and materials for the growing child. The learning is immediate and continuous, individual and emotional, variable and fast paced, but it is an educational process resulting in a broad base of knowledge and ability. The child who arrives at the school door comes equipped with a foundation of learning provided by the family.

Understanding the role of parents and other family members is important, since society is expected to manage the child's education for a major portion of the growing years. There are some areas of overlapping responsibility and a number of political and social conflicts, but the roles of home and school are both significant to the child's learning and socialization. Unfortunately, the family's contribution to the educational process is seldom appreciated. While some children appear to be poorly prepared for school experiences, the majority are ready for the curricular and social demands made upon them. In addition, parents are usually respectful of the teaching role assumed by the society and are ready to support the school's efforts. Where children are in attendance at child care programs or where private arrangements are made, the family comes to share its earliest teaching role with others long before entry into kindergarten and the primary grades. At this point in history, with an apparent increase in infant, preschool, and school-based early-childhood programs, greater knowledge about the family's teaching-learning activities is needed in order to balance the child's educational experiences with professionals. Home-school relationships also can be expected to improve when everyone adopts a sensitive approach to parent programs that takes into account the education already being provided by family members in the child's home.

THE EDUCATIONAL HOME ENVIRONMENT

Children's homes have physical, social, and psychological characteristics. The people present, the activities that go on, the materials available for play—these features of the home environment have an effect on the child's behavior and learning. The specific ways in which these influences are felt and for how long is not, as yet, very clear. Indeed, the home and family can be said to comprise a system of influences where different effects are interwoven. Children participate in these interactions, and each brings a unique temperament and set of abilities, a personal style, and special interests to every situation. The result is a complex and unique child-rearing environment for each infant or preschooler. The child's education is part of this picture; education, that is, in which socialization, basic skills, attitudes toward learning, and so forth all contribute to general competence.

From birth onward most children spend a relatively large proportion of their day studying the people, objects, and activities around them. They look, touch, examine, and react to their parents, toys, and all the interesting and mundane activities that go on around them. Such experiences may not seem educational, but there is a good deal of information and understanding being retained by the child. It is a slow, cumulative process, one limited by the child's immature intellectual and physical capacities. Gradually the baby and the preschooler gain enough understanding that it becomes obvious something is being learned. The infant smiles at a favorite rattle or repeats a sound; the preschooler figures out a puzzle solution or describes yesterday's puppet show. Each time, parents and teachers may feel somewhat surprised and pleased at this evidence of competence learned partly through their efforts.

At least three authorities in education and child development have investigated and described some important features of early education within the family. Each theorist has focused upon what it is that adults, particularly mothers, do to teach children during the course of their days together. Since the primary focus in this chapter is the home as an educational setting, only material relating to this parenting function will be discussed (see other chapters for behavior, personality, care, and so on).

Bettye Caldwell and Associates

Dr. Caldwell published the "Inventory of Home Stimulation" in 1970 following a series of studies about how the home environment might contribute to the child's developmental status. The scale contains several subscales, each of which reflects an important feature of parental behavior and the child's physical surroundings. In relation to mothers' behaviors, beneficial characteristics seem to include emotional and social responsivity to the child (vocalizing, explaining, expressing ideas, praising, and showing affection); the avoidance of restriction and punishment (no shouting, spanking, scolding, or undue interfering with the child's activities); and involvement in the child's play (talking, encouraging, structuring, and emphasizing the use of mature toys). In terms of the physical environment, developmentally helpful features include organization of the home (few hazards and regular sitters; trips to stores, clinics, and other outings; and a place for the child's belongings); the provision of appropriate play materials (toys for physical and learning activities, role play, stories, and music); and opportunities for variety (father involvement, visitors, and use of books). While this scale is used primarily for research purposes, it nonetheless provides some interesting notions of the kind of learning and support families can provide that may aid the child's development in the first years of life.

Jean Carew and Associates

In a small book entitled *Observing Intelligence in Young Children* (Carew et al., 1975) and a later research study concerning young children's daily experiences (Carew, 1980), Jean Carew and her associates describe how mothers assume educational roles with their children. They organize the home environment so that youngsters can engage in educationally relevant activities and can share these with other family members. They model procedures for doing things about the house, and children watch them closely. They informally observe their child's behavior, making interpretations about the child's interests, abilities, and temperament. They serve as facilitators, making suggestions, providing materials, and praising the child's efforts. Mothers also restrict some of their toddlers' activities, in moderate degrees and without punitiveness for the most part. They assume a participant role in some activities, and this involvement tends to help them understand the child's growth and to attempt to influence it as needed. This participation could be intellectual, social, or physical. Mothers occasionally function as teachers in giving information, correcting mistakes, posing a question, and reading to the youngster. Finally, some mothers also fulfill roles as entertainers, playmates, and conversers, all cheerful involvements they obviously enjoyed together. This overview of the mothers of well-developing children emphasizes how naturally the educational process is carried out in some homes. Carew's later work focuses on the value of parental structuring and mediation of children's experiences during the day, to make them into intellectually valuable and educational play times.

Hope Leichter

A rather broad and fascinating account of education in the family is described in the book *The Family as Educator*, an edited volume by Leichter (1975) taken from a conference on this subject. It emphasizes the value to children of educational encounters within the family. The model Leichter proposes for this process is one that is broad, extensive, complex, and open, with multiple causes and effects, levels, and areas. It is continuous over time but shifting in patterns and membership. The system can, however, be scanned for significant influences in the child's development. Leichter describes six important educational spheres influenced by the family: language interactions that require children to respond to codes, questions, and narratives; organization of time and space in the home so that family members' interactions and comfort are manageable; the development of memory in relation to ongoing experiences from one time to the next; evaluation and labeling of the child's activities and characteristics; educational coaching or mediation of experiences outside of the family, such as school and television; and the teaching of values related to sex roles, attitudes, and so forth. The outcomes of these activities can be seen in the child's cognitive style, language ability, test skills, and personality.

Leichter also describes three other, often overlooked aspects of education in the family. One is the education of parents by their children. This would include a range of experiences from child bearing and its impact on the parents to the effect of children's developmental problems on parents' esteem and confidence. A second aspect is the education of siblings by siblings. The daily power relationships, verbal exchanges, guidance, and sibling teaching influence children's self-definition and their relationships with their mothers and fathers. Third is the education between parents themselves. Their division of labor in homemaking, child rearing, and children's education; their occupations; and their outside encounters around the children provide for their own learning and development as adults. Over the long term this can influence the educational environment provided in the home.

The work of these authorities provides some guidelines for the information offered to parents about helping their young children to develop well. In many ways these descriptions are not surprising; they are certainly not new to early education and child development specialists. However, the data base provided in these analyses can help to keep parent-education program staff focused on the details of home-based learning.

Several other important aspects of education in the home will be discussed in the next sections. The content is derived from a wide variety of sources, including that of Caldwell, Carew, and Leichter. In order to maintain a smooth flow of discussion there will be less of an emphasis on documentation by author and publication, with more of a focus on an integration of the writings of many professionals on these topics. Some of the content is original, but much of it is contained in parent-education materials of many different kinds. This format is expected to be practical, to inform the reader, and to permit use of the material in an applied program. Five major areas will be presented. Basic skills familiar to teachers and schools will be described as these are taught in potentially optimal home environments. The child's socialization for interactions with others and attitudes related to learning are then presented, followed by a section on special challenges faced by some families. A final portion of the chapter describes how parents continue to play a significant role in the child's education after the youngster is enrolled in a school program.

BASIC SKILLS

In many families the child's home-based education in the early and middle years provides not only the social skills required by the larger society and the attitudes conducive to learning, but a variety of basic school-related skills as well. Parents are their children's first teachers in many ways, including a role implied by the old-fashioned didactic sense of the word. A great many homes serve as valuable learning centers. Parents' instruction may be more informal, irregular, and emotional, but the content areas bear a strong resemblance to basic early childhood education curriculum resources.

Physical Skills

It may seem rather obvious to point out, but family members do spend a great deal of time and energy in the early years teaching their children basic physical skills. Babies learn to sit up, crawl, and walk in their homes. The toddler learns bladder-bowel control and self-feeding. Preschoolers become practiced in tricycle riding; swinging; climbing and other balance skills; self-dressing; and fine-motor skills such as holding a pencil, using scissors, and manipulating small pieces of toys. In middle childhood, parents typically help their youngsters begin to develop skills such as playing a variety of games with balls, riding a two-wheel bicycle, and many other specialized activities ranging from roller skating to skiing. These motor abilities serve as a foundation for the school's physical education program (basketball, track, soccer, football, volleyball, and so on). They also prepare the child for small-muscle activities involving dexterity in the fingers and hands, for example, writing letters and words or completing math and science projects using small pieces of equipment.

Vocabulary and Speech

A second rather obvious set of skills taught in homes that has far-reaching consequences for the child is the development of language. Family members play a vital role in the first years of life in teaching words and phrases; the construction of sentences; the uses of language; the refinement of concepts expressed in words; and the enjoyment of language by way of books, stories, and reading. The child develops his vocabulary in relation to the words used during day-to-day activities and casual conversations. As the child's understanding of words grows and vocabulary expands, many parents begin to require clear expressions and explanations from the youngster. They press the child to use language to deal with needs, feelings, and information. Most family members take great pride in seeing these skills mature, and even the child's mistakes are enjoyed. By the end of the preschool period, the communicative and cognitive skills represented by language abilities are quite mature, and by middle childhood they seem most remarkable. Most families are effective in supporting this spiral of increasing competence and complexity in dealing with language. In some communities, there may be dialects and idiomatic expressions evident in the child's speech that may or may not present problems in school; however, for the most part, the preschool child is able to use the skills gained at home to manage a wide variety of new academic and social challenges.

Information and Memory

As an infant, the child is able to process information through the senses. Gradually, what is seen, heard, felt, smelled, and tasted is remembered. When new information comes along, it also is processed by the child, whose memory capacity matures throughout the preschool and middle childhood years. In homes, family members often provide the growing youngster with small doses of simplified information. By the end of the preschool period, children may have a rather impressive wealth of knowledge about objects, people, and events. Some information is more popular than others. Competent young children tend to know a lot, relative to their age, about animals, vehicles, seasons, songs, characters in popular stories and television series, their own possessions, and any other special hobbies and interests of their families. The amount and nature of their knowledge will reflect, to a large extent, whether and how much their parents, siblings, and neighbors, have described, explained, and presented information to them.

Preschoolers are renowned for their inquisitiveness. When adults take the time to respond to these curiosities as they are expressed, they extend the child's knowledge base at the best possible moment—when the child is eager to know. Activities outside the home may add considerably to this information because both child and adult are exposed to new ideas. Daycare and nursery-school enrichment programs also tend to stimulate interest in new, previously unexplained places, substances, events, people, and so on. Teachers also deal with misconceptions and with ideas that are very incomplete. They attempt to provide clarification and may be quite skillful in reducing the size and scope of a concept to match the child's limited understanding.

Counting and Logic

Basic skills in these areas are more a part of daily experience than is often realized. Children deal with amounts, sizes, time, patterns, money, and rules from the toddler age onward. Babies know a big from a little truck; two year olds can match some patterns on a wrapper or select two candies; and preschoolers gain rapidly in their abilities to count, sort, and deal with concepts of time, amount, and shape during their play activities. Children's logical ability, or capacity to reason beyond what the senses perceive, is still quite limited. Their repeated exposure to these kinds of activities in homes and early childhood programs helps to build later understanding. At mealtimes and on shopping trips, in play and brief teaching exchanges, young children often take an interest in mathematics. They very much enjoy demonstrating the concrete and observable math operations such as counting, adding, measuring, or sorting. It is a very real skill to them that can be used in most any play activity. Parents who are able to teach and observe these growing skills in such informal situations are contributing to the growth of logic and mathematics, even though these terms are reserved for the later school years.

The Reading Process

If the process of learning to read is viewed as a long-term, developmental accumulation of skills and attitudes, then the child's early experiences at home and in preschool are very much a part of the reading process. Over the years from about age one and a half to age six, children are typically exposed to a wide range of activities that relate to reading. Toddlers, for

example, may spend time with parents leafing through picture books and pointing out favorite scenes, while parents articulate the words for each. During the three- and four-year-old period, children often listen to a great many stories. They attempt to use alphabet games and write and read their names, may ask about letter sounds and how particularly interesting words look, and may play school with other children. Some youngsters become quite adept at reading store signs and grocery can labels. They may begin by pretending to read a favorite memorized story, then gradually turn their attention to decoding the printed words. While there is a wide variation in how much these prereading activities are encouraged and used as learning sessions from one home to the next, in many cases such a gradual building up of the composite skills leads the child comfortably into reading itself. For some youngsters the process is rapid and satisfying, while, for others, even with parent support, there is much less motivation to reach that end product.

The involvement of family members in helping children to develop these skills is not supported by some professionals. They fear that parents will place too much pressure on the child or that they will use teaching-learning strategies that conflict with the methods preferred in the school setting. The many different approaches to teaching reading that have been described in the literature demonstrate that there are many avenues to take. It may be the case that some techniques are quite suitable for parents to use and rather natural to the home setting. The language-experience approach, for example, where children's own expressions are written down for use as reading materials, can be part of the families' repertoire. Some letter-sound decoding strategies and whole-word recognition methods also seem to be consistent wih the kind of informal activities parents might do with children at home. Certainly, building a positive attitude toward books and reading, sharing stories in the comfort and intimacy of the living room, and avoiding pressured or structured teaching have traditionally been recommended. Other approaches could be developed as well, for use in homes by parents whose children seem interested in and capable of beginning the reading process and who already demonstrate a healthy, balanced set of developmental, personal, and social skills. From this foundation, school-based programs can continue to teach the child increasing advanced reading competencies.

Science and Inquiry

The changes that children can observe in weather and seasons, in substances that are heated and frozen, and in plants and animals that grow and die are all mysteries of science that delight and intrigue them. Parents can teach a great many science-related concepts to their children when at home or out for simple excursions in the neighborhood. Toddlers can see and feel snow, rain, and sun. Preschoolers may study a growing flower or collect pebbles. Children who are permitted to help in the garden and kitchen may gain a good deal of understanding about fruits and vegetables and what is needed to eat them for supper. A variety of these informal science studies and experiments are well suited to home settings and relaxed parent-child interactions.

Parents also teach more abstract concepts about the life cycle when they answer questions and explain, in simple terms, about babies, human development, and death. Opportunities also exist for thinking about mechanical energy and the properties of substances. Objects may be taken apart and put together, to study their mechanical features. Children may dismantle a three-piece metal coffee pot and eventually repair loose seats on their bicycles. Magnets and battery-powered circuits, the properties of water and sand in the sink and backyard, watching nature films—all are activities that parents may share with children while enriching the child's knowledge and understanding.

History and Culture

In some families children are taught a great deal about their religious and cultural heritage; their families' histories; and a measure of information concerning their city, state, and country. Most preschoolers are capable only of managing rather simple explanations, but the groundwork is laid by family members in thinking about the child's relationships to others. Young children are already aware that their friends may have different religious observances. They may know something about their grandparents' earlier days or how their own parents behaved at such an age. Families who participate frequently in local community activities, who bring their children to visit their workplaces, or who take tours of their cities are providing their youngsters with basic information in the area of social studies and human relationships. These experiences also generate feelings of family pride and the child's relatedness to others. Some of this can be part of the child's school experience. Favorite foods, craft items, special events, story books, and so forth can be shared. Other aspects of history and culture may remain a private concern of the family, whose traditions should be respected by schools.

Creativity and Imagination

While there may be a great deal of discrepancy from one home to the other in resources and interest in artistic skills, many families are able to provide children with a degree of exposure to the creative process. Pretend play, fantasy, dreams, original expressions, and imaginative ideas are part of the child's early development. Spontaneous dramatic play, with the child assuming the role of another person (often a family member, hero, or story character), is part of most preschoolers' experiences. Some of this play is rich in the use of props and dress-up clothing, but many youngsters require only a tiny toy car, doll, or stuffed animal to engage in fantasy. Most homes also contain varied opportunities for music and dance experiences; from radios to children's phonographs, even toddlers react with pleasure to the sounds of music and rhythm. Crayons, paper, small paint kits, wood, and craft materials of many types may be available to children at home. Water and chalk designs might be seen on any street. All of these materials and activities can support the development of creative thinking at home and school.

SOCIAL SKILLS

Preschool education has often been thought to provide a social base for the child's later schooling. Adjustment to a group, separation from parents, some exposure to academic learning, the development of an overall motivational system or a "learning-to-want-to-learn" attitude, are all thought to be important precursors to formal schooling. The family fulfills a critical role in building and maintaining these social skills and learning attitudes, especially in relation to feelings about oneself and others and behaviors around tasks and learning activities. These, in turn, influence whether and how children embrace the total school experience, from social exchanges to group instruction.

The socialization process is particularly important, as successful relationships require confidence, independent care of self, and some control of emotions. These are often taught by parents and provide the base upon which teachers can help each child to develop more mature skills in the group situations that characterize a major portion of the child's day in a school or early-childhood program.

Confidence

When parents and children interact successfully with one another, both may come away with a sense of pride and satisfaction that in turn makes them feel secure, confident, and valued. This confidence about one's social and personal self is an important source of motivation for the child. Good feelings about oneself tend to encourage learning and dealing with challenges that present themselves. The secure baby, for example, ventures into exploratory play with toys and safe household objects. The confident preschooler struggles to complete a thoughtfully designed block building. The first grader who has a good sense of self-esteem is less likely to get overly discouraged with mistakes in decoding words and sentences from a reading primer. Feelings of confidence are developed when the child receives feedback from parents in the form of attitudes and behaviors providing evidence of competence. Expressions of love and demonstrations of affection also help. Pride in the child's efforts, even if not fully successful, helps the child to want to try more challenges. Being positive and emphasizing the child's newest interests and successes also build esteem. In short, this regard for children is a good investment in their education because it can strongly influence their attitudes about a variety of learning activities, making tasks interesting, manageable, and satisfying. Those who have difficulty with their feelings about themselves may require special efforts by adults to rebuild their confidence.

Management of Self

The young child's beginning mastery of self-care, in both the physical and social senses, is a major milestone in the early childhood years. Achieving some measure of independence in dressing, eating, toileting, getting responsibly from place to place, looking after one's possessions, and expressing one's needs are all part of the child's self-management. For the most part, it is mothers, fathers, siblings, and other family members who gradually, over the first four years, teach children these skills. Even though the young child continues to require frequent coaxing, reminders, and supervision, the average preschooler is quite capable of negotiating somewhat independently about the home, neighborhood, and nursery school. Parents often feel quite proud of these accomplishments, as indeed they should. Each represents an extended series of teaching and learning episodes in which parents have demonstrated, instructed, and praised the child for these growing abilities. There are immediate and long-term rewards as well. Such independence reduces parents' responsibilities to the extent that the need for constant physical care giving is eased and, with it, some emotional pressure. The child is now able to spend time away from the home, in neighborhoods and nursery schools. The child also gains. The posture of independence that is easily recognized in the competent preschooler serves the child well. It opens up a world of experience that comes more directly to the child than when it is translated by the family. The child who can manage somewhat independently out in the world is exposed to a wider variety of people, places, and events, with less need for direct adult mediation.

Emotional Control

From infancy to the end of the preschool period, children have generally learned a great deal about harnessing some of their emotions. They develop strategies for expressing their feelings in ways that can lead to the fulfillment of the original need. They can manage some conflict by finding distractions and substitutions or by giving in, walking away, arguing verbally, or seeking adult assistance. Frustrations are often less intense because physical and social skills offer alternative solutions to a difficult problem. Happiness can be expressed with humor and affection or with great bursts of physical joy. Fear and sadness can be overcome with soothing conversation. From the baby, who is essentially at the mercy of rising and falling emotions, to the more controlled but nonetheless expressive preschooler, a very long educational distance has been traveled. Family members, and professionals if the child has attended toddler and preschool programs, can accept a good deal of credit for guiding the child to a more comfortable and mature emotional state. It is a learning process that persists throughout life, but the strides made in the early years are often significant.

Children who are able to channel their emotions or express them in ways that permit adult assistance are poised for a great deal more learning. Such children can accept and work with the behavioral limits established by schools and families. Some correction and guidance from teachers and neighbors can be managed with good grace. The requirements of group living can be negotiated, such as taking turns, sharing resources, attending to a schedule of activities, waiting for assistance, and dealing with the inevitable conflicts of interest and style that are part of being a group member. Most young children, even as early as toddlerhood, derive some satisfaction from expressing positive feelings and concern to others. Children who have some control over their own feelings are often able to put aside some immediate needs in order to comfort a playmate, help another child with a project, or express love for the teacher. These acts of kindness may stimulate the kind of positive emotions that guide a preschooler into an optimistic, outgoing world view.

Peer Participation

As children spend a few hours each day with one or more playmates, they begin to develop attitudes and skills that become a part of their general social style with peers. Each child and his respective peer group is different, however, and the young child is challenged repeatedly to both protect personal interests and enjoy the contributions of friends. Parents help children to negotiate these situations long before enrolling them in a nursery school or other program. Tolerating another child's infringements or inviting a friend to play both require a positive attitude toward other youngsters that is communicated by parents. When conflict occurs parents often help the child to try to recognize the other person's view as well as her own. Parents emphasize compromise, turn taking, sharing, and occasionally separating oneself from others as strategies for successful living with playmates. Grabbing, fighting, name-calling, and so forth are discouraged and sometimes punished. Verbal resolutions or "talking it out" are supported in many homes and neighborhoods.

Children also learn a great deal of information and some task-related activities from peers. During the popular dramatic or pretend role-play games of early childhood, many kinds of information and some physical skills are transmitted. Toddlers and preschoolers learn to participate at least to a minimal degree in these playtimes, with all the give and take, communication, sharing of ideas, and learning that occur in such situations. The child who has acquired some abilities and pleasures in participating with peers is likely to continue to enjoy friendships, games, and special activities with other children. Parents who help in the early years are contributing to the child's development in this important area.

ATTITUDES RELATED TO LEARNING

Children's feelings about learning, persisting, accepting instruction, and using resources are developed, in part, through experiences in the home. The infant who tries to locate a noise, the toddler who tries to take apart toys, and the preschooler who insists on having new books read to him are all demonstrating positive attitudes toward learning. Parents who respond by expressing interest, enthusiasm, and praise, or who provide new ideas or assistance in getting around obstacles, are helping the child to acquire an appetite for learning. This approach to children's investigation, curiosities, or persistent questions is sometimes hard on families and not always easy to maintain. Exploring about the house can create problems for everyone in the family, and the child in the classroom whose interests are different from others is a challenge to a teacher. For the most part, however, a curious, inquisitive attitude enables children to learn throughout childhood.

Interest in Learning

Children who are interested in learning new things and understanding the materials and activities around them are motivated learners. They are the children who find learning enjoyable, who initiate activities, and who ask questions and are willing to investigate what they do not know. Such children demonstrate an interest, drive, or motivation to learn and succeed. School tasks come relatively easy to them because their motivation is high. Families can help to create this kind of attitude through supportive responses to the child's developing skills. They provide answers to questions, show enthusiasm and praise successes, obtain needed books and materials, and help with difficult tasks. While children vary widely in their own approaches and adaptation to home and school learning opportunities, most youngsters can be expected to develop a solid interest in learning when family members support their curiosity and provide new activities. During the preschool period there is also a great deal more flexibility in the content and style that children can elect to learn. When the curriculum is more predetermined, as it is in later school years and in some homes, then children's interest in learning may decline and other motivators will need to be found. Parents and teachers can often share ideas about this and develop a plan for recapturing that child's interest.

Task Persistence

In the early years children differ a great deal in how they respond to an assigned or self-selected task. Once their motivation is clear and their attention focused, the challenge of the "work" involved in seeking out and completing a given activity may be embraced or rejected. Toddlers, for example, are often observed flitting from one task to another without completing any one of them. Preschoolers may avoid activities that require slightly more advanced physical or intellectual skills, preferring less complex materials. Grade-school youngsters may give up too quickly in their reading or math groups when new operations are presented. Children who are able to persist and who select and enjoy tasks tend to feel satisfied with them and willing to take on new school experiences. In the home setting, mothers and fathers help to develop this attitude by keeping children focused on what they are doing, demonstrating interest in the outcomes of their activities, following up on unfinished tasks, and modeling persistence themselves, even in the face of minor frustrations. For some children who may have an easy-going temperament or enjoy reaching an end product, task persistence is relatively easy to maintain. For others, parents and teachers may need to seek solutions that minimize distraction and rejection and maximize attention and persistence.

Learning from Others

Just as young children create and expand their understanding through their own interests, exploration, and persistence, so they also learn from other people. Toddlers, for example, are famous for their attempts to imitate what they observe in their parents and friends. They repeat words and phrases, they follow parents about the house, they carefully copy the same banging of playdough observed in a friend. In short, they are willing and eager to accept the modeling provided by other persons, be they large or small. Such interest in the activities of others provides to the child an important learning mode. As toddlers reach the preschool years they are capable of more detailed duplications. Songs, fingerplays, stories, block buildings, pretend play, climbing, and tumbling can all be learned by watching other children and then attempting to do the very same. The process occurs at home, in school, and in the neighborhood. Parents tend to support enthusiastically the positive learning from others, especially when there is a clear teaching motive.

Children do not always immediately reproduce the learning. Parents may hear themselves repeatedly explaining and demonstrating, or pointing out the fine job that they expect. Toward the end of the preschool period, however, children often quite enjoy the one-to-one instruction they can obtain from an adult or another child, particularly when the child invites this and the person who assumes the educational role does not overwhelm or create pressure for immediate success. Accepting this kind of instruction from others, if extended to teacher-child relationships, can result in a good deal of later learning.

Of course, some behavioral learning that is modeled by others is not constructive or useful, or it is misconstrued by the child. Parents and teachers find some modeled behavior to be pollutive in its effect. The child who repeats unsuitable language uttered at home or on the street or the youngster who attempts a dangerous antic demonstrated by an older child are each likely to receive strong negatives from adults. But that is another facet of learning from others: Some of what is seen has to be rejected. Some learning helps while other learning hinders. Accepting instruction from others requires that the child contribute something as well. This could be an alteration, an embellishment, a shift in time and place, or an outright veto.

Finding Resources and Solutions

Some children find even simple problems overwhelming; some fail to use available resources that could help them resolve some difficulty. Other children seem to think, reason, and search for or otherwise find ways around any obstacles they encounter. As parents deal with the problems their children present to them, they may point out the routes available to resolving a difficulty. Their explanations help to create the attitude that resources and solutions can usually be discovered if you take the time to find them. A child who has that kind of approach to experience is likely to learn a great deal more about everything she does. Initially, working in this way with a young child requires much in the way of time, patience, and creativity from family members. A child who is in distress, for example, has to be calmed and the problem communicated, sometimes requiring detective work from parents to determine the causes and potential solutions. Then the child's choices have to be outlined in simple language. The end result of this process, however, may very likely contribute to the development of a rational problem-solving approach and use of adult and other resources by the child in dealing with both social and learning problems.

SPECIAL CHALLENGES

The child-rearing activities of families give shape to the process of socialization, the development of positive attitudes, and the teaching of basic skills. In this way, parents help to lay important educational foundations for children. When these things are done well, child, family, and school are all pleased. There may be minor problems, temporary setbacks, some confusion about role responsibilities, and even some pattern of minimal versus greater success in particular areas. For the most part, however, the preceding descriptions outline the best that can be accomplished in the home setting.

In some families, however, there are special challenges—unique problems or promises—presented by the child or the parents, and these influence the child's education in the home. Children may demonstrate special talents or abilities, special learning difficulties, lack of interest and persistence, or a preference for particular activities outside of the parents' range of priorities and abilities. Families and homes may not be able to provide learning opportunities, and emotional supports may exert too much pressure or control, may be overburdened with economic or social problems, may be quite unaware of the child's interests or their own educational potential, or may elect to leave all learning responsibilities in the hands of teachers. Some problems occur in particular parent-child relationships. A temperamental mismatch between a parent and child may interfere with many attempts to create a comfortable learning environment. An overly anxious parent or youngster may make the other person reject opportunities for sharing. A tired, working parent and an active, sociable child may not be able to find the time to interact together. In all these situations, mothers, fathers, and children may find themselves especially challenged or handicapped. Extraordinary efforts may be required to meet such challenges. Examples of some of these outstanding efforts will be discussed here.

Children with Learning Problems

Whether a child is formally identified as having learning difficulties such as dyslexia or some degree of mental retardation, in the early years parents may discover they have to cope with the special challenges of working with this child at home. The youngster whose development moves along slowly in the early years is one example. The other is a child who demonstrates a marked imbalance in one area of growth or the other. The slow learner needs patient, sequenced, simplified instruction from parents and siblings. Extra precautions may need to be taken to avoid confusion and irrelevance in the youngster's accumulation of information. Special motivations such as praise during the child's attempts to accomplish something and some assurance of success often help. Parents who have worked with their slow children and who are able to accept and even love their special qualities soon learn the value of these strategies. If the child is not eligible for a special intervention program or if parents elect to use normal preschool programs in the early years, the family may assume extra teaching responsibilities for the youngster. Professionals may be able to help them to provide these learning experiences.

The child whose development is above the norm in one area and below the norm in the other also requires extra support and assistance from family members. Areas of need may be difficult to work with because the tendency is to admire and respond to strengths. The physically skillful youngster may wish to avoid activities that challenge weaker cognitive domains. The child with advanced language skills may ignore puzzles or creative activities. A child with outstanding preacademic skills whose social growth is lagging may begin to reject friends who want to play differently. Sometimes a child's weaknesses may be criticized without acknowledging his abilities in other areas. Family members may help to balance these difficulties when they become noticeable. Sometimes parents do this without realizing what is happening; for example, when their two and one half year old is not talking enough, they may institute measures such as more stories, questions, and table conversation. Again, if a child is attending school, teachers can often make specific recommendations.

Gifted and Talented Children

Families with children who show signs of special abilities and interests also tend to experience difficulties in providing an educational home environment. Such youngsters, contrary to popular myth, are not easily managed. They may be frustrated and socially immature. Their perceptions may often be at odds with others around them. There may be a pattern of isolation, impatience, and self-criticism. The projects and activities they choose to undertake may absorb them to the exclusion of other kinds of learning, and when their intellectual understanding exceeds their skill abilities it may be difficult for them to cope with the routine, rote tasks needed for dealing with reading, mathematics, and similar subjects. In the case of artistically talented children, a great many outside resources may have to be gathered to guide instruction and provide role models.

Parents who recognize special abilities and talents in their children often find themselves pulled in several directions. On the one hand, they make efforts to support the child's strength, even when the routes to this are confused; and they may witness a good deal of frustration as the child struggles with her successes and failures. On the other hand, they often have to find ways to motivate the youngster to attend to skill areas in which she is lacking. Gifted children may have relative delays in social and physical development, for example. At the preschool level, these children may refuse the robust playtimes enjoyed by their peers, preferring adults who can provide intellectual challenges. They may reject self-expressive activities because their products are not as mature as they wish them to be. Parents often need to search for appropriate playmates who can "keep up" with their youngster's continual ideas and inventions. Creatively talented children have similar needs for friends with comparable interests.

As their children attend preschool programs, parents of the gifted and talented may need to work closely with professionals to pinpoint the child's special needs. Most teachers wish to see youngsters develop a balanced set of skills. Some may find the very bright child to be disruptive or too much of a challenge. The special attention and planning that are needed in the families of handicapped children or slow learners may very well be needed in these families as well. Mothers and fathers may have derived useful methods with their gifted children during the years at home, and they tend to have abundant data about the child's abilities. These can be valuable resources for the teacher.

FAMILIES' RELATIONSHIPS TO SCHOOLS

As families fulfill their role in providing an educational home environment in the child's early years, the professionals in schools and early-childhood centers have parallel responsibilities. To build upon the foundation laid by parents, or to supplement this in areas not provided for at home, requires real knowledge of what has occurred and respect for the families' continuing role in helping their children. All teachers, at some point or another, rely upon parents to follow up, extend, or support their work with children. Such a relationship does not develop without some investment of time, energy, and respect on the part of the school. The specifics of establishing and maintaining mutually satisfactory parent-teacher and home-school relationships have been discussed at length in other chapters. Here it is important to emphasize that professionals should keep in mind all of the teaching and learning that occurs in families and use this knowledge in working with children and their parents.

From the point of view of the family, much of the responsibility for educational experiences shifts to the school when children enter first grade or when they attend full-day educational programs earlier. However, parents never relinquish all of the teaching role. In addition to transmitting the values supported by the family and helping the child learn skills and gather information that schools do not routinely handle, parents continue to provide an educational environment at home. Opportunities and materials, socialization skills, healthy learning attitudes, basic skills, and special challenges are part of the family experience throughout childhood and, for some, into adulthood. In addition, family members may directly support the school's learning curriculum in several ways.

Homework Recognition and Assistance

By far one of the most familiar and traditional roles of parents with school-aged children is that of checking homework. In the early years this may simply take the form of looking over the products children bring home from the program and, in some cases, adding to it or sending back to school additional drawings, printing, and the like that the youngster might attempt at home. The painting, clay sculpture, or Mother's Day gift may be recognized by parents as evidence of the child's involvement and progress in the program. Children often enjoy duplicating these projects with their families. At older ages, the products tend toward the academic. Some papers are finished at home, such as a drawing related to a story or a costume for a play. In the primary grades children's mastery of reading, writing, and mathematics may require a good deal of work brought home and returned to school. Not only do parents need to supervise this activity, correct mistakes, and occasionally teach methods for study, but they have to help children organize their homework time and make decisions about the quality of the work that is accomplished.

Participation in School Matters

Mothers and fathers contribute to the child's schooling by sharing their children's learning, their teachers' perceptions, and the school's projects. Almost every weekday evening parents may spend time listening to the child's descriptions of learning and social activities at school. This sharing enables them to keep track of the curriculum and the child's skills in working with peers in the school setting. The information they gain in this way is often quite extensive, especially if they are familiar with the classroom environment and the teachers' goals. Report cards and conferences with teachers also involve families in the child's education. These sharing sessions can be informative for parents and for teachers. The child's academic progress and behavior are examined with an eye toward making adjustments and delivering praise. Often parents' assistance is solicited for both the positives and negatives. Areas of doubt are explained, and parents may obtain information that helps at home.

Questions and Criticisms

One important role played by parents that is seldom appreciated for its potential to help children is that of asking hard questions about the child's education in the school setting. The issues that arise might include slow progress through a curriculum, superficial or imbalanced treatment of a subject, too much or too little practice or repetition, poor grades in areas of known ability, questionable marking systems, instructional groupings based on inappropriate criteria, overly large class sizes, patterns of confusion on homework assignments, and unrealistic goals. Most teachers and administrators are not comfortable with these issues, but they can be very significant for particular children and families. Open, honest, and respectful questioning and even criticism are part of the parents' continuing responsibility in working with schools to help their children receive a good education.

Resources

To support the child's education fully, parents may need to obtain special resources for their children. In the early years this may include sending empty grocery containers to school for a unit on the supermarket, or gathering leaves for a fall collage. In kindergarten and first grade, parents may need to purchase a variety of easy reading books, alphabet games, or counting toys. In the primary grades, the child might need frequent trips to the library for resource books, extra paint and paper for posters, or parental assistance in developing skills in a particular sport or gathering materials for a long-term hobby. The resources family members can obtain for children can influence significantly the quality of their school learning. These aids and tools may very well provide the extra information and understanding needed to master a concept, skill, or task fully.

SUMMARY

To summarize this chapter on families and the child's education, it can be said that mothers and fathers launch and help to maintain their children's learning careers from infancy through the early primary grades. They do this in a variety of ways, covering many important attitudes and curriculum areas. These are presented in Table 10. The challenge to the early childhood and elementary teacher is to build upon these specific learning in the child and to continue to involve the family in clearly educational activities.

PROGRAM SUGGESTIONS

1. Using the ideas from studies of the home environment, have parents examine their own experiences with their children for a one-week period. Discuss their findings.

Table 10
Parents' Contributions to Children's Education

Areas	Parents' Contributions
ATTITUDES	The care and handling of children's needs
	The nurturance of developmental competence
	The management of the home and family
	The growth of self-confidence
	An interest in learning
	Persistence in completing tasks
	Interest in learning from others
SKILLS	Language structure and use
	Memory and recall
	Emotional control and redirection
	Self-management and independence
	Logic and counting
	Prereading composite skills
	Inquiry and investigation
	Cultural expectations
	Creative processes
	Peer relationships
INFORMATION	Vocabulary and labels
	Ideas and concepts
	Books, stories, characters
	Natural events and substances
	History and family
	The locations of information
SCHOOL RELATIONSHIPS	Home-school assignments
	Participation in school activities
	Questions and criticisms
	School resources and support

2. Ask parents to select two basic skills that they value, from the eight areas presented early in this chapter, then have them list four specific activities they use with their children to build these skills.
3. Invite two teachers to discuss the activities they use to develop the socialization skills identified in this chapter.
4. Identify four parents whose children have both positive and negative attitudes toward learning in particular areas or subjects. Discuss ways in which these may have developed and are being handled.

5. Arrange a visit from an expert on helping children to complete and enjoy their homework.
6. Ask parents to identify special challenges and problems they experience in helping their children to learn. Be sure to include the potential conflict between the early teaching of academics and the child's need to develop a balanced competence.
7. Identify recent articles that are critical of public education and use these to lead a discussion of this role of parents and community members.
8. Ask parents to describe their best experiences and successes in handling the child's education at home and school during each developmental period. Develop a chart of these to demonstrate the value of the parents' activities.

References

Adcock, D., & Segal, M. *Two years old: Play and learning.* Rolling Hills Estates, CA: B. L. Winch and Associates, 1979.

Adler, A. *What life should mean to you.* Boston, MA: Little, Brown, 1931.

Allport, G. W. *Personality: A psychological interpretation.* New York: Holt, Rinehart and Winston, 1937.

Allport, G. W. Traits revisited. *American Psychologist,* 1966, *21*, 1–10.

Almy, M., & Genishi, C. *Ways of studying children,* rev. ed. New York: Teachers College Press, 1979.

Andrews, S. R., Blumenthal, J. M., Bache, W. C., & Weiner, G. *The New Orleans model: Parents as early childhood educators.* Paper presented at the biennial meeting of the Society for Research in Child Development, Denver, CO, 1975.

Apple, M. Economics and control in everyday school life. In M. Apple (Ed.) *Ideology and curriculum.* London: Routledge and Kegan Paul, 1979.

Arnstein, H. *The roots of love.* Indianapolis, IN: Bobbs Merrill, 1975.

Auerbach-Fink, S. Mothers' expectations of child care. *Young Children,* 1977, *32*, 13–21.

Auerbach, S. *Choosing child care.* New York: E. P. Dutton, 1981.

Axline, V. *Play therapy.* New York: Ballantine, 1978.

Babcock, D., & Keepers, T. *Raising kids O.K.* New York: Grove Press, 1976.

Badger, E. The infant stimulation/mother training project. In B. Caldwell & D. Stedman (Eds.) *Infant education: A guide to helping handicapped children in the first three years.* New York: Walker, 1977.

Bakker, C., & Bakker-Rabdau, M. *No trespassing: Explorations in human territoriality.* San Francisco, CA: Chandler and Sharp, 1973.

Baldwin, A. *Theories of child development.* New York: John Wiley, 1967.

Barker, R. C. *Ecological psychology.* Stanford, CA: Stanford University Press, 1968.

Becker, W. C. *Parents are teachers.* Champaign, IL: Research Press, 1971.

Bee, H. *The developing child.* New York: Harper & Row, 1975.

Beller, E. K. *Clinical process.* New York: Free Press, 1962.

Beller, E. K. Adult-child interaction and personalized day care. In E. Grotberg (Ed.) *Day care: Resources for decisions.* Washington, DC: Office of Economic Opportunity, 1972.

Beller, E. K. Early intervention programs. In J. Osofsky (Ed.) *Handbook of infant development*. New York: John Wiley, 1979.

Belsky, J., & Steinberg, L. The effects of day care: A critical review. *Child Development*, 1978, *49*, 929–949.

Berger, E. *Parents as partners in education: The school and home working together*. St. Louis, MO: C. V. Mosby Co., 1981.

Bigner, J. *Parent-child relations: An introduction to parenting*. New York: Macmillan, 1979.

Biller, H., & Meredith, D. *Father power*. New York: David McKay Co., 1974.

Blank, H., & Klig, S. The child and the school experience. In C. Kopp and J. Krakow (Eds.) *The child: Development in a social context*. Reading, MA: Addison-Wesley, 1982.

Bluma, A., Shearer, M., Frohman, A., & Hilliard, J. *Portage guide to early education*. Portage, WI: The Portage Project, CESA, 1976.

Boss, M. *Psychoanalysis and daseinsanalysis*. New York: Basic Books, 1963.

Bower, T. G. R. *A primer of infant development*. San Francisco, CA: W. H. Freeman, 1977.

Bradley, R., & Caldwell, B. Early home environment and changes in mental test performance in children six to thirty-six months. *Developmental Psychology*, 1976, *12*, 93–97.

Brazelton, T. B. *Infants and mothers: Differences in development*. New York: Delacorte Press, 1969.

Brazelton, T. B. *Toddlers and parents: A declaration of independence*. New York: Delacorte Press, 1976.

Brazelton, T. B. *On becoming a family*. New York: Merloyd Lawrence, 1981.

Briggs, D. *Your child's self-esteem: The key to his life*. Garden City, NY: Doubleday, 1970.

Bromwich, R. *Working with parents and infants: An interactional approach*. Baltimore, MD: University Park Press, 1981.

Bronfenbrenner, U. *Is early intervention effective?* Washington, DC: Office of Child Development, 1974.

Bronfenbrenner, U. Contexts of child rearing: Problems and prospects. *American Psychologist*, 1979, *34*, 844–850.

Brooks, J. *The process of parenting*. Palo Alto, CA: Mayfield, 1981.

Brown, B. (Ed.) *Found: Long-term gains from early intervention*. Boulder, CO: Westview Press, 1978.

Brutten, M., Richardson, S., & Mangel, C. *Something's wrong with my child*. New York: Harcourt Brace Jovanovich, 1973.

Caldwell, B. The inventory of home stimulation. Little Rock, AR: University of Arkansas, 1970.

Caldwell, B., & Stedman, D. (Eds.) *Infant education: A guide for helping the handicapped in the first three years*. New York: Walker, 1977.

Callahan, S. *Parenting: Principles and politics of parenthood*. Baltimore, MD: Penguin, 1974.

Caplan, F., & Caplan, T. *The power of play*. Garden City, NY: Andros, 1973.

Caplan, F., & Caplan, T. *The parenting advisor*. New York: Doubleday, 1976.

Carew, J. Experience and the development of intelligence at home and in day care. *Monographs of the Society for Research in Child Development*, 1980, *45*.

Carew, J., Chan, I., & Halfar, C. *Observing intelligence in young children.* Englewood Cliffs, NJ: Prentice-Hall, 1975.

Cataldo, C. The parent as the learner: Early childhood parent programs. *Educational Psychologist*, 1980, *15*, 172-186.

Cataldo, C. (Ed.) *Learning in the home.* Vols. 1 & 2. Early Childhood Research Center, SUNY at Buffalo, 1980-1981.

Cataldo, C. *Infant and toddler programs.* Reading, MA: Addison-Wesley, 1983.

Cataldo, C. Infant-toddler education: Blending the best approaches. *Young Children*, 1984, *39*, 25-32.

Cataldo, C., & Geismar, L. Preschoolers' views of parenting and the family. *Journal of Research and Development in Education*, 1983, *16*, 8-14.

Cataldo, C., & Salzer, R. Early childhood program benefits and middle-class families. *Child Study Journal*, 1982, *12*, 45-56.

Cazden, C. (Ed.) *Language in early childhood education.* Washington, DC: National Association for the Education of Young Children, 1977.

Chance, P. *Learning through play.* New York: Gardner Press, 1979.

Charlesworth, R. *Understanding child development.* Albany, NY: Delmar, 1983.

Chase, R., & Rubin, R. (Eds.) *The first wondrous year.* New York: Macmillan, 1979.

Child Care Information Exchange. Selecting a center: How parents decide. *CCIE*, 1982, 29-32.

Chomsky, N. *Aspects of the theory of syntax.* Cambridge, MA: MIT Press, 1965.

Church, J. *Understanding your child from birth to three.* New York: Random House, 1973.

Clarke-Stewart, A. Parent education in the 1970's. *Educational Evaluation and Policy Analysis*, 1981, *3*, 47-58.

Clarke-Stewart, A. *Daycare.* Cambridge, MA: Harvard University Press, 1982.

Cochran, M., & Brassard, J. Child development and personal social networks. *Child Development*, 1979, *50*, 601-616.

Cohen, D., & Stern, V. *Observing and recording the behavior of young children,* 2nd ed. New York: Teachers College Press, 1978.

Comer, J., & Poussaint, A. *Black child care: How to bring up a healthy black child in America.* New York: Simon and Schuster, 1975.

Croake, J., & Glover, K. A history and evaluation of parent education. *The Family Coordinator*, 1977, *26*, 151-158.

Crow, G. *Children at risk.* New York: Schocken Books, 1978.

Dale, P. *Language development: Structure and function.* Hinsdale, IL: Dryden Press, 1972.

Dinkmeyer, D., & McKay, G. *Systematic training for effective parenting.* Circle Pines, MN: American Guidance Service, 1976.

Dodson, F. *How to parent.* New York: Signet, 1970.

Dreikurs, R., & Grey, L. *A parent's guide to child discipline.* New York: Hawthorne Books, 1970.

Dreikurs, R., & Soltz, V. *Children: The challenge.* New York: Duell, Sloan & Pearce, 1964.

Dunn, J. *Distress and comfort.* Cambridge, MA: Harvard University Press, 1977.

Elkind, D. *A sympathetic understanding of the child: Birth to sixteen,* 2nd ed. Boston, MA: Allyn and Bacon, 1978.

Elkind, D. *The hurried child.* Reading, MA: Addison-Wesley, 1981.

Erikson, E. *Childhood and society.* New York: Norton, 1950.

Faber, A., & Mazlish, E. *Liberated parents: Liberated children.* New York: Avon, 1975.

Figley, C. R., & McCubbin, H. I. *Stress in the family: Coping with catastrophe.* Vol. II, New York: Brunner/Mazel, 1983.

Fowler, W. *Daycare and its effects on early development.* Toronto: The Ontario Institute for Studies in Education, 1978.

Fowler, W. *Infant and child care: a guide to education in group settings.* Boston, MA: Allyn and Bacon, 1980.

Fraiberg, S. *The magic years: Understanding and handling the problems of early childhood.* New York: Charles Scribner, 1968.

Fromm, E. *The sane society.* New York: Holt, Rinehart and Winston, 1955.

Galinsky, E. *Between generations: The six stages of parenthood.* New York: Times Books, 1981.

Galinsky, E., & Hooks, W. *The new extended family: Daycare that works.* Boston, MA: Houghton-Mifflin, 1977.

Gardner, R. *The parents' book about divorce.* Garden City, NY: Doubleday, 1977.

Gesell, A., Ilg, F., & Ames, L. *Infant and child in the culture of today: The guidance of development in home and nursery school.* rev. ed. New York: Harper & Row, 1974.

Giffin, M. Assessing infant and toddler development. In B. Weissbourd & J. Musick (Eds.) *Infants: Their social environments.* Washington, DC: National Association for the Education of Young Children, 1981.

Ginott, H. *Between parent and child: New solutions to old problems.* New York: Macmillan, 1968.

Golden, M., Rosebluth, L., Gross, M., Policare, H., Freeman, H., & Brownlee, E. *The New York City Infant Day Care Study.* New York: Mental and Health Research Association, 1978.

Gonzalez-Mena, J., & Widmeyer, D. *Infancy and caregiving.* Palo Alto, CA: Mayfield Pub. Co., 1980.

Goodson, B., & Hess, R. The effects of parent training programs on child performance and parent behavior. In B. Brown (Ed.) *Found: Long-term gains from early intervention.* Boulder, CO: Westview Press, 1978.

Goodwin, W., & Driscoll, L. *Handbook for measurement and evaluation in early childhood education.* San Francisco, CA: Jossey-Bass Publishers, 1980.

Gordon, A. K., & Klass, D. *They need to know: How to teach children about death.* Englewood Cliffs, NJ: Prentice-Hall, 1979.

Gordon, I. *The infant experience.* Columbus, OH: C. E. Merrill Pub. Co., 1975.

Gordon, I. Parenting, teaching and child development. *Young Children,* 1976, *31,* 173–183.

Gordon, I., Guinaugh, B., & Jester, R. The Florida parent education infant and toddler programs. In M. Day & R. Parker (Eds.) *The preschool in action* (2nd ed.). Boston, MA: Allyn & Bacon, 1977.

Gordon, I., Olmstead, R., Rubin, R., & True, J. How has Follow Through promoted parent involvement? *Young Children*, 1979, *34*, 49–53.

Gordon, T. *P.E.T. Parent effectiveness training: The tested new way to raise responsible children.* New York: Peter H. Wyden Inc., 1970.

Gray, S., & Wandersman, L. The methodology of home-based intervention studies. *Child Development*, 1980, *51*, 993–1009.

Green, M. *First-aid handbook for childhood emergencies.* New York: Bantam Books, 1977.

Greenspan, S. *Psychopathology and adaptation in infancy and early childhood.* New York: International Universities Press, 1981.

Grollman, E. *Talking about death: A dialogue between parent and child.* Boston, MA: Beacon Press, 1970.

Grollman, E. *Talking with families about divorce.* Pittsburgh, PA: Family Communication Inc., 1981.

Guilford, J. P. *The nature of human intelligence.* New York: McGraw-Hill, 1967.

Hall, C. S., & Lindzey, G. *Introduction to theories of personality.* New York: John Wiley, 1985.

Hall, C. S., & Lindzey, S. *Theories of personality*, 3rd ed. New York: John Wiley, 1985.

Harris, T. *I'm O.K.–You're O.K.: A practical guide to transactional analysis.* New York: Harper & Row, 1969.

Hartup, W. Peer relations. In C. Kopp & J. Krakow (Eds.) *The child: development in a social context.* Reading, MA: Addison-Wesley, 1982.

Heatherington, E., & Parke, R. *Child psychology.* New York: McGraw-Hill, 1975.

Heber, R., & Garber, H. The Milwaukee project: A study of the use of family intervention to prevent cultural-family retardation. In B. Z. Friedlander, G. M. Sterritt & G. E. Kirk (Eds.) *Exceptional infant: Assessment and intervention (Vol. 3).* New York: Brunner/Mazel, 1975.

Heffner, E. *Mothering.* Garden City, NY: Doubleday, 1978.

Hess, R., Bloch, M., Costello, J., Knowles, R., & Largay, D. Parent involvement in early education. In E. Grotberg (Ed.) *Day care: Resources for decisions.* Washington, DC: Office of Economic Opportunity, 1971.

Honig, A. *Parent involvement in early childhood education.* Washington, DC: National Association for the Education of Young Children, 1975.

Honig, A., & Lally, R. *Infant caregiving: A design for training*, 2nd ed. Syracuse, NY: Syracuse University Press, 1981.

Horney, K. *Our inner conflicts.* New York: Norton, 1945.

Huntington, D. Supportive programs for infants and parents. In J. Osofsky (Ed.) *Handbook of infant development.* New York: John Wiley, 1979.

Johnson, D. L., Kahn, A. J., & Leler, H. *Final report: Houston parent child development center.* Houston, TX: University of Houston, 1976.

Jung, C. G. *Analytical psychology: Its theory and practice.* New York: Pantheon Books, 1968.

Kagan, J., Kearsley, R., & Zelazo, P. *Infancy: Its place in human development.* Cambridge, MA: Harvard University Press, 1978.

Karnes, M. *Small wonder! Activities for baby's first eighteen months.* Circle Pines, MN: American Guidance Service, 1979.

Katz, L. Mothering and teaching—some significant distinctions. In L. Katz (Ed.) *Current topics in early childhood education Vol. III.* Norwood, NJ: Ablex, 1981.

Kempe, R., & Kempe, C. *Child abuse.* Cambridge, MA: Harvard University Press, 1978.

Keniston, K., and the Carnegie Council on Children. *All our children: The American family under pressure.* New York: Harcourt Brace Jovanovich, 1977.

Kennedy Foundation. *Let's-play-to-grow.* Washington, DC: Kennedy Foundation, 1977.

Kiester, E., & Kiester, S. *The Better Homes and Gardens new babybook.* Des Moines, IA: Meredith, 1979.

Kiley, D. *Nobody said it would be easy: Raising responsible kids and keeping kids out of trouble.* New York: Harper & Row, 1978.

Kilmer, S. Infant-toddler group care: A review of research. In L. Katz (Ed.) *Current topics in early childhood education Vol. 1.* Norwood, NJ: Ablex, 1979.

King, N. Play in the workplace. In M. Apple & L. Weis (Eds.) *Ideology and practice in schooling.* Philadelphia, PA: Temple University Press, 1983.

Koch, J. *Total baby development.* New York: Wyden Books, 1976.

Lamb, M. (Ed.) *The role of the father in child development.* New York: John Wiley, 1976.

Lamberth, J., Rappaport, H., & Rappaport, M. *Personality: An introduction.* New York: Alfred Knopf, 1982.

Laosa, L. The sociocultural context of evaluation. In B. Spodek (Ed.) *Handbook of research in early childhood education.* New York: The Free Press, 1982.

Lazar, I., Hubbell, V., Murray, H., Rosche, M., & Royce, J. *The persistence of preschool effects.* Washington, DC: Department of Health, Education and Welfare, 1977.

Leichter, H. (Ed.) *The family as educator.* New York: Teachers College Press, 1975.

LeShan, E. *Natural parenthood: Raising your child without a script.* New York: New American Library, Signet Books, 1970.

Levenstein, P. The mother-child home program. In M. Day & R. Parker (Eds.) *The preschool in action* (2nd ed.). Boston, MA: Allyn & Bacon, 1977.

Lewin, K. *Field theory in social science: Selected theoretical papers* (*D. Cartwright, ed.*). New York: Harper & Row, 1951.

Lightfoot, S. *Worlds apart: Relationships between families and schools.* New York: Basic Books, 1978.

Lillie, D., Trohanis, L., & Goin, W. (Eds.) *Teaching parents to teach: A guide for working with the special child.* New York: Walker, 1977.

Lorenzo, L., & Lorenzo, R. *Total child care.* New York: Doubleday, 1982.

Margolin, I. *Governor's conference on families.* Albany, NY: Governor's Office, 1980.

Maslow, A. H. *Motivation and personality* (2nd ed.). New York: Harper & Row, 1970.

Maslow, A. H. *The farther reaches of the human mind.* New York: Viking, 1971.

McClinton, B., & Meier, B. *Beginnings: Psychology of early childhood.* St. Louis: C. V. Mosby, 1978.

McGillicuddy-DeLisi, A., & Sigel, I. Parental constructs of child development, teaching strategies, and children's development. In J. Joffe & L. Bond (Eds.) *Facilitating infant and early childhood development.* Hanover, NH: University Press of New England, 1983.

Mead, D. *Six approaches to child rearing: Models from psychological theory.* Provo, UT: Brigham Young University Press, 1976.

Moody, E. *Growing up on television.* New York: Times Books, 1980.

Morrison, G. *Parent involvement in the home, school and community.* Columbus, OH: Charles Merrill, 1978.

Murray, H. A. *Some basic psychological assumptions and conceptions.* Dialectica, 1951, *5*, 266–292.

Mussen, P., & Eisenberg-Berg, N. *Roots of caring, sharing and helping: The development of prosocial behavior in children.* San Francisco, CA: W. H. Freeman, 1977.

Nash, J. *Developmental psychology: A psychological approach.* Englewood Cliffs, NJ: Prentice-Hall, 1970.

Nedler, S., & McAfee, O. *Working with parents: Guidelines for early childhood and elementary teachers.* Belmont, CA: Wadsworth, 1979.

Neugarten, B., & Weinstein, K. The changing American grandparent. *Journal of Marriage and the Family,* 1964, *26*, 199–206.

Osofsky, J. *Handbook of infant development.* New York: John Wiley, 1979.

Painter, G. *Teach your baby.* New York: Simon and Schuster, 1971.

Patterson, G., & Gullion, N. *Living with children: New methods for parents and teachers.* Champaign, IL: Research Press, 1969.

Peters, D., & Sibbison, B. Considerations in the assessment of day care needs. *Child Care Quarterly,* 1974, *3*, 166–176.

Piaget, J. Piaget's theory. In P. H. Mussen (Ed.) *Carmichael's manual of child psychology* (Vol. 1). New York: John Wiley, 1970, 703–732.

Piaget, J., & Inhelder, B. *The psychology of the child.* New York: Basic Books, 1969.

Pickarts, E., & Fargo, J. *Parent education: Toward parental competence.* Norwalk, CT: Appleton-Century-Crofts, 1971.

Porter, C. *Voices from the preschool: Perspectives of early childhood educators.* Buffalo, NY: State University, 1980.

Powell, D. The interpersonal relationship between parents and caregivers in day care settings. *American Journal of Orthopsychiatry,* 1978, *48*, 680–689.

Powell, M. *Assessment and management of developmental changes and problems in children,* 2nd ed. St. Louis, MO: C. V. Mosby, 1981.

Rabin, A. Motivation for parenthood. *Journal of Projective Techniques,* 1965, *29*, 405–411.

Ramey, C., Holmberg, M., Sparling, J., & Collier, A. An introduction to the Carolina Abcedarian project. In B. Caldwell & D. Stedman (Eds.) *Infant education: A guide to helping handicapped children in the first three years.* New York: Walker, 1977.

Rapoport, R., Rapoport, R., & Strelitz, Z. *Fathers, mothers and society: Perspectives on parenting.* New York: Vintage Books, 1980.

Read, K., & Patterson, J. *The nursery school and kindergarten.* New York: Holt, Rinehart and Winston, 1980.

Robertson, J. Grandparenthood: A study of role conceptions. *Journal of Marriage and the Family,* 1977, *39,* 165–174.

Rogers, C. R. *On becoming a person: A therapist's view of psychotherapy* (2nd ed.). Boston, MA: Houghton Mifflin, 1970.

Rosenthal, R., & Jacobsen, L. The disadvantaged child. In J. Frost & G. Hawkes (Eds.) *The disadvantaged child: Issues and innovations,* 2nd ed. New York: Houghton Mifflin, 1970.

Roupp, R., Travers, J., Glantz, F., & Coelen, C. *Children at the center: Final report.* Cambridge, MA: Abt Associates, 1979.

Rubin, K., & Ross, H. (Eds.) *Peer relationships and social skills in childhood.* New York: Springer-Verlag, 1982.

Rubin, Z. *Children's friendships.* Cambridge, MA: Harvard University Press, 1980.

Rutherford, R., & Edgar, E. *Teachers and parents: A guide to interaction and cooperation.* Boston, MA: Allyn & Bacon, 1979.

Rutter, M. *Maternal deprivation reassessed,* 2nd ed. Baltimore, MD: Penguin Books, 1981.

Rynders, H., & Horrobin, J. Project EDGE: The University of Minnesota's communication stimulation program for Down's syndrome infants. In B. Friedlander, G. Sterritt, & G. Kirk (Eds.) *Exceptional infant: Assessment and intervention (Vol. 3).* New York: Brunner/Mazel, 1975.

Salk, L., & Kramer, R. *How to raise a human being.* New York: Random House, 1969.

Samuels, M., & Samuels, N. *Well baby book.* New York: Simon and Schuster, 1979.

Schaffer, H. R. *Mothering.* Cambridge, MA: Harvard University Press, 1977.

Shapiro, E. Playing together. In Bank Street College of Education, *The pleasure of their company.* Radnor, PA: Chilton, 1981.

Sheldon, W. H. *The varieties of human physique.* New York: Harper & Row, 1940.

Sheldon, W. H., & Stevens, S. S. *The varieties of temperament.* New York: Harper & Row, 1942.

Sigel, I., Secrist, A., & Forman, G. Psychoeducational intervention beginning at age two: Reflections and outcomes. In J. Stanley (Ed.), 2nd edition, *Compensatory education for children ages two to eight.* Baltimore, MD: Johns Hopkins University Press, 1972.

Simon, S., Leland, W., Howe, H., & Kinschenbaum, H. *Values clarification: A handbook of practical strategies for teachers and students.* New York: Hart, 1972.

Singer, D., Singer, J., & Zuckerman, D. *Teaching television: How to use TV to your child's advantage.* New York: Dial Press, 1981.

Singer, R., & Singer, A. *Psychological development in children.* Philadelphia, PA: W. B. Saunders, 1969.

Skinner, B. F. *Science and human behavior.* New York: Macmillan, 1953.

Skinner, B. F. *Verbal behavior.* New York: Appleton-Century Crofts, 1957.

Smart, M., & Smart, L. *Families: Developing relationships.* New York: Macmillan, 1976.

Sparling, J., & Lewis, I. *Infant learning games.* New York: Walker, 1979.

Sparling, J., Lowman, B., Lewis, I., & Bartel, J. *What parents say about their information needs.* Chapel Hill, NC: Frank Porter Graham Child Development Center, 1978.

Spock, B. *Baby and child care.* New York: Simon and Schuster, 1976.

Sponseller, D. Play and early education. In B. Spodek (Ed.) *Handbook of research in early childhood education.* New York: The Free Press, 1982.

Stein, S. *New parents' guide to early learning.* New York: New American Library, 1976.

Stevens, J. Parent education programs: What determines effectiveness: *Young Children,* 1978, *33,* 59–65.

Stevens, J. The National Day Care Home Study: Family day care in the United States. *Young Children,* 1982, *37,* 59–66.

Stevens, J. & Matthews, M. *Mother/child, father/child relationships.* Washington, DC: National Association for the Education of Young Children, 1978.

Sullivan, H. S. *The interpersonal theory of psychiatry.* New York: Norton, 1953.

Sutton-Smith, B., & Rosenberg, B. *The sibling.* New York: Holt, Rinehart and Winston, 1970.

Sutton-Smith, B., & Sutton-Smith, S. *How to play with your baby.* New York: Hawthorn, 1974.

Swan, S. *Home made baby toys.* Boston, MA: Houghton Mifflin, 1977.

Taylor, K. *Parents and children learn together,* 3rd ed. New York: Teachers College Press, 1981.

Thomas, A., Chess, S., & Birch, H. G. *Temperament and behavior disorders in children.* New York: New York University Press, 1968.

Tjossem, T. (Ed.) *Intervention strategies for high risk infants and young children.* Baltimore, MD: University Park Press, 1976.

Tough, J. *Listening to children talking.* London: Ward Lock Educational, 1976.

Turnbull, A., & Turnbull, R. *Parents speak out.* Columbus, OH: Charles Merrill, 1978.

U.S. Department of Health and Human Services. *A parent's guide to day care.* Washington, DC: 1980.

Wallerstein, J. S. *Surviving the breakup: How parents and children cope with divorce.* New York: Basic Books, 1980.

Watrin, R., & Furfey, P. *Learning activities for the young preschool child.* New York: Van Nostrand, 1978.

Weber, C. U., Foster, P. W., & Weikart, D. P. *An economic analysis of the Ypsilanti Perry Preschool Project.* Ypsilanti, MI: High/Scope Educational Resources Foundation, 1978.

Weissbourd, B. The family support movement: Greater than the sum of its parts. *Zero to Three*, 1983, 4(1), 8–10.

Weissbourd, B., & Musick, J. S. (Eds.) *Infants: Their social environments.* Washington, DC: National Association for the Education of Young Children, 1981.

Wesley, F. *Childrearing psychology.* New York: Behavioral Publications, 1971.

Westin, J. *The coming parent revolution.* Chicago, IL: Rand McNally, 1981.

White, B. *The first three years of life.* Englewood Cliffs, NJ: Prentice-Hall, 1975.

White, B., & Watts, J. *Experience and environment: Major influences on the development of the young child.* Englewood Cliffs, NJ: Prentice-Hall, 1973.

White, B. L. *The Harvard preschool project.* Paper presented at the biennial meeting of the Society for Research in Child Development, Santa Monica, CA, 1969.

Willemsen, E. *Understanding infancy.* San Francisco, CA: W. H. Freeman, 1979.

Willis, A., & Riccuiti, H. *A good beginning for babies.* Washington, DC: National Association for the Education of Young Children, 1975.

Wolfgang, C. *Helping aggressive and passive preschoolers through play.* Columbus, OH: Charles Merrill, 1977.

Zigler, E., & Valentine, J. (Eds.) *Project Headstart: A legacy of the war on poverty.* New York: Free Press, 1979.

Index

Abcedarian Project, 88
Acceptance, self-esteem and, 81, 206
Accommodation, definition of, 143
Activities management in parenting, 39–41
Adaptation and mutuality approach, 81
Adcock, D., 83
Adler, A., 211
Adult development, 55–56
Adult relationships, 42–44, 53–57
Adult roles in play, 161–166
Aggression, expression of, 221–222
Allport, G. W., 213–214
Andrews, S. R., 92
Anger, children's expression of, 221–222
Apple, M., 151, 152
Applied behavior analysis, 77, 193–194
Assertiveness training, 79, 194–195
Assimilation, definition of, 142
Attachment, children's need for, 203–205
Auerbach, S., 135, 136–137
Authority in behavior control, 193–195

Babcock, D., 81, 196
Badger, E., 88
Bakker, C., 79, 194
Barker, R. G., 212–213
Basic skills learned at home, 236–241
Becker, W. C., 77, 193
Behavior, children's, 172–200
  as communication, 173–174
  and conflict, 176–178
  and development, 178–179
  and discipline, 180–189, 198 *tab.*
  distinguishing feelings from, 184–185
  and distress, 176–178
  management of, *see* Behavior
    management
  and social skills, 174–175
Behavior control, 77, 193–195
Behavior management, 36–37, 77, 189–198,
  199 *tab.*

Behavior-oriented approaches, 76–79
Berger, E., 69
Bigner, J., 29, 30
Biller, H., 29
Birth order, 46, 216–217
Blank, H., 65–66, 69
Blended families, 147, 148
Bluma, A., 87
Bonding process, parent-child, 203–205
Boss, M., 213
Brazelton, T. B., 81
Briggs, D., 81, 197
Bromwich's Interaction Program, 89
Brookline Project, 85
Brooks, J., 76, 195

Caldwell, B., 233–234
Cantalician Family-Infant Program, 91
Career changes in families, 55
Caplan, F., 74, 76, 82, 152, 197
Carew, J., 234
Cataldo, C., 45, 144, 152
Chance, P., 150–151, 154
Child(ren)
  behavior, *see* Behavior
  benefits for, from parent-education
    program, 15–17, 16 *tab.*
  care of, *see* Child care
  emotional needs of, *see* Children's
    emotional well-being
  parenting skills needed, *see* Parenting
    skills
  peers of, 45–48, 57–63
  personality development of, *see*
    Personality development
  social needs of, *see* Social skills learning
  in triad with family and professionals,
    20–25
  value acquisition by, 28, 35–36
Child abuse, 44, 149

Child assessments in parent-education program, 108
Child care
developmental patterns, 137–142
developmental problems, 143–146
developmental transitions, 142–143
within the family and center, 127–133
family crises and uniqueness, 147–149
family needs and concerns, 28–29, 34–35, 136–137
food and nutrition, 53, 74–76, 129
health and fitness, 28, 34–35, 74–76, 129–130
safety and shelter, 127–129
selecting supplementary care arrangements, 135–136
self-care by children, 130–131
self-protection by children, 131–132
special place of child in the family, 132–133
supplementary, 133–137
Child care providers, interaction with families, 68–69; *see also* Day care services; Schools
Child developmental patterns, 137–142
Child developmental problems, 143–146
Child developmental transitions, 142–143
Child development approaches to child rearing, 82–84
Child development assessment scales, 138
Child health care, 28, 34–35, 74–76, 129–130
Child nutrition, 53, 74–76, 129
Child-proofing the home, 34, 36, 128
Child-rearing approaches, 73–84
acceptance and esteem, 81
adaptation and mutuality, 81
assertiveness, 79, 194–195
behavior management and control, 36, 77, 189–198
behavior-oriented approaches, 76–79
child development, 82–84
child study information, 74
developmental curriculum, 83–84
developmental guidance, 83
health and nutrition information, 74–76
interpersonal communication, 80
limit setting, 78–79, 186–187
parent-family development, 84
personality and mental health approaches, 79–81
personal support, 79–80
play participation, 82–84
problem-solving, 76–77, 188, 192

references for, 75 *tab.*
special family interactions, 76, 147–149
theory information, 76
values and morality, 80–81, 192–193
Children's coops, 93
Children's education within the family, 28–29, 54, 232–254
attitudes related to learning, 245–247
basic skills, learning, 236–241
educational home environment, 233–236
families' relationship to schools, 250–252
parents' contributions, 253 *tab.*
social skills, learning, 241–244
special challenges, 147–150
Children's emotional well-being, 37–39, 53, 201–206
attachment and security, 203–205
expression and management of feelings by children, 219–229
self-esteem and security, 205–206
showing love, 202–203
Children's peer relations, 45–48, 57–63
characteristics of, 58–59, 58 *tab.*
dominance patterns in, 62
expected benefits of, 58 *tab.*, 59–61
and moral development, 61
potential problems in, 58 *tab.*, 62–63
Children's personality development, *see* Personality development
Children's play, *see* Play
Children's rights, 149–150
Child sexual abuse, 149
Child Study Association, 4
Church, J., 81
Clarke-Stewart, A., 135, 136–137
Classroom participation programs in parent education, 111 *tab.*, 116–118
Classroom settings, influence of, 66–68, 179
Cochran, M., 56
Comfort, expression of, 224
Communication, 173–174, 204
Communications approach to behavior management, 191–192
Community resources, family use of, 41–42
Confidence learned at home, 242
Conflict, children's behavior and, 176–178
Conflict resolution approach, 188, 192
Counseling models for parent education, 14–15, 89–90, 111 *tab.*, 118–119
Counting learned at home, 238
Creativity learned at home, 241
Crow, G., 144
Cultural influences, 206, 218, 241

Daycare services, 10–11, 33, 37, 68–69, 133–135
family needs and concerns, 136–137
selecting, 135–136
Decision-making approach, 192–193
Dependency, expression of, 221
Developmental curriculum approach to child rearing, 83–84
Developmental guidance approach to child rearing, 83
Developmental psychologists, 8
Dinkmeyer, D., 80, 191, 194
Disadvantaged children, 5, 147[1]
Discipline, 180–189, 198 tab.
accepting uneven results, 185
and conflict resolution, 188
consistency in, 183–184
definition of, 180
and development of social skills, 187
dilemmas in, 183–185
distinguishing feelings from behavior, 184–185
to encourage responsibility and fairness, 189
flexibility in, 183–184
issues related to children and adults, 180–183
positive and negative feelings, expressing, 184
primary goals of, 185–186
and problem solving, 188
reasons for, 185–189
and self-esteem, 206
and setting limits, 186–187
to teach consequences of behavior, 188–189
Distress, behavior and, 176–178, 220
Divorce rates, 43
Dodson, F., 74, 76
Dreikurs, R., 78, 194

Educational needs management as parenting skill, 39–41
Educational skills training models for parent education, 86–87
Education networks, 67–68; see also Schools
Effective Parenting Information for Children (EPIC), 86
Elkind, D., 79, 83, 175
Emotions
and behavior management, 195–197
learning control at home, 243–244

Environmental factors in child's behavior, 179–180
Erikson, E., 38, 210, 211–212
Existential theory, 213
Extended family, 27

Faber, A., 195
Family
children's peers, 57–63
definitions of, 26
grandparents, 63–65
parents' peers, 52–57
schools and, 65–71, 250–252
self-sufficiency of, expectation of, 50–51
and society, 49–52
socioeconomic status, 49–50, 66, 215–216
triad with child and professionals, 20–25
Family crises, child care/development and, 147–149
Family Focus, 92
Family functions, 28–29
Family organization, 26–29
Family relationships, 42–48
child-child, 45–48; see also Children's peer relations; Sibling relations
parent-child, 44–45
parent-parent, 42–44
Family roles, 28
Family types, 27–28, 147–148
Fear, expression of, 220–221
Feelings, 184, 219–229
vs. behavior, 184–185
role of language in, 226–229
Field-environmental theory of personality, 212–213
First-aid training, 129
First grader (6–7-year-old), development of, 141, 146
Florida Parent-Education Program, 87
Footsteps (program), 86
Foster homes, 28, 147
Fraiberg, S., 79
Frank Porter Graham Child Development Center (Univ. of N. Carolina), 88
Freud, S., 209–210, 212
Fromm, E., 211

Galinsky, E., 56, 84
General parent-education programs, 7–9
General parent-support programs, 13–14
Gesell, A., 83, 174, 175
Gifted children, 249–250
Ginott, H., 78, 80, 195

Gordon, I., 87
Gordon, T., 76, 83, 191
Grandparents, 43, 63–65
Green, M., 129
Greenspan, S., 144
Group programs in parent education, 109,
   110 *tab.*, 112–113, 122
Guilford, J. P., 209

Handicapped-child families, 147
Handicapped Children's Early Education
   Programs, 90
Happiness, expression of, 224–225
Hartup, W., 45, 47, 60
Head Start, 10, 85
Health concerns with children, 28, 74–76,
   129–130
Heatherington, E., 68
Heber, R., 90
Hess, R., 45
High-risk for developmental difficulties, 6,
   10, 50
Hi-Scope programs, 88–89
History learned at home, 241
Home-visiting programs for parent
   education, 110 *tab.*, 114–115
Homework, parents' role in, 251
Horney, K., 211
Hurt, expression of, 222

Ideographic theory of personality, 213–214
Imagination learned at home, 241
Independence, self-esteem and, 206
Infant (to 1 year), development of, 139, 145
Information learned at home, 237–238
Inquiry learned at home, 240
Intelligence in personality, 217
Interpersonal communication approach, 80
Intrafamily behavior management, 36–37

Jealousy, expression of, 222–223
Johnson, D. L., 92
Jung, C. G., 210, 212

Karnes, M., 83, 197
Katz, L., 29
Keniston, K., 51
Kennedy Foundation, 83, 91
Kiley, D., 79, 194
Kindergarten child (5–6-year-old),
   development of, 140–141, 146
Koch, J., 83

Language
   and feelings, 226–229
   learned at home, 237
Laosa, L., 45
Learning-disabled child, 248–249
Learning-oriented programs, 8
Leichter, H., 29, 47, 235
LeShan, E., 79, 81
Levenstein, P., 86
Lewin, K., 212–13
Life changes for parents, 55
Lightfoot, S., 66
Limit-setting approach, 78–79, 186–187
Logical consequences approach, 77–78, 194
Logic learned at home, 238
Love, expression of, 202–203, 223–224

Maslow, A. H., 196, 213
Mastery, expression of, 225–226
Mead, D., 76
Media, 8, 155 *tab.*, 160–161, 219
Memory training at home, 237–238
Mental health approaches to child rearing,
   79–81
Mental health education resources, 8
Milwaukee Project, The, 90
Modeling
   in children's peer relations, 60–61, 63
   as parenting skill, 35–36, 246–247
Models, *see* Child-rearing approaches; *see*
   Parent-education program models
Morphological theory of personality, 208
Mothers' Project, The, 89–90
Motivated learning, instilling, 245
Murray, H. A., 213
Mussen, P., 80

Nedler, S., 69
Needs, children's expression of, 205–206
Neo-Freudian theory of personality, 211
Neugarten, B., 63–64
New Talker (2–3-year-old), development of,
   139, 145
Nuclear family, 27
Nursery schools in parent-education
   programs, 10–12
Nutrition of children, 53, 74–76, 129

Painter, G., 83
Parent(s)
   and behavior management, 189–198, 199
   tab.

benefits to, from parent-education
  programs, 15, 16 *tab.*, 18
child care concerns, *see* Child care
and children's behavior, 172–180
disciplining children, 180–189, 198 *tab.*
evaluation of program progress, 106–107
as home-school liaison, 12–13
loss of interest in program, 121
personal development of, 44, 55–56
perspectives and roles in education
  program, 103–104
as policy makers and advisors, 11–12
recruitment and involvement in program,
  100–103
showing love, 202–203
time with children, adequate, 54
Parent advisory groups, 102
Parent-child centers, 92–93
Parent-child relations, 35–39, 44–45
  see also Parenting skills
Parent cooperatives, 10, 11
Parent counseling programs, 14–15, 89–90,
  111 *tab.*, 118–119
Parent education
  current trends in, 5–7
  definition of, 3–4
  effectiveness of, 15–21
  history of, 3–7
Parent-education program(s)
  classroom participation programs, 111
    tab., 116–118
  current beliefs about, 19–20
  development of, 3–25
  establishing purposes of, 96–97
  follow-through, lack of, 122–123
  formats, 109–119, 110–111 *tab.*
  general, 7–9
  general parent-support programs, 13–14
  group programs, 109, 110 *tab.*, 112–113
  home-visiting programs, 110 *tab.*, 114–115
  impact study of, 108
  parent counseling, 14–15, 111 *tab.*,
    118–119
  parent participation/observation, 10–11
  parent roles in, 5–6, 103–104, 120
  parents as home-school liaison, 12–13
  parents as policy makers, 11–12
  parent training, 9–10
  privacy concerns in, 121–122
  problems in, 119–123
  procedures for, 95–108
  progress and evaluation in, 105–108

rapport and respect in, 104–105
recruitment and involvement of parents,
  100–103, 120
research on, 15–19, 16 *tab.*
staff of, 97–100, 105–107, 120–121
types of, 7–15
Parent-education program models, 84–94
  counseling and rehabilitation, 89–90
  educational skills training, 86–87
  general information and involvement,
    85–86
  problem prevention, 87–89
  selecting, 96–97
  social support for parents, 92–93
  special education, 90–91
Parent-education program staff, 97–100,
  105–107, 120–121
Parent Effectiveness Training (PET), 77,
  191–192
Parent-family development approach, 84
Parenting, developmental stages in, 55–56
Parenting role, 29–31, 51–52
Parenting skills, 32–42
  areas of, 33 *tab.*
  attention to emotional-social needs,
    37–39
  learning from peers, 52–54
  management of activities and educational
    needs, 39–41
  management of intrafamily behavior,
    36–37
  modeling, 35–36
  overview of, 32–33
  providing basic care and protection,
    34–35
  use of community resources, 41–42
Parenting style, influence of, 218
Parent interviews, 107
Parent meetings, 70–71, 101
Parent networks, 56–57, 101
Parent participation/observation, 10–11
Parent report forms, 107
Parents' peers, 53–57
Parent-support programs, 13–14
Parent-to-parent relations, 13–14, 42–44
Parent-training programs, 9–10
Patterson, G., 77
Peers relations
  of children, 45, 57–63, 244
  of parents, 53–57
Personality approaches to child rearing,
  79–81

Personality development, 207–219
  birth order and, 216–217
  culture and, 218
  field-environmental theory of, 212–213
  ideographic theory of, 213–214
  intelligence and, 217
  morphology/physiology theory of, 208
  neo-Freudian theory of, 211
  parenting style and, 218
  peer relations and, 60
  personal differences in, 215–219
  person-centered theory of, 210
  person-environment interaction theory of,
    214
  psychoanalytic theory of, 209–210
  psychosocial stage theory of, 211–212
  reinforcement theory of, 208–209
  schooling and media, influence of, 219
  sexual status and, 216
  socioeconomic status and, 215–216
  temperament and, 217
  trait-factor theory of, 209
Personal-support approach to child rearing,
    79–80
Person-centered theory of personality, 210
Person-environment interaction theory of
    personality, 214
Physical skills learned at home, 236–237
Piaget, J., 214
Play
  adult roles in, 161–166
  affectionate, 155 tab., 157
  and behavior management, 197–198
  communicative, 155 tab., 159
  definition of, 151–155
  exploratory, 155 tab., 156
  imaginative-constructive, 155 tab., 157
  as learning and development medium, 153
  media, 155 tab., 160–161
  nature of, 151–154
  organized games, 155 tab., 160
  as pleasurable pastime, 152–153
  skill, 155 tab., 156
  social-interaction, 155 tab., 158–159
  as socializing medium, 153–154
  social-pretend, 155 tab., 158
  toys and, 167–171
  types of, 154–161
Play participation approach to child
    rearing, 82–84
Play-to-Grow, 91
Policy makers, parents as, 11–12
Portage Project, The, 87

Poverty and child care, 147
Powell, M., 144
Power struggles, 43, 46
Preschoolers (4–5-year-olds), development
    of, 140, 145–146
Pride in children, 205, 226
Problem prevention models for parent
    education, 87–89
Problem-solving approach, 76–77, 188, 192
Professionals in triad with child and family,
    20–25; see also Parent-education
    program staff
Project Edge, 90–91
Protective parenting approach, 79, 194–195
Psychoanalytic theory of personality,
    209–210
Psychosocial stage theory of personality,
    211–212
PTA, 4, 9, 11–12

Rabin, A., 30
Ramey, C., 88
Reading learned at home, 238–240
Recruitment of parents for education
    programs, 100–103, 120
Rehabilitation model for parent education,
    89–90
Reinforcement theory of personality,
    208–209
Rejection, expression of, 222
Rights of children, 149–150
Rogers, C. R., 196, 210
Rutter, M., 136
Rynders, H., 90

Safety concerns with children, 127–129
Salk, L., 79
Schools
  activities in, 69–71
  after-school activities, 69–70
  benefits to, from parent-education
    programs, 16 tab., 18
  curriculum planning, 69
  families and, 65–71, 250–252
  as microsystems, 66
  parent-teacher conferences, 70–71
  and personality development, 219
  power relationships, 43
  resources of, using, 41–42
  settings of, 66–68
  teachers and child care providers, 68–69
Science learned at home, 240

Second-grade child (7–8-year-old),
    development of, 141–142, 146
Security, children's need for, 203–206
Self-awareness approach, 195–197
Self-care by children, 130–131
Self-concept in children, 205
Self-confidence, expression of, 225–226
Self-control in children, 205–206
Self-doubt, expression of, 222
Self-esteem, 81, 206
    approach to behavior management,
        195–197
    children's development of, 205–206
    expression of, 226
Self-management learned at home, 242–243
Self-protection by children, 131–132
Sexual status, influence of, 216
Shapiro, E., 155
Sheldon, W., 208
Shelter for children, 127–129; see also Child
    care
Sibling relations, 45–49, 176–178
Simon, S., 80, 192
Singer, D., 161
Single-parent families, 27, 43, 147–148
Smart, M., 29, 30, 47
Social skills learning, 37–39, 57, 60–61,
    174–175, 187, 191–193, 241–244
Social support models for parent education,
    92–93
Society
    and families, 49–52
    and schools, 65–66
Socioeconomic status (SES), influence of,
    49–50, 66, 215–216
Sparling, J., 83, 197
Special education models for parent
    education, 90–91
Special education schools, 10
Special family relationships, 76, 147–149
Spock, B., 75–76
Sponseller, D., 155
Spouse relations, 42–44

Stein, S., 83
Stepparents, 148
Sullivan, H. S., 211
Sutton-Smith, B., 46, 47, 83
Systematic Training for Effective Parenting
    (STEP), 80, 191

Talented children, 249–250
Task persistence learned at home, 245–246
Teachers, see Schools
Teenage parents, 147
Temperament in personality differences, 217
Tension, expression of, 223
Toddler (2–3-year-old), development of,
    139, 145
Toys and play, 167–171
Trait-factor theory of personality, 209
Transactional analysis approach, 81,
    195–196

Value acquisition, 28, 35–36
Value-clarification approach, 80–81,
    192–193
Verbal Interaction Project, 86–87
Vocabulary learned at home, 237

Watrin, R., 83, 197
Weber, C. U., 88
Weissbourd, B., 56, 89, 92
Well-being, expression of, 224; see also
    Children's emotional well-being
Wesley, F., 77
Westin, J., 79
White, B., 83, 175, 197
White, B. L., 85
Willis, A., 175
Wolfgang, C., 83

Young child (3–4-year-old), development of,
    139–140, 145

Zigler, E., 85

About the Author

The late **Christine Z. Cataldo** held an Ed.D. degree in Early Childhood Education from the State University of New York at Buffalo, where she was Associate Professor in the Department of Learning and Instruction, and Director of the Early Childhood Research Center. She was an active member in the Society for Research and Child Development, the Association for Childhood Education International, and the National Association for the Education of Young Children. Dr. Cataldo authored *Infant and Toddler Programs: A Guide to Very Early Childhood Education*, coauthored *What's the Hurry? Developmental Activities for Able and Handicapped Children*, was the author of numerous articles in professional journals, and presented widely in the areas of infant and toddler programs, and parent education. Her research interests included preschool children's views of parenting, effects of early education intervention programs, and children's uses of computers and software. She was a consultant to daycare centers and early intervention programs, a number of large toy and computer software manufacturers, and was the mother of two children.

DATE DUE

OCT 26 '89			
MAR 21 '91			
APR 8 '91			
SEP 21 '91			
OCT 13 '91 NOV 7 '91			
NOV 27 '91			
OCT 02 '92			
APR 11 '94			
OCT 09 '94			
NOV 30 '95			
OCT 28 '96			
NOV 22 1996			
GAYLORD			PRINTED IN U.S.A.